AT HOME IN FRANCE

EATING AND ENTERTAINING WITH THE FRENCH

CHRISTOPHER PETKANAS

Photographs by JEAN-BERNARD NAUDIN

Foreword by Marie-Hélène de Rothschild

PHOENIX ILLUSTRATED

FOR MY MOTHER AND FATHER

First published in 1990 by
George Weidenfeld & Nicolson Ltd

This paperback edition first published in 1999 by
Phoenix Illustrated
Orion Publishing Group,
Orion House,
5, Upper St. Martin's Lane
London WC2H 9EA

Distributed in the United States of America by
Sterling Publishing Co., Inc.
387 Park Avenue South,
New York, NY 10016-8810

British Library Cataloguing-in-Publication Data
A catalogue record for this book is available from the British Library
ISBN 0753807084

Designed by Sarah Sears, with help from Lindsey Rhodes and Benn Linfield
Typeset by Keyspools, Globorne, Lancs
Printed and bound in Italy by L.E.G.O., Vicenza

Half-title page: Luncheon preparations *chez* Nad and Christian Laroche, Boulogne

Frontispiece: The cookbook collection of Nad Laroche, Boulogne

Contents page and facing: The end of the grape harvest at Château Le Tertre
Roteboeuf in Saint-Emilion is traditionally celebrated with an outdoor *fête* for the
grape pickers.

Foreword (page 8): In the house of Jean and Irène Amic on the rue de Grenelle, Paris, a
table dressed with fine linen, porcelain, crystal and English silver from The White
House, London. (Flowers by Henri Moulié.)

Foreword (page 10): At Château de La Chaize in the Beaujolais, an eighteenth-century
rafraîchissoir, or wine glass cooler, by Charles-François Hannong. The crimson-
purple flowers are typical of *faïence de Strasbourg*.

ACKNOWLEDGEMENTS

THIS BOOK DEPENDED on the owners of eighteen extraordinary houses, people who were generous with their time and generous with their enthusiasm. They did much more than simply allow their houses and tables to be photographed and described, and I thank them. Special gratitude is extended to Irène Amic and Jean-Louis Riccardi, and I greatly appreciate the participation of the Baroness Guy de Rothschild. For the interest she took in the book in the early stages and for taking the first pictures that proved the idea was a good one, I am grateful to Virginia Liberatore.

At Weidenfeld and Nicolson, Michael Dover set the project in motion, and Sarah Sears was an exceptionally attentive editor. Encouragement and indispensable help were given by the following friends, who made whatever was important to me important to them: Kenneth Paul Block, Dominique Jackson, Peter O'Brien, Sally Rennison and Morton Ribyat. Emelie Tolley was a stranger when I contacted her for advice before the book was begun; remarkably open, she offered great support.

In addition, I would like to thank the following people who contributed to the book in important ways or made realizing it easier: Anne Sterling Alsina for testing many of the recipes, Colette Barcia, Constance Borde, Pascal Bouchet of the Ecole Hôtelier de l'Hermitage, Gérard Cariou, Jean-Luc Clouerac, Henri and Josette Colla, Jean-Pierre Démery and his family, for developing my taste for Provence, Henri and Micheline Dos Ramos, Nadine Frey, Richard Hussey, Dominique Gontard, Jacques Hugonot, Olga Hugounenq, Bernard and Michelle de Jouffroy-Gonsans, Odette Jung, Henriette Meynardi, Jean-Marie Lardet, Chef Jean-Louis Le Gall of the restaurant Le Roc'h-Ar-Mor on Ile d'Ouessant, Nicole Lesauvage, Amy, Grace and Zora Li, Benn Linfield, Patricia McColl, Henri Moulié, Jean-Luc Poujauran, Lindsey Rhodes, Joel Rosenthal, Chef Reine Sammut of the restaurant La Fenière in Lourmarin, Gregory Usher and Jérome Vital-Durand.

Appreciation is due to the following for quotations that appear in the text: Samuel Chamberlain, *Clementine in the Kitchen*, David R. Godine, Boston, 1988; Betty Fussell, *Masters of American Cookery*, Times Books, New York, 1983; L'Oncle Hansi, *Mon Village*, Editions du Rhin, Mulhouse, 1988; Henry James, *A Little Tour in France*, Penguin Books, London, 1985; Jacques Médecin, *La Cuisine du comté de Nice*, Julliard, Paris, 1972; James Pope-Hennessy, *Aspects of Provence*, Penguin Books, London, 1982; Roderick Cameron, *The Golden Riviera*, Weidenfeld and Nicolson, London, 1975; Waverley Root, *The Food of France*, Vintage Books, New York, 1977; Steven Spurrier, *French Country Wines*, Willow Books, London, 1984; Alice B. Toklas, *The Alice B. Toklas Cook Book*, Harper & Row, New York, 1954; Laurence Wylie, *A Village in the Vaucluse*, Harvard University Press, Cambridge, 1957; Marie-France Boyer, 'Rock Folly' and 'Seasons Greetings' from *The World of Interiors*, London, October 1986 and January 1987 respectively; Nancy Mitford, 'Portrait of a French Country House' from *The Sunday Times*, 1961; Robert Parker, *The Wine Advocate*, Monkton, Maryland; Henri Pellerin, 'Le Manoir de Querville' from *Le Pays d'Auge*, Lisieux, July 1955; Jancis Robinson, 'Philosophy of Wine, A Real Find' from *A la Carte*, London, February 1987.

The author and publishers are also grateful for permission to reproduce or adapt the following recipes: 'Gâteau à l'orange de grand-mère Blanc' from *Ma Cuisine des Saisons* by Georges Blanc, Robert Laffont, Paris, 1984; 'Gâteau renversé à l'ananas' (which appears as Gâteau aux cerises non-dénoyautées) from *Les Carnets de cuisine, recettes pour débutantes grandes et petites*, by Marianne Comolli, Hachette Pratique, Paris; 'Velouté de céleri au Stilton' from *Madame Figaro*, Paris; 'Beignets de pommes' excerpted from *Les Meilleurs Desserts* © Gründ, with the kind permission of the publisher; 'Mélange aromatique' and 'Pigeonneaux aux épices et légumes confits' (which appear as Mélange d'aromates marocains and Pigeons frottés aux aromates marocains, cuits aux citrons confits) by Jacqueline Saulnier from *Marie-Claire*, Paris, May 1988.

CONTENTS

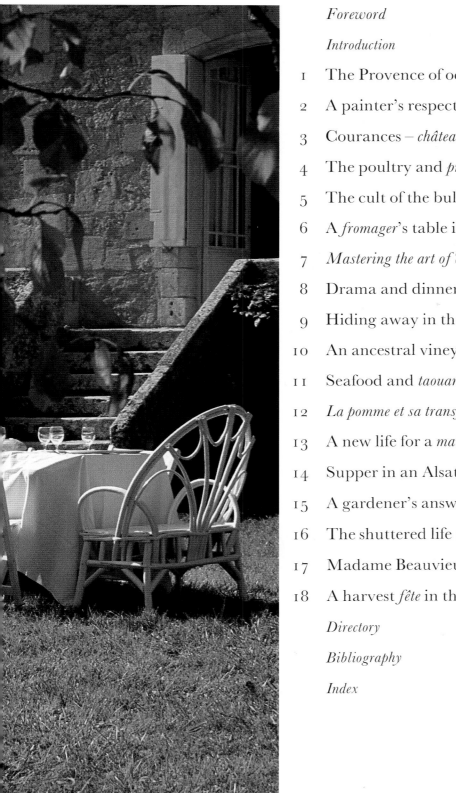

FOREWORD

'There are three different sorts of cooking,' says the first man, 'with garlic, with butter, or with cream.'

'Wrong,' says the second. 'There is country cooking, bourgeois cooking and grand cooking.'

'Wrong again,' retorts the third. 'There is French cooking, Chinese cooking and Moroccan cooking.'

'No,' comes the chorus from those who advocate a simpler approach, 'there are only two sorts: men's and women's, or rather traditional and innovative, or old and new, if you prefer.'

'There is good cooking,' concede the pacifists in the company at length, 'and the rest!'

GENERAL de Gaulle put his finger on the problem when he protested, in so many words, 'How can a man be expected to govern a country which produces more different types of cheese than there are days in the year?'

The answer may be found in the pages of this book, one of the chief virtues of which is that it manages to reconcile such deeply entrenched attitudes. In the realm of cooking, as in the art of entertaining or of interior decorating, there are no rules and no laws. Entertaining is not a skill that can be learned, like reading. Three centuries ago Pascal observed, with his customary candour, that 'true eloquence transcends eloquence'; and true elegance, as the French have learned from the English, has nothing whatever to do with the vagaries of fashion.

So does this imply that anything is acceptable? Quite the contrary: there is a secret to be discovered, and a key with which to unlock it. The secret is the realization that the art of entertaining, like true courtesy, requires us to put the pleasure of others before our own. The key is harmony, the natural fruit of simplicity and sympathetic surroundings. Just as the art of good speaking depends on the right combination of words and circumstances, so the art of preparing good food demands careful attention both to cooking times and to the balance of flavours, while the art of entertaining lies in a judicious mixture of decorum and harmony.

The keyword is harmony. The harmony that there should always be between what one is and what one does: while nothing could be more delicious than a proper country spread, there is something inappropriate and even ridiculous about elegantly refined food served in a simple rustic setting, and vice versa.

The harmony that should exist between the region and the dish: nobody goes to New York to eat cassoulet, for the very good reason that the sausage does not come from

Toulouse or Castelanaudary as it should, any more than they go to Berlin for a *cocido madrileño* or to Tokyo for a couscous.

The harmony that a skilful host or hostess should know how to create, in the echoing colours of flowers and table napkins, for instance, or in the play of candlelight on glasses of ruby or golden wine, or the flashing brilliance of diamond rings.

The harmony that should suit the content of a meal to its presentation: the subtlest of wines will lose all its delicacy if served in an opaque goblet, even if it were made of gold, while *foie gras* loses nothing when served with hunks of country bread.

And finally the harmony that should reign between what one is eating and one's state of mind. I forget which journalist it was who, while sitting at Point's waiting for his fellow diners to arrive, ordered a glass of water. Then, changing his mind, 'No, bring me a glass of champagne. It would be a pity to waste such a beautiful thirst!'

There is a famous French saying: 'Good cooking is when things taste of what they are.' Similarly, the art of entertaining lies in doing so according to one's temperament. If you are baroque by nature,

entertain in the baroque style; or if you tend more towards the restraint of the eighteenth century, then let your entertaining be more classical in inspiration. Do not be afraid to express your own character, be it ceremonious or romantic, passionate, dashing or languorous.

But those who are small in spirit, who are mean, narrow-minded or timid, should leave entertaining to others. For, however rich or poor one is, certain ingredients are essential: a pinch of madness, two dashes of refinement, three grains of effort – and a few heartbeats. If your heart is not in your entertaining you will never be able to follow the example of those French hosts and hostesses who are worthy of their gallant past, and who know how to serve a truly exquisite meal – or, as they would say, *mettre les petits plats dans les grands*.

Let us leave the last word to one of the great masters of the art of good living. Talleyrand, Prince of Bénévent, while busily engaged in re-apportioning the world at the Congress of Vienna, was heard to cry (his appetite perhaps whetted by his work), 'I've no use for written instructions. Send me my saucepans!'

Marie-Hélène de Rothschild

Hôtel Lambert, Paris
April 1990

INTRODUCTION

'The French like to say that their food stems from their culture and that it has developed over the centuries.'

Alice B. Toklas, *The Alice B. Toklas Cook Book*

'Impossible to convey the prettiness of these rooms, with their old-fashioned furniture, amateur watercolours and double taffeta curtains, pink and white.'

Nancy Mitford, *Portrait of a French Country House*

ON THE bullet train from Avignon to Paris, I was asked by a French woman – middle class and about sixty years old – what had taken me to Provence. I said I was writing a book about *l'art de recevoir*, a book that would explore 'the art of receiving', or 'entertaining', as practised by the French, and that would place the private French table in the greater context of the entire house. The woman on the train was very surprised by my subject.

'Do you really think that there is such a thing in France as *l'art de recevoir*?' she asked. 'Do you really think the French eat and entertain better than other people?'

After living in France for almost nine years, and having eaten in many houses where the food and setting are indeed worthy of each other, the answer is 'yes'. Throughout the country – in Alsace as in Bordeaux, in Brittany as in the Auvergne – the food, the table at which it is served, and the larger setting provided by the house achieve a union that is peculiarly French. It is a recipe realized with *haute cuisine* and *cuisine rustique*, on Napoleonic Sèvres and dishes from the sale shelves at Monoprix, in châteaux and farmhouses, by *comtesses* and *paysans*. It is a recipe with magic and charm.

Today, the French are doing nothing to ruin their reputation as a people who find it natural and sensible to spend long easy hours *à table*, even when there is no special occasion. When there is an event – a baptism, friends or family invited for lunch, dinner or the weekend – the element of ceremony without fuss, of form without bother, becomes deliciously exaggerated. A leg of lamb is ordered from the butcher, *foie gras* is taken excitedly from the larder, jugs of lilac and coverlets put out in the guest rooms. There is an atmosphere of care, respect and attention that is all the more engaging for being automatic.

'In France,' says the food historian Philip Hyman, 'the whole notion of *fête*, that food can be entertainment, is one of the things that keeps it alive. And yet,' he worries, 'the celebration too often takes people's attention away from the food in front of them. What is the point of serving nice young green beans if no one notices them?'

While lunch in other Western countries has been whittled down to a nasty sandwich eaten while polishing off at least two other tasks, in France it remains a serious meal. This puts the French at table more often, and always, as Alice B. Toklas specified, with wine. When she wrote in 1954 that

'The French drink wine with their lunch as well as with their dinner', it was something of a revelation to her British and American readers. But it is still worth noting today. Wine is served no matter how modest or spontaneous the meal and no matter whose table you are sharing. The French themselves do not notice especially, but wine gives their meals shape and rhythm while introducing a sense of ritual. This is true of the *premier cru classé* in a château in Burgundy, the *vin de pays* in a farmhouse in the Lot, and the *gros rouge* on a building site in Paris.

Some of the best food served in private houses in France today is the result of teamwork – a household demanding good and interesting things to eat and a talented staff dedicated to making them. France, of course, is not the only society with the structure and wealth that allows for one class of people to engage another in its kitchens, but the natural interest the French have in food makes them especially good employers of cooks and chefs. The *maîtresse de maison* stands over her cook counting the number of times the *pot-au-feu* is degreased (three), and raps him lightly on the knuckles when the

cabbage is too finely shredded – 'It was never meant to be *chiffonnade*.' In this way the old and luxurious tradition of systematically moulding a cook to a family's palate is still practised with some extravagance. Indeed, there remains at least one very public titled French woman who travels between her five residences with an extended retinue that always includes her chef. Every year she tours a different region of France with her chauffeur in search of specialist suppliers – of honey, truffles, chocolate, olive oil.

Other houses of means grimly illustrate the saying that the 'better' the house in France, the worse the food. As in so many restaurants, the distracting splendour of the setting hoodwinks people into thinking that the food will be equal to it. It is a short distance from here to that vast category of French people who take infinite care laying their tables but who are seemingly indifferent about the menu. But one is grateful for their beautiful tables nevertheless.

The difference between eating in a smart French house and a humble one is the difference between a salad Niçoise made with peeled and seeded tomatoes

ABOVE: *At Château de Courances, the Chambre des Fables, so-named for its* boiseries *painted with scenes from La Fontaine's* Fables.

and one that dismisses such refinements as foolish. One of the bonuses of eating in the modest houses which never leave family hands are the inspired accidents of decoration – a pair of heavy gold rep draperies hanging in the middle of a wall to frame a seventeenth-century Dutch school painting of the Crucifixion.

True to the postcard image, many of these country tables are still supplied largely with ingredients grown and gathered within a few yards of the farmhouse door. Happily, the same excellent ingredients are available to anyone who shops at local markets, where *paysans*, gap-toothed and bereted for the tourists, are found selling a few impeccably raised chickens, a couple of dozen discs of *chèvre*, an armful of tender lettuce, or a bag of *haricots* and a bunch of coriander. The countryside represents what is best in food in France today but also what is worst. For standing in the shadow of these markets are the inevitable *grandes surfaces*, hypermarkets where in one stop it is possible to buy a loin of pork, have your shoes re-soled, photocopy your tax return, and acquire a new pair of fashion jeans.

The pillar of French home cooking, the average *'boeuf bourguignonne'* household, has been threatened since the last war when, for the first time, women went to work in offices and factories in large numbers. Today, scholars say these households are disappearing in the ever-widening gulf separating people who spend money and time to eat well at home and those who do not. The first group is smaller, braver and the subject of this book. Among them are examples of sociologist Françoise Sabban's 'ten to fifteen per cent of women of the *petite bourgeoisie* living in French cities who buy fresh ingredients, still know how to cook, and take time to do it.'

The woman on the bullet train was surprised by my subject but still interested. She described her house in Eyga-lières, a village that had been a neolithic settlement before being occupied by Romans despatched to divert the local spring waters to Arles. She spoke about her kitchen garden, the herbs she cultivated, her view of the Alpilles mountains and twelfth-century Chapelle Saint-Sixte, the situation of her outdoor dining table under a canopy of vines, the beautiful old tiles in her Provençal kitchen. Then she invited me to lunch. There were the normal protestations about how it would not be anything special – just whatever happened to be in the garden, *une petite grillade*, the local *pinard*, some fruit. But I will go, knowing it will be good.

BELOW: *At Le Castelas, a dairy farm in the Vaucluse.*

I The Provence of ochre and *aïoli*

AS THE OWNER of a fashionable Paris antique shop selling exquisite and rather offbeat bits and pieces, Dorothée d'Orgeval is as sophisticated and cunning as one could want her to be. But she is also a *terrienne*, a woman of the soil, whose soil is Provence. Her father's family are *originaires* of Roussillon, the village in the Vaucluse whose unique russet charm has been its own undoing, and Roussillon is where Dorothée d'Orgeval spent much of her childhood.

ABOVE: *A 1920s* cabane, *seen from just outside Dorothée d'Orgeval's front door at the very top of Roussillon, would have been built by village people who wanted a garden to cultivate and a cool shaded place to escape to on especially hot days. Mme d'Orgeval's own house was originally used by her family for much the same reason. Ochre was mined from hills like this one for centuries before a synthetic product from America replaced it on the marketplace.*

LEFT: *The stone slab that serves as a dining table was originally part of the Roman way that passed through the Lubéron. Before Dorothée inherited it, the table furnished her great-grandfather's farm in the valley below the village. Many of the chairs under the canopy of leafy lilac are classic Lloyd Looms.*

15

ABOVE: *The apéritif table is packed with lupin seeds, aubergine caviar,* fougasse aux gratons, *brine-cured green olives of Les Baux Valley, small black olives from Nyons, conserved tomatoes, tapenade, broad beans, anchovies and capers, and hummus. The bottles contain* Vin d'orange, *fennel-flavoured water and almond syrup.*

LEFT: *'"Secretions that are too bitter or too listless escape from tissues thus sharply attacked",' writes Samuel Chamberlain in* Clementine in the Kitchen, *quoting an expert on the effect of showering the live snails with salt and vinegar. Of the shells, he adds, '"Wash and wipe [them] as you would handle precious bits of porcelain."'*

She says that in the late 1950s if you ordered a whisky in the local bistro, your order went unnoticed. In those days it was a narrow glass of pastis or a *ballon* of rosé or nothing. And tea was considered too exotic and posh an item to be stocked by the town *épicerie*. Even now she says that the idea of *un vrai Provençal* drinking a cup of tea is ridiculous.

There are still people in Roussillon today who remember Dorothée's great-grandfather, 'And for me that counts,' she says, 'that's important.' The absolutely original house in which she now lives with her husband Jean, and their daughters Priscille and Domitille, was used only in summer when Dorothée was growing up – a *maison d'été* 275 metres up at the very top of the village. A second, smaller

and more manageable place nearby served her family for the rest of the year.

In the Roussillon Dorothée first knew there were no photographers to dodge. You got out of bed, walked into town to buy bread for breakfast, and no day-trippers documented it. The villages of the Petit Lubéron – calcareous mountains east of Avignon that incise themselves on your memory forever – were still happy to be thought of as unfashionable, if they were thought of at all. No one took any notice when the Impressionist scholar John Rewald bought a place in Ménerbes, or when Tiffany design director Van Day Truex moved in down the road, or when Marc Chagall or Bernard Dufour started painting in Gordes. Neither Parisians nor government ministers had caught

RIGHT: *Glazed tiles in the green so characteristic of Provence are still produced by François Vernin of Carreaux d'Apt in Bonnieux nearby. The kitchen gives on to the garden where Sacha Pitoëff made* Le Paradis Retrouvé *in 1952. Roussillon is also distinguished for having sheltered Samuel Beckett during the war. The playwright harvested grapes at the local Bonnelly vineyards, which he cited in* Waiting for Godot; *the d'Orgevals table wine is from the same property.*

on (although Jack Lang eventually discovered Bonnieux and bought a place there), and *le Train Grand Vitesse* was still years away. But when it finally did arrive in 1982, it changed the face of the Lubéron for ever. The whole area became 'chic', perilously expensive and even slightly sinister. And it became *La Vallée des Piscines* – Swimming Pool Valley.

In the nineteenth century it would have been impossible to imagine such frantic interest. Then it was the Riviera or nothing. Quarantined on the coast in 1834 during the cholera epidemic, Lord Brougham invented it as a resort, leaving the English with no appetite for places like Avignon and Aix, let alone an inconvenient curiosity like Roussillon. 'Even towards the end of the last century,' James Pope-Hennessy wrote in *Aspects of Provence*, 'the most obvious and unavoidable cities of Provence were being treated by these travellers as mere incidents of the southward journey – places with possible hotels and picturesque inhabitants, places you could glimpse from the railway-carriage window, and could rely upon to give you a thrilling foretaste of pleasures to come.' What these travellers wanted was the sea, they wanted their villas and their cool, dense gardens. Inland Provence was a bore.

Not today. The crumbly sandstone hills of spectacularly and variously coloured ochre surrounding Roussillon have since then become a substantial attraction, causing the village to suffer more than others in the Lubéron. *Chaussée des Géants* (Giants' Way) and *Aiguilles du Val des Fées* (Needles of the Vale of the

LEFT: *A collection of bottles, including hand-blown ones from the last century, in the* cave *below the kitchen. Jean d'Orgeval will fill them with Gigondas wine bought in bulk from Paul Jaboulet Aîné.*

ABOVE: *While meat is grilled in the* potager, *or small hearth, in the far corner of the kitchen, an oven is hidden in a niche behind the small round table watched over by a 1930s* terre vernisée *sculpture. The steps lead up to the main room where a Louis XIII four-poster is glimpsed at the far end. Stairs behind the closed door lead to the* cave.

RIGHT: *A Restoration* tôle *tray and a nest of casseroles in the traditional* jaspé *earthenware of Vallauris on the coast. In the 1950s when the Roussillon house was not equipped with a stove, vegetable* gratins *cooked in these vessels were walked down to the village* boulangerie *for baking.*

Fairies) are the storybook names given to two cliffs with jagged vertical slices, or 'needles', projecting from their faces. Act Two of the performance staged by nature includes the crest of Mont Ventoux floating snowily in the distance, and a general preponderance of pine, juniper, scrub oak, herbs and the scarlet motif that signals Provence, poppies. The air is thick with resin, lavender and rosemary.

While very little ochre was quarried in Roussillon in the nineteenth century, by 1914 foreign markets and new machinery had transformed mining into a crucial activity. Production was practically wiped out by World War I, however, and though former levels of output were later matched, the Depression and then World War II had the same crushing effect. The levelling blow was dealt when the authentic Vauclusian ochre – ochre that had coloured so much house paint – was supplanted by an artificial product from America. The other traditional activity to which Roussillon might then have turned, the raising of silkworms, had not been viable since the 1860s. The combination of disease and competition from different parts of the world during that decade left

the women of the village with bales of mulberry leaves but with no voracious silkworms to consume them.

Dorothée d'Orgeval throws up a stiff back to the visitors who throng Roussillon to imbibe a bit of this history; if she did not, they would not only grill her about why she is painting her door that particular shade of green, but would invite themselves in for a drink as well. Inside they would discover a house whose novelty is the result of a subtle and compassionate give-and-take between the house and its *maîtresse*. Designed for fun and repose, comfort was never the reason you went there, yet today it is immensely comfortable. *Il y a tout ce qu'il faut*, including a kitchen that announces its owners as people who care profoundly about cooking and eating, and a glamorously fitted bathroom that lands you in Morocco. It is a house that was never destined to welcome anyone except at those times of year for which the Midi is famous, but if you were offered the keys in January you would go, *rapidement*, with no worry of draughty mistrals.

The house had *its* way regarding the rooms, or room, for if you do not count the

ABOVE: *A late nineteenth-century French pine* épicerie *cupboard stands against a wall coloured with the natural but increasingly scarce ochre of Roussillon. Whereas there were four* épiceries *in the village when Mme d'Orgeval was growing up, now there is only one.*

OPPOSITE: *Dorothée d'Orgeval says that equipping the WC with enamelled pitchers is a reflex that comes from living in a house where water has not always been plentiful. In Roussillon in the early part of the century, people either stored rain in cisterns, or collected water from the village fountain, or bought it from men who climbed up through the town with donkeys hauling barrels on wheels. Running water reached Roussillon, piped from the mountains, in 1912.*

kitchen and bathroom there has only ever been one – a sprawling, unbroken space of one hundred square metres. Three arched French windows give onto the garden, and planted giddily at one end of the room with no explanation is a hulking Louis XIII four-poster with its original yellow raw silk hangings and coverings. This is where the d'Orgevals sleep. When they want to feel less exposed they draw the curtains, and when it is especially hot, or they are giving a dinner party and want to give the room a different and fresher and cooler look, they exchange the bedcover for a bright white one.

If you want to win automatic disfavour with Dorothée, tell her how Provençal her house is. 'Provençal is not what I sought and it's not what this place is. On the contrary, it was done in a very anarchic way. Everything is mixed up. I don't like change – I am very constant, and the carcass of the main room hasn't altered since I was a child. My memory is of a place in a vague state of disorder with different areas, nooks and corners. The furniture in the house is mainly seventeenth century and it too has been here as long as I can remember. We've made it a bit more comfortable, adding things that are not necessarily the best, and sometimes we even wonder if it wasn't somehow better before. And yet when my mother visits she says it hasn't changed. The table, the sofa, the chairs, the dishes, the American garden swing, the rose bushes that give us petals for jam-making – they're all the same.'

Above all, Dorothée says that she quashed any impulse to create a *résidence secondaire*, 'furnishing it the way people do old agricultural properties around here, as if they were houses and not farms. They plant flowers carefully around the olive trees, and the grass is always perfectly maintained – very bad taste that, and what anguish. In any case, the vacation house in France is part of an *état d'esprit* I don't share; my idea of a *maison secondaire* is one that demands a completely different way of life. I am as happy in Roussillon as I am in Paris. I live in both places. But we don't pretend that this is a real house because it's not structured like one. There isn't a salon, bedrooms, dressing rooms, a smoking room. And the way we eat is completely different – I would never serve *aïoli* in town!'

When Dorothée says that the main room in Roussillon remains as she first knew it, a wide-open space with casually defined areas of interest and function, she neglects to say that she has ushered out the disorder. Above a table piled with boxed insects pinned behind glass and books on every aspect of Provence and its history sits an old draper's display case. The collection of Provençal pottery it contains – Apt, Uzès, Aubagne, Vallauris – is regarded by experts as being one of the finest in private hands. Across the room, pulled around the fireplace, are a folding steel camp bed, an eighteenth-century grey-painted chaise longue covered in coarse yellow silk, and a pair of Louis XV *fauteuils à la bonne femme*, or Provençal grandmothers' armchairs, so-called because of the wide welcome they give to wide old *mémés*. Cushions made from antique *boutis*, native hand-blocked and hand-stitched quilts, are placed over the traditional rush seats of these chairs. And between the draper's case and the bed hangs a provincial painting of a shooting trophy – a hare and a duck and flowers. Below it a rigidly carved Louis XIII walnut buffet is peopled with religious figures trapped under bell jars. These startled frozen figures, together with an oak prie-dieu and a string of beads dangling from a footed pole, give this corner of the room an atmosphere of pretty devotion. A decorator could easily say her prayers here.

No matter how civilized and comfortable the house becomes, however, Dorothée says it will always be a kind of excuse for the garden, which is planted with trees chosen for their ornamental value as well as their value in the kitchen – jujube, cherry, apricot, greengage, pear, olive and quince. Towards the thirteen traditional Provençal Christmas desserts the garden contributes dried red figs and quince that is made into jelly and jelly squares. Herbs are also plentiful: santolina for its lovely lavender smell, mint, thyme and fennel. Feathery fennel branches are stuffed into a bottle of water in summer for a cool and faintly perfumed drink. An acacia tree offers delicate flowers to dip in batter and fry, and reaching up from behind benches and around cypresses are great eye-filling patches of mauve, bronze and flame-coloured irises. The round, squat stone folly with a canal-tiled roof was added to close the perspective at one end of the garden, providing a place for napping or playing cards after lunch.

Although the festive look of the lunch pictured here might suggest a special occasion to people unfamiliar with

OPPOSITE: *Only a few steps away the d'Orgevals own a second house, a house reserved for their children and friends. Two guest rooms there are separated by a raw plaster wall 1 metre (40 inches) thick. An embroidered picture and trumpet of spun glass hang over a cast-iron bed.*

the region, Dorothée says that it could not be more ordinary or more typical. Certainly there is a lot to eat and drink. For apéritifs there is not just *vin d'orange* and pastis *pur*, but also pastis that when mixed with mint syrup becomes a drink known as a *perroquet*; when combined with almond syrup becomes a *mauresque*; and that when mixed with grenadine becomes a *tomate*. Among the hors d'oeuvres crowded onto a table with all these bottles are *anchoïade*, a spread of anchovy fillets with olive oil, vinegar and garlic; *tapenade*, a pounded mash of capers, black olives and anchovies; and *fougasse aux gratons*, a local lattice-like bread made with duck crackling and puff pastry, as here, or with baguette dough.

If it is midsummer and the sun is high and unforgiving, the pastis and hors d'oeuvres will have done their job, blasting the way for the *aïoli monstre*. Aïoli here refers only to the thick globs of garlic mayonnaise made with best-quality olive oil and turned by hand in a mortar with a pestle. Food processors are no good; too much air is introduced into the *pommade* and the result is dull and fluffy. An *aïoli* must wobble. With it the d'Orgevals serve the compulsory poached salt cod, potatoes cooked in their jackets, whole unpeeled carrots, green beans, artichokes and hard-boiled eggs simmered in the same aromatic liquid as the escargots. All of these are served warm with industrial quantities of well-iced Côtes du Ventoux rosé from the vineyards of Alain and Aimé Bonnelly in the Roussillon *commune*. A drawing of the stepped village decorates their label. Anthony Burgess's words come back: 'Provence, all sun, garlic, charming rogues, and hot-blooded girls, is wine turned into geography.'

Provence is also goat's cheese – seven kinds lined up on a giant ceramic banana leaf. Dessert, coolly rational after the fire-breathing *aïoli*, is a platter of fresh yellow peaches peeled and halved and presented in a pool of chilled strawberry *coulis*. Then, coffee.

Despite the time, specific ingredients and even skill required to prepare this lunch, Dorothée says that it has as much to do with gastronomy as a common plate of *steak-frites*. 'There is no such thing as *gastronomie provençale*; it's a very rustic, ordinary, poor cuisine you eat every day. It's simple food you eat in the open air – you can't just have a plateful and then disappear to the office. It's not very considered and not very refined – *la cuisine raffinée* is something and somewhere else in France. The locals eat *aïoli* more regularly than we do and in a simpler, more ordinary way that takes less time – with fewer vegetables, say. It's even served at school. While the same locals have exuberant temperaments, I can't really say that they're hospitable. Whatever else they may be, the French are not people who tap you on the shoulder and say, "Come on, come and eat with us."'

In *Village in the Vaucluse*, his dissecting study of Roussillon published in 1958, American sociologist Laurence Wylie wrote that Peyrane, his name for Roussillon, 'lies on the road to nowhere. Except for the National Highway No. 100 which crosses only the tip of the commune, its roads lead only to and from the village. If you are going to Peyrane you are not simply passing through on your way elsewhere. You must have some reason for going there.' This is not true today. Most people go just to look. But Dorothée d'Orgeval has one of the reasons why Wylie thought people would always need to go to Roussillon.

MENU
for 10

LE GRAND APÉRITIF PROVENÇAL DU ROUSSILLON

Pastis
Perroquets, Moresques, Tomates
Pastis with mint syrup, almond syrup and grenadine
Eau fraîche infusée au fenouil
Cold water infused with fennel

AUBERGINE PURÉE, LACY PUFF PASTRY WITH DUCK CRACKLING,
ANCHOVY SPREAD, CAPER AND OLIVE SPREAD, HUMMUS,
CONSERVED GREEN TOMATOES, BLACK OLIVES FROM NYONS,
GREEN OLIVES CURED IN BRINE FROM LES BAUX VALLEY,
BROAD BEANS, LUPIN SEEDS, CELERY, ANCHOVY AND CAPER ROLLS

———

L'AÏOLI MONSTRE DE DOROTHÉE D'ORGEVAL

MORUE POCHÉE, ESCARGOTS, CAROTTES, POMMES DE TERRE,
OEUFS DURS, ARTICHAUX, HARICOTS VERTS
GARLIC MAYONNAISE WITH POACHED SALT COD, SNAILS, CARROTS,
POTATOES, HARD-BOILED EGGS, ARTICHOKES, GREEN BEANS

Bonnelly Père et Fils   Côtes du Ventoux rosé

———

PÊCHES JAUNES DU VERGERS DE VAUCLUSE
À LA MENTHE FRAÎCHE ET SES COULIS DE FRAISES
YELLOW PEACHES FROM THE ORCHARDS OF THE VAUCLUSE
WITH FRESH MINT AND STRAWBERRY SAUCE

———

Café

L'AÏOLI MONSTRE DE DOROTHÉE D'ORGEVAL

Tradition requires that an *aïoli*'s accompaniments be served warm – a potential headache for the cook. One solution is to keep the artichokes, potatoes and carrots hot as they become ready, in a large strainer set over a large pot of simmering water on the back of the stove. Both the fish and eggs go into their pots 10 mins before serving, and the snails are removed from their warm cooking liquid and returned to their shells at the last minute. The beans are prepared in advance and doused with boiling water just before serving.

A note on salt cod: 'Green' salt cod denotes fish that is salted only, as compared to a second variety that is both salted and dried. Of the two, 'green' is considered better for hot dishes, though both must be soaked for 12–24 hours in a good quantity of cold water changed a number of times. Packed in brine, a third kind has excellent flavour and texture and requires only a brief bath – 3 hours – before poaching. To be sure the cod is thoroughly desalted, cut a small piece and taste the middle.

BELOW: *A copy of* L'Aïoli *newspaper dated 27 November 1893 and printed in Avignon, shows a young Arlésienne pouring olive oil into a mortar in the preparation of* aïoli. *The availability of* escargots *after a storm is a good excuse in Provence to make this garlic mayonnaise.*

ANCHOÏADE

Powerfully fishy.

170 g (6 oz) tinned anchovy fillets
4 cloves garlic, peeled, crushed and finely
  chopped
60 ml (2 fl oz/¼ cup) olive oil
1 tbs red wine vinegar

Mash the anchovies, combine with the garlic, and then stir in the oil and vinegar to make a smooth paste. Allow to stand at room temperature for an hour or so. Serve with celery stalks, *fougasse* and/or small rounds of grilled bread.

TAPENADE

A true *tapenade* should be pounded in a mortar with a pestle to release all the uncompromising flavours of these archetypally Mediterranean ingredients.

200 g (7 oz) oily black olives, pitted
1 tbs capers, drained
60 g (2 oz) tinned anchovy fillets
1–2 tbs olive oil
1 tbs lemon juice
1 tbs cognac

Pound the olives, capers and anchovies. Trickle in the olive oil as for a mayonnaise, stirring continuously. Mix in the lemon juice and cognac. Serve as you do *anchoïade*.

For the *aïoli*:
16 firm, meaty, unblemished garlic cloves,
  peeled
a pinch of coarse salt
2 egg yolks at room temperature
475 ml (17 fl oz/2 cups) olive oil
juice of 1 lemon
a pinch of cayenne pepper or a few drops
  Tabasco (optional)
For the accompaniments:
50 large snails, fresh or canned
for fresh snails:
  coarse salt
  vinegar
  5 black peppercorns
  1 onion, stuck with cloves
  1 carrot, peeled and quartered
  1 bulb fennel with its feathery tops,
  quartered
10 medium artichokes
2 tbs olive oil
juice of 1 lemon
salt
10 medium waxy potatoes, scrubbed
3 bay leaves
10 small carrots, peeled if necessary
600 g (1¼ lb) salted and dried cod, desalted
  (see introduction above for desalting
  information)
10 eggs

For the aïoli:

1. Using a marble mortar and wooden pestle, pound the garlic and salt to a paste. Incorporate the yolks until the mixture is pale yellow. As for a mayonnaise, trickle in the oil, turning the pestle slowly and continuously. When half the oil has been added, stir in the lemon juice and 1 tsp warm water, then continue with the remaining oil. Taste for salt, adding

the cayenne or Tabasco if desired. Do not chill.

For the accompaniments:

2. If using tinned snails, drain, rinse and wrap in damp cheesecloth. If you are using shells, fill them with the snails. Place the snails in the strainer.

If using fresh snails, degorge them of their potential toxins by starving them for several days in a covered shoe box punched with holes and left out of doors. Rinse in cold water, transfer to a bowl and sprinkle generously with coarse salt and vinegar. Set aside for 2–3 hours, discarding any snails that do not move. Rinse in several changes of cold water, place in a pot of cold water and simmer for 15 mins. Rinse again until the water runs clear. When cool, pull the snails out of their shells. Trim away any unpleasant black bits and return to the pot with the peppercorns, onion, carrot, fennel and enough salted water to cover. Simmer, skimming off impurities, for approx 2 hours, or until tender. While the snails are cooking, scrub the shells and dry them in a low oven. Remove the snails with a slotted spoon and return them to their shells.

3. Holding down each artichoke so that the stem projects over the edge of a work surface, push down on the stem to break it off at the top and pull out the fibres that attach it to the base. Fill one large or several smaller non-reactive pots with enough water to cover the artichokes and add the oil, lemon juice and salt. Bring to a simmer, add the artichokes in one layer and cook for 20–30 mins, or until tender. Drain upside down.

4. Place the potatoes and bay leaves in a large pot of cold salted water and boil until tender. Drain.

5. Plunge the carrots and beans into separate large pots of salted, rapidly boiling water and cook until just tender. Drain and plunge immediately into separate bowls of iced water. Drain as soon as the vegetables are cool. Dry the beans on a hand towel and reserve. Add the carrots to the strainer.

6. Place the desalted cod in a pot of cold water to cover and heat to just below simmering. Poach the fish, never allowing the surface of the water to break, for approx 10 mins, or until tender. Drain, picking out the obvious bones.

7. Transfer a bit of the snails' cooking liquid to another pan. Add the eggs and enough water to cover. Hard boil and then drain, and serve the *aïoli monstre*.

ABOVE: *After the garlicky excesses of an* aïoli, *these simple peaches, served with a* strawberry *coulis, are welcome and refreshing. As strawberries become available in the Lubéron in May and peaches not until July, Mme d'Orgeval prepares the sauce as a conserve and stores it.*

2 A painter's respect for a *maison de maître*

O F EVERYTHING André Breton might have found most beautiful at Le Pradié, he had no trouble settling on a patched-up hole in the kitchen chimney breast. Once the opening for a stovepipe, it was filled with plaster by Le Pradié's owner, painter Bernard Dufour, who then drew a man's face around it. The big white circle became the mouth, and the man was called 'Charles O'. Lunching with the artist and his wife Martine in 1966, Breton was fascinated by Dufour's fresco.

ABOVE: *Sempervivum and hollyhocks in the back garden. Bernard Dufour, who trained as an agricultural engineer, practises what he calls 'medieval landscaping' at Le Pradié. 'With a baroque labyrinth, clipping the hedges and clearing away the bigger branches is my only work.' M. Dufour has also planted more than a hundred trees – chestnuts, ashes, acacias, willows, junipers and cypresses – in the 6-hectare (15-acre) park.*

LEFT: *In the dining room, nineteenth-century mesh-backed garden chairs are pulled up around a walnut table designed by Bernard Dufour. The doorway to the right leads to the souillarde, or scullery. The lamp clamped to the table is from Espace Lumière, Paris, while the two-piece fruitwood cupboard behind it is Empire. The face on the plaster of the chimney breast was drawn by the owner and much admired by André Breton. The fireplace itself is actually held up by what Bernard describes as 'a very old and rare shepherd's coat stand'.*

A PAINTER'S RESPECT FOR A *MAISON DE MAÎTRE*

Other visitors have found other things they want to label 'most beautiful' at Le Pradié. One writer recalls long, cool August afternoons resting in a hammock strung up inside the tiny vaulted oratory, where the shelves are filled with a collection of birds' nests. Another writer describes his walks through the baroque labyrinth of attentively clipped box. And yet another writer remembers the good port consumed around a Charles X billiard table, an accessory crucial to the concept of life in the bourgeois French country house. The table at Le Pradié returns balls to players through the yawning mouths of chased lions' masks.

Why all the writers? 'It's simply that Bernard does not like the work of other painters,' says Martine Dufour. Toasted as an architect and interior designer in the 1960s and fallow in the 1970s, Martine is now hugely famous all over again. 'Alechinsky came once but, as I say, mostly it's always been just writers – Jacques Henric and Pierre Guyotat, Claude Ollier and Alain Robbe-Grillet, Guy Scarpetta and Alain Jouffroy. We prefer writers.'

Numerous paintings by Bernard Dufour are hung throughout Le Pradié, recounting the emotional history of his rapport with the house and the sensual history of his rapport with Martine. Born in 1922, he trained as an agricultural engineer before turning to painting in 1945. Three years later Bernard exhibited for the first time, and successfully, at the Salon de Mai. After a non-figurative period during which he produced mostly landscapes, in 1960 his work became more

LEFT: *An artichoke fashioned in* tôle *posed on an ikat cloth. The window frame is painted the traditional blue of the Aveyron.*

ABOVE: *Le Pradié, designed by an Italian architect for a French lawyer, is located in the* département *of the Aveyron in the southwest. Built in 1810, the limestone house is surrounded by plane trees which were planted at about the same time.*

representational and began to include hazy, reflective nudes and rather melancholic self-portraits.

Martine hatched one trend after another throughout the 1960s from a Paris boutique she called Pascal. In 1961 it was American patchwork quilts, hunted down and shipped over regularly by the sister of her friend Dorothea Tanning, the wife of Max Ernst. In 1963 it was minerals – minerals as decorative objects. André Breton and the Egyptian surrealist poet Joyce Mansour sent Martine to buy them from a man doing business from a *chambre de bonne* in Paris. And in 1968 it was steel furniture. But the events of May that year turned Martine against her bourgeois patrons, and Pascal closed in 1971. When

she resurfaced it was without a shop but with a new clientele drawn principally from the arts.

When the Dufours began shopping for a house in 1961, they were living in a flat linked to Pascal on rue Jacob, 'and we wanted space,' Martine remembers. They wanted a hulking great château, not the more romantically scaled *maison de maître* with farm buildings they eventually chose. 'We were young, we were good looking, we flew around the countryside in a stylish little convertible, and to us space meant a château. Our meetings with *notaires* were always the same. Bernard would say, "I'm a painter, my wife here runs a smart Paris boutique, and we want to buy a house."'

ABOVE: *M. Dufour's 1955 abstract painting hangs beside a Directoire fruitwood food-safe with screened sides that permit the circulation of air. Rustic local pottery is meant for storing oil and condiments.*

ABOVE RIGHT: *Filling a butterflied and rolled loin of pork, a* crème *inspired by pesto replaces basil with parsley, pine nuts with walnuts, and olive oil with walnut oil. The Château-Mouton Rothschild 1951 bears a label by the Hungarian artist Marcel Vertès.*

OPPOSITE: *The billiard room, furnished with a monumental Charles X table from Normandy, is immediately to the right on entering Le Pradié. The sculpted mantelpiece and painting above it are both by Bernard Dufour.*

Although the Dufours knew they wanted to live in the southwest – Bernard's family is from Toulouse – they agreed to confine their search to three *départements*: the Lot, the Ozère, and the Aveyron. In each *département* they identified the biggest cities, and in each city they identified the *notaire* with the inside track. There were rendezvous and they were shown what was for sale. It was all very precise, very systematic, and very gay. They gave themselves fifteen days.

In a short time the idea of a château began to seem less attractive. All the ones they visited either had poor views or were *too* hulking and attached to abandoned villages. Then, in the Aveyron, which lies northeast of Toulouse, they were led to Le Pradié. The house was sold to the Dufours instantly and the *notaire* had had to do no selling. Martine was won, charmed, 'because Le Pradié is exactly the house one draws as child: square, symmetrical, with the door in the middle and all the windows aligned.' It also reconciled the

couple's preferences – hers for stunted, scratchy vegetation on a wild, arid plateau with Bernard's for Dorothy Perkins roses flourishing in a green valley. Neither could quite believe their good luck when they discovered that while Le Pradié was set on *causse*, or calcareous tableland, the property also incorporated a small, well-watered hollow with caverns and grottoes. Bernard would later write a book, *La Pierre et la Seigle*, delineating the two terrains of the Aveyron and the culture and people they shape. Caussenards, those who live on the rocky *causse*, have no alternative but to raise sheep, while the Ségali, who live on the more fertile *ségala*, grow rye.

There is no trace of the two mills that once turned on the site of Le Pradié. The medieval one belonged to the Knights Templar, while the sixteenth-century one was the property of Galiot de Genouilhac, a weapons manufacturer and *maréchal de France* under François I. Nothing is known of M. Ser, the lawyer who commissioned the house, except that he liked it so much that he ordered an identical one – only three times as big – to be built in the neighbouring Lot. With its typically Aveyronnais roof of scalloped slate tiles, Le Pradié was not actually completed until 1810, yet in spirit, size and proportion it is very much an eighteenth-century house. Martine says that building and decoration styles usually took a while to reach the provinces, but that once they did, they lingered. They were also adapted to suit a narrower budget and a rural setting. The staircase *chez* the Dufours is in wood rather than stone, and there is no ornamentation around the windows.

From the outside Le Pradié looks like a classic four-up and four-down – precisely what it is not. No two rooms are the same size. Designed by an architect from northern Italy who was working in France, the house is for Martine the work of someone with '*un sens de la vie très bien*. Le Pradié is perfectly conceived. The idea of having no two rooms alike could not be more sympathetic, or intelligent, or rare. It is one of the ways we know that it was designed by an architect. The embrasures even follow the orientation of the sun, which is remarkable. On the north side they fan out to admit the greatest quantity of light, while on the south side they are perpendicular. And instead of firedogs to hold logs in the fireplace, there are two big stones that are part of the actual masonry – a typical feature of the villas north of Venice and one I've adopted when I build now myself.'

When the Dufours explain their prudent, restrained, almost anonymous ap-

LEFT: *A fragment of a 1973 painting by the owner in the oratory.*

ABOVE: *The most popular guest room at Le Pradié; interior* oeil de boeuf *windows frame an alcove covered with eighteenth- and nineteenth-century* toile de Jouy *printed with pastoral farm scenes.*

RIGHT: *Breakfast is taken at a bistro table on the terrace jut outside the oratory. The modern cast-iron copies of Russian 'fern' chairs were made in England. Breakfast includes walnut tarts, bowls of tea, and an assortment of the jellies and jams – blackcurrant, redcurrant, apricot, strawberry, apple, plum, quince – M. Dufour makes every summer.*

proach to the decoration of Le Pradié, they sound like dissenters. Who, after all, has ever heard of a French couple who are revolted by the idea of a *maison de famille*? None of the furniture belonged to *grand-maman*; there are no powdery aunts taking ages over tea in the salon; and there are no children streaking through the hall. The house is not only completely unsentimental but completely un-pretty. Nor are Bernard and Martine interested in undertaking a lot of work or leaving their mark; they do not want to shake things up. They are going to let sleeping beauty sleep.

'The *paysans* who lived at Le Pradié in the years before us never changed anything,' says Bernard. 'The doors and windows function now in just the same way as they did in 1810.'

'Because transforming and renovating houses is part of my métier', says Martine, 'I find it very difficult doing the same kind of work for myself. It's the property next door that interests me professionally, not my own. I loved the idea of having nothing to do at Le Pradié. Besides, we were seduced by the place just as it was. We adored its wild Visconti quality.'

In a bizarre but friendly arrangement, the Dufours shared Le Pradié for that first summer of 1961 with the *paysans* who sold it to them. 'They were finding it difficult to leave, so Bernard and I took a bedroom and the room that is now his office and they had the rest,' says Martine. 'For two months we lived together and ate our meals together without any problem. I knew so little about the country then that when the cockerel climbed on top of the hen I screamed because I thought he was trying to kill her! It was September when our friends finally did go; a tractor pulled up in front of the house and they piled on their beds and the few things they owned. The *paysans* in the Aveyron are poor because the land does not give them back very much at all.'

If the land were richer, the Aveyron would probably have its own entry between 'avapana' and 'azarole' in *Nouveau Larousse Gastronomique*. Instead, the difficult limestone soil has shaped a cuisine that is poor, simple and extremely limited, with an unhealthy emphasis on *charcuterie*: *lard gras*, *lard maigre*, ham, stuffed goose and duck neck, *saucisson*, *saucisse*, and *fritons*, which refers to either rough *rillettes* or a chunky pâté made with offal. According to Bernard, these products,

once first-rate, have slid in quality because the pigs are no longer slaughtered young. Other local specialities include *foie gras*, *tripoux*, or rolled tripe packets, boiled stuffed hen, lamb, and *aligot*. To make *aligot*, fresh Cantal is beaten over heat into potato purée until the cheese melts and forms ribbons.

At Le Pradié it is the painter who cooks – for the lunch pictured here, a glisteningly aesthetic salad of steamed summer vegetables (*ratatouille*, in fact, without the tomatoes); butterflied loin of pork filled with a pesto-like mixture of parsley, walnuts and walnut oil; potatoes in their jackets; and slightly crunchy strips of succulent Swiss chard. Dessert is a mountain of three fresh red fruits, and the wines are two for which Bernard has designed labels.

Château Vignelaure 1985, a Côteaux d'Aix-en-Provence, is decorated with his paintings of two symbols of the region, the *cigale plébéienne* and the *citron de Provence* butterfly. Vignelaure has had great success with the Cabernet Sauvignon grape, a variety now permitted to comprise sixty per cent of the total grapes used in reds of this *appellation*. Critic Steven Spurrier has written that it gives 'an intense colour and a blackcurrrant-cedary bouquet that is unusual in the wines of Provence'.

Bernard was also commissioned by Château Mouton-Rothschild, though his drawing of a nude woman holding a cluster of grapes did not adorn an especially good vintage – 1963. Fortunately, however, the seventy-two bottles he received as payment included, among other years, the far better 1951. With a label by Marcel Vertès, it is served and savoured with the roast. Mouton-Rothschild is legendary, with a commitment to excellence that is unmatched in the Médoc.

While Bernard looks after the wine, Martine looks after the guests, creating an easy atmosphere of comfort she associates with the English rather than the French: 'To me, *l'art de recevoir* is something very Anglo-Saxon. When you arrive at someone's house in England, they immediately try to do everything they can for you, which is not the case in France. As a child growing up in Paris, it was unnatural for me to invite a friend home. To feel at home among the French on their own ground you have to stay longer and become part of the family. You've got to insinuate yourself into the surroundings. In France, I would say, it takes time.'

OPPOSITE: *The Aveyron is a region of* charcuterie. *For* cou de canard farci, *the tube of skin around a duck's neck makes a neat and convenient casing for a forcemeat of duck, pork, liver, lard, shallots and* purée de foie gras. *A great deal of fat is required to cook the neck* en confit, *or submerged in fat, as this one has been. A different, slightly roasted flavour is obtained by simply cooking the neck uncovered in the oven.*

MENU
for 8

Porto autour de la billard
Port around the billiard table

COU DE CANARD FARCI, UNE FARCE RELEVÉE DE FOIE GRAS
DUCK NECK WITH A *FOIE GRAS*-ENRICHED STUFFING

LÉGUMES D'ÉTÉ À LA VAPEUR 'LE PRADIÉ'
STEAMED SUMMER VEGETABLES

Château Vignelaure 1985
Côteaux d'Aix-en-Provence rouge

ROULADE DE PORC RÔTIE FOURRÉE
DE CRÈME DE NOIX AU PERSIL
ROAST PORK ROLL WITH A WALNUT
AND PARSLEY CREAM FILLING

SAUTÉ DE BLETTES À L'HUILE DE NOIX
SWISS CHARD SAUTÉED IN WALNUT OIL

ASSORTIMENT DE POMMES DE TERRE
EN ROBES DES CHAMPS
ASSORTED POTATOES IN THEIR SKINS

Château Mouton-Rothschild 1951   Pauillac

SALADE VERTE AUX FEUILLES DE BASILIC
GREEN SALAD WITH BASIL LEAVES

UNE SALADE AUX TROIS FRUITS ROUGES
A SALAD OF THREE RED FRUITS

Château de Carles 1983   Fronsac

Café

Château de Jau 1987   Muscat de Rivesaltes

RIGHT: *Bernard Dufour was one of forty-three artists invited by Château Mouton-Rothschild between 1924 and 1987 to produce a work especially for its label. For the 1963 vintage he painted a nude woman holding a cluster of grapes. The accompanying text –* 'Ainsi, quand des raisins, j'ai sucé la clarté' – *is from* 'L'Après-midi d'un faune' *by Stéphane Mallarmé.*

COU DE CANARD FARCI

In the traditional cuisine of the southwest, every part of the duck or goose is used. In this dish, the skin around the neck makes a natural sausage-shaped casing for a forcemeat. (Unless you are working with a force-fed goose or duck, however, you will need the necks of two ducks for the amount of filling given here.) If ducks with their necks attached are not available, the skin from the breast can be sewn up to form the same tubular shape.

1 duck weighing 1–1.5 kg (2–3 lb), dressed
2 tbs cognac
50 g (2 oz) back fat (fatback), diced
450 g (1 lb) lean pork, minced
100 g (3½ oz) purée de foie gras (optional)
2 shallots, finely chopped
1 tbs vegetable oil (plus 2 tbs if you are roasting the neck)
salt and freshly ground pepper
1 litre (1¾ pints/5 cups) duck fat (if you are cooking the neck en confit)

1. Remove the wings and legs from the duck and cut through the skin around the breast to obtain one large squarish piece. Separate the skin from the meat around the edges with your fingers. Towards the centre of the breast the skin is attached more firmly and must be cut away carefully with a short-bladed knife without making any holes. Trim the skin into a square, fold in half with the inside facing

out, and sew up the long side and one end with a needle and thread. Turn the casing right-side out and reserve.

2. Remove and reserve the liver. Bone the legs and thighs, trimming away all tendons. Cut the meat into small cubes and marinate in the cognac for 1 hour. Pass it through a mincer (meat grinder) fitted with a medium disc, together with the liver and fat. Combine with the pork and optional *foie gras*.

3. Sauté the shallots in 1 tbs oil until soft and translucent, cool, and combine with the minced meat and seasoning. Poach or pan-fry a spoonful of the forcemeat and taste for seasoning. Using a piping bag, fill the skin casing completely. Sew up the open end and preheat oven to 165°C (325°F) if you are cooking the neck in fat, and to 180°C (350°F) if you are roasting it.

4. For the first method, melt the fat slowly in a deep earthenware dish, submerge the neck and cook for 3 hours. Leave in the fat to cool completely. For the second method, rub the neck with 2 tbs oil and roast, basting often with water or stock, for approx 1 hour, or until the juices run clear. For best results, chill overnight, remove the skin, slice and serve.

LÉGUMES D'ÉTÉ À LA VAPEUR 'LE PRADIÉ'

Steaming this traditional medley of vegetables brings out their vibrant colours and individual flavours. Using perfectly fresh, umblemished produce is crucial.

5 cloves garlic, peeled
1 bunch fresh thyme
3 sprigs fresh rosemary
2 bay leaves
¼ tbs black peppercorns
4 small red or purple onions, cut into wedges
2 medium courgettes, cut into medium slices
3 medium bell peppers (red and green), cut into thick slices
2 small aubergines, cut into medium slices
3 tbs red wine vinegar
125 ml (4½ fl oz/½ cup) olive oil
salt and freshly ground pepper

1. Slice 4 of the garlic cloves in half and place with the herbs and peppercorns in the bottom of a large steamer filled with water. (A large pot fitted with a bamboo steamer works well.) Bring to the boil, add the onions and steam for 5 mins. Add the

ROULADE DE PORC RÔTIE FOURÉE DE CRÈME DE NOIX AU PERSIL

1 boneless centre-cut loin of pork weighing approx 1.5–2 kg (3–4 lb), trimmed and butterflied
90 ml (3 fl oz/6 tbs) walnut oil
salt and freshly ground pepper
1 bunch flat-leaf parsley, finely chopped
100 g (3½ oz/¾ cup) walnuts, finely chopped
4 cloves garlic, peeled and finely chopped

1. Preheat oven to 190°C (375°F). Lay the pork out flat, sprinkle with 1 tbs of the oil and season. Combine the parsley, walnuts, garlic, seasoning and all but 1 tbs of the remaining oil. Spread evenly over the meat, roll into a neat roast and tie securely with string. Rub the pork with the

courgettes and peppers and steam until tender but not soft. Transfer to a serving platter.

2. If your steamer is aluminium, line it with cheesecloth to prevent the aubergines darkening. Steam the aubergines, checking for done-ness after a few minutes; they will cook very quickly. They are ready when soft to the touch of a fork. Add to the platter.

3. Crush the remaining garlic in a garlic press and whisk the garlic purée into the vinegar and seasoning. Trickle in the oil whilst continuing to whisk. Drizzle over the vegetables, toss, and serve at room temperature.

remaining oil and season. Roast, seam-side up and basting often, for 35–45 mins, or until the juices run clear.

2. Transfer the meat to a serving platter and let rest for 10 mins in a warm place. Remove string, slice and cover. Pour off the fat from the roasting pan, deglaze with a little water and reduce until syrupy. Spoon over the pork slices and serve.

BELOW: *Created by Bernard Dufour, this dish is a light variation on* ratatouille *that does not include tomatoes. The vegetables are steamed over herbs and dressed with garlic vinaigrette.*

SAUTÉ DE BLETTES À L'HUILE DE NOIX

A neglected vegetable that is perfectly suited to this fragrant oil of the southwest.

8–10 stalks Swiss chard, trimmed, with leaves and stalks separated
4 tbs walnut oil
salt

Cut the chard into medium pieces, keeping the stems and leaves separate. Heat the oil and sauté the stem pieces until softened. Add the leaves and salt and continue to cook until the leaves are tender. Arrange the chard around the pork and serve.

3 Courances – *château pas cher*

T HE FRENCH do not really approve of Château de Courances – too untidy, too many gewgaws, too irreverent. Too un-French!

'A lot of people say it's very pretty but that they wouldn't dare,' says Lauraine de Ganay, who heads one of three independent Ganay households installed at Courances, the Louis XIII château near Fontainebleau. 'It's not beige and beige and beige like a lot of French houses.'

'I suppose this kind of house in France is usually more purist,' says her mother Philippine, who has the title of Marquise. 'I think I've included many more things than one normally finds in French châteaux, don't you? *Country Life* called it "French grandeur with English messiness". That sounds right to me.'

ABOVE: *The pretty west wing of Courances is occupied by Lauraine de Ganay's sister Anne-Marie. The canal is part of the elaborate pattern of water effects on the estate which are fed by many natural springs. The ornamental lake on the other side of the house is the site of elaborate family picnics that take place ceremonially from Easter onwards.*

LEFT: *Lauraine de Ganay had her revenge on the French decorating establishment by swamping the dining room with Laura Ashley wallpaper and fabric. A semi-professional cook with no formal training, she made the* bavarois, *served with blackcurrant sauce, using rhubarb from the château* potager. *Only the stalks of rhubarb are ever eaten; the fan-like leaves contain a poisonous acid that is employed as a bleaching and cleaning agent.*

Courances started to earn that un-holy description in 1974 when, on the death of her father-in-law, Philippine and her husband Jean-Louis moved 'upstairs' from the west wing to rather more luxurious apartments in the main, central part of the château. The grandeur had already been organized – richly carved walnut *boiseries* and lavishly upholstered Napoleon III chairs and sofas combined with furniture produced under every Louis from Louis XIII to Louis XVI. 'All the good stuff was here,' says the Marquise, walking through the *couloir des invités* with a walkie-talkie that keeps her in touch with the front gate, through which paying visitors pass. 'I just added the bits and pieces, the fringes, the cushions, the carpets – all the things one *could* add with a good base. Courances was always comfortable; I made it cosy.'

The padded sense of warmth, ease and 'messiness' she contributed took a little money and a lot of mettle: flea-market cast-offs and variety-store baubles are gaily tossed in with the good stuff in spaces of otherwise imposing formality and elegance. According to Lauraine's

sister Anne-Marie, who owns the Juste Mauve interior design shop in Paris, Philippine is 'a genius with houses'. Her talent for making a room mean more than the sum of its furniture is always traced to her mother the Duchesse de Mouchy, and to the Marquise's aunt and uncle, the art patrons Marie-Laure and Charles de Noailles.

'Mummy loves those thick gold plastic rococo frames, the kind that usually come with a picture of a stag on a shiny background,' says Lauraine. 'You wouldn't give it to your maid, but she gets out her paintbox, gives it an antique or malachite finish, and frames a worthless old watercolour. If she needs a mount for a picture she'll take the marbled back cover of a gardening catalogue and make it out of that. When fancy invitations arrive on heavy decorative paper, she cuts them up and uses them to cover matchboxes in the salon. Instead of having an ugly matchbox you have a pretty one. No one can believe that the fabric and paper in the dining room in my part of the house is Laura Ashley. Everybody thinks Laura Ashley is just for bathrooms and

ABOVE: *By placing the bed she inherited from her paternal grandmother on a platform, Lauraine de Ganay made sense of its heroic proportions. The lamp belonged to her other grandmother, the Duchesse de Mouchy, the one with the flair for decorating.*

OPPOSITE: *In the more formal and imposing of two salons in Philippine de Ganay's apartments, the rich cloth covering a table was cut down from a woman's dress dating from the time of Louis XV. Placed around the eighteenth-century Chinese lamp are a baton of star anise, a Louis XVI paperweight in the form of dolphins, an alabaster hand found in the park by one of the Marquise's daughters as a child, and an antique Greek bronze.*

children's rooms. But Mummy and I have got the Braquenié that all French people buy coming out of our ears.'

Philippine's many entertaining impertinences encourage at Courances a way of life calculated to please an extended family that includes packs of unfailingly polite but unstoppable children. The mirror basin in the garden designed or inspired by Le Nôtre serves as a swimming pool; rooms are raced through; furniture flopped into; and hide-and-seek played in the deep folds of long draperies. Everything is used, fondled, admired, enjoyed. 'It may look like a castle,' says the dress designer Karl Lagerfeld, 'but Courances is really just a very well-lived-in family home.'

It follows that the culinary tradition at the château is one of *cuisine bourgeoise de femme*, as Lauraine describes it, not *grande cuisine de chef*. Lurdès Quintanillo, the Portuguese cook who runs the kitchen for the Marquise, is also her frighteningly efficient housekeeper and a very accomplished flower arranger.

'As children we ate very good, basic, plain French cuisine – good, but not sophisticated,' says Lauraine. 'Soufflés, skate *au beurre noir*, which we eat more sensibly today *aux fines herbes à la crème* – you see the sort of thing. My mother hates pompous food, which might explain a lot of it. We also had things like gazpacho and savoury pies, which are not at all French. Ninety-nine per cent of the French hate the kind of plain fruit gelatin that's eaten for dessert in America and we loved it. As the Ganays don't have a reputation for being mad on food, I'm thought of as the crazy caterer in the family. Mummy always asked why the hell I did a Spanish degree if I was going to end up in the kitchen. It bores her so she's quite astonished and amused that one of her daughters turned to cooking.'

For fifteen years, beginning in 1971, Lauraine ran a successful one-woman catering business out of her rue de la Pompe apartment, offering dishes unavailable from any other prepared-foods operation or shop in Paris. One did not go to Lauraine for anything as banal as *chaud-froid de poulet*. One went to her for pâté of smoked salmon, buttery carrot mousseline, *snob au chocolat* – a dessert she likens to eating truffles with a spoon – and her bestselling *porc à l'ancienne* – an autumnal ragout of pork, red wine, shallots, raisins, honey, dill and mint.

'The French, and I'm talking about the French with a capital "F", are very narrow-minded when it comes to food,' says Lauraine. 'They have no originality and no creativity. When they entertain at home they either have their own chef and it's good and pompous, or you see from a mile away that it's from one of those big catering outfits like Lenôtre. A lobster all tied up in a starched napkin or some bird in two inches of jelly looking like it's about to fly out the window – all that can be very good, but *merci, non*. The kind of catering I did just isn't part of the French food mentality. Although the French are less complicated than they used to be, there still aren't twenty-five people in Paris doing what I used to do the way there are in London. It is still impossible to imagine the equivalent of a Mrs Snooks arriving with the food for a private bank luncheon.'

Lauraine's clients, many of whom were friends as well, had some trouble understanding how she could be selling her cooking services for a dinner which she was also meant to attend. But for the chef there was no conflict. She would deliver the food, chose the serving dishes, change her dress, and grab a cocktail. Rather than use the French word *traiteur* and risk being slotted in with Lenôtre, she would tell people she was a caterer. 'By that they thought I meant I was the *chef d'orchestre* with a team of minions working under me. People had a hard time realizing that it was the Comtesse de Ganay of Château de Courances who was actually whipping the *crème Chantilly*.'

From the outside Lauraine's share of Courances is regarded as the rather unlovely link between her parents' quarters and the graceful one-storey wing now occupied by her sister Anne-Marie. Except for this link the château one sees today was built by Gilles Le Breton for Claude Gallard, who acquired the estate in 1662 and who was counsellor and secretary to Louis XIII. When the present Marquis's great-great-grandfather the Baron de Haber bought it in 1870 the house had been abandoned for forty years. The Baron did good and bad things for Courances, 1,250 acres of which are now farmed for corn, wheat and sugar beet. He employed the architect Destailleurs to restore the château and Achille Duchêne to work on the gardens. But this being '*l'époque des splendeurs*', he also ordered dubious '*embellissements*': a more substantial building marrying the two parts of the house, and a huge double staircase

OPPOSITE: *An assortment of 'printed' wafers, rye crackers and a whole-wheat roll is discovered by each guest as he takes his place for dinner. The marquetry table of mixed fruitwoods was bought by the Marquise Philippine de Ganay at the* marché aux puces *at Saint-Ouen just outside Paris and, in a pattern now familiar to her family, stored until it could be put to use. The bone butter knives were bought by Lauraine de Ganay in China, and the celadon Limoges porcelain is from Casa Pascal, a seconds shop in Paris.*

based on the one at Fontainebleau and grafted clumsily onto the façade.

'The second half of the nineteenth century was a disastrous time of very bad taste in France,' says Lauraine. 'People with money thought their houses were not grand enough. As a result, mine are the largest rooms in the château. But the nicest houses in France belonged to people who were broke at that time.'

Married to her second cousin Serge, Lauraine moved into Courances in 1987 when her grandmother's apartments became available after her death. The space she inherited was painted 'that dirty-looking *vert Louis XVI*' and hung with 'wishy-washy' tapestries, reflecting the slow life and dusty taste of a genteel old lady whose greatest need was privacy – hardly suitable for Lauraine and her young brood. The brightest yellow was splashed on the walls in the bathroom with art nouveau tiles, and the famous Laura Ashley fabric put up where the tapestries used to hang in the oak-panelled corridor, which also serves as the dining room.

The small unglamorous kitchen where Lauraine prepared the meal shown here was formerly a maid's room. The first course, *clafouti* of haddock, can also be made with odd bits of leftover salmon, the difficult-to-use tail – or even a tin of tuna. The wine, Chevalier de Malle, is a dry white she chooses for the sweet *arrière-goût* of the same estate's Sauternes, Château de Malle. The main course, served with tricolour tortellini, was created by Lauraine as a way of using game from the freezer in summer. Wild duck and pheasant are simmered in aromatic vegetable broth, boned and tossed with fresh tarragon and cider vinaigrette. Serge de Ganay has a small interest in the accompanying wine, Les Forts de Latour, stepchild of the great Pauillac, Château Latour. A *2ème cru classé*, Les Forts is made from the grapes of younger vines inside the walled Latour vineyards as well as from those grown outside them. But the style of the two wines is similar: big and well-built.

The entire menu, including the *bavarois* made with rhubarb from the

ABOVE: 'Couloir des invités' *refers to the fact that all the rooms off the long corridor are guest rooms. Philippine de Ganay gave each of the six bookcases on the window side of the gallery a different* trompe l'oeil *finish. The pictures on the walls are a typical mixture of the good – Serrebriakoff, Walter Gay – and the worthless.*

potager, or kitchen garden, conforms to Lauraine's creed that 'everything's got to be ready before I have my bath.

'The various apartments within a château like this one don't generally have dining rooms near the kitchen; they're at the other end of the house, so it's not as if the *maîtresse de maison* can look after her meal and guests at the same time. The only thing I agree to do once people have arrived is reheat.'

The speciality at the château's formal game dinners – tuxedos for the men, long dresses and best jewellery for the women, Philippine's brother's Château Haut-Brion on the table – is the thinly sliced liver of a wild boar killed the same day. When Lurdès the cook gets it the liver is still warm from the animal's body. 'Most people don't take it the first time it's passed around, but then they taste their neighbour's and have a helping of their own,' says Lauraine. 'Fried black like a steak, it's not the prettiest thing to look at, but it's tastier and finer than calves liver. And I don't know anywhere you can eat it besides Courances. We also marinate the leg of the boar for a week in an

earthenware crock with red wine, herbs and vinegar. But game when it's too high, forget it. If you can smell it coming through the kitchen door, it's ready for the bin.'

The shooting season for pheasant, wild duck, hare and rabbit at the château begins in mid-October and a month later for stag and boar. 'The wild boar shoot here is absolutely A-1, first rate, really the best,' says the Marquise. Photographs showing twelve guns around a tableau of eighty boar document the record held at Courances. 'Unfortunately, there are no partridges left and the pheasant shoot is normal. For dinner on shooting weekends there is a butler for each of the four tables of eight, an arrangement that makes *placement* very easy. I can put Anne-Marie with one guest of honour, Lauraine with another, like that. But I think *l'art de recevoir* is changing in France, or at least I hope it is. French people who try to maintain the pompous grandeur of the old days are pathetic. If you can't have a butler, and all you've got is a poor little Spanish maid struggling around the table with a huge silver dish, isn't it more chic

BELOW: *When the death of the Marquise Hubert de Ganay made apartments in the château available to Lauraine, she converted her grandmother's oak-panelled bedroom into a salon and furnished it with an enthusiasm learned from her mother. People who make a game of following the evolving decoration of Courances are able to spot pieces once found in other parts of the house.*

to have a buffet? In England, even in grand houses, they know how to do things simply and well. You bring your own dirty plate through, that kind of thing.'

Shooting weekends at Courances set the standard for country house living in France. In the morning, trays filled with pretty old silver and blue and white 'Mettlach' breakfast china from Villeroy and Boch are carried up to the guest rooms. The Marquise takes such care with the books she puts out, titles that demonstrate what keen anglophiles the Ganays are, it is all too easy to miss the first drive. How to choose between a first edition Nancy Mitford (who knew Courances) and an Anita Brookner? *Carnets d'un Bécassier* and Nevil Shute? Isabel Colegate and the autobiography of Consuelo Vanderbilt Balsan? Hemingway and *Cocktails & Laughter, the Albums of Loelia Lindsay*? If none of these pleases, there is this month's *Harpers* or *Tatler*, or today's *Herald Tribune* or *Figaro*.

On the dressing table there is a shoehorn, a sewing kit, and a shrivelled orange stuck with cloves nestling in a bowl of pot-pourri. A writing table across the room is furnished with a sheaf of stationery, postcards of the house and park, and a guide to the Essonne. Hanging beside the full-length mirror is a good nylon clothes brush. Alka-Seltzer, aspirin, mineral water and boiled sweets from Dalloyau are set out on a sprigged porcelain tray on the dresser, and a fluffy Glen Cree mohair blanket is folded at the end of the chaise longue. While the bedside table is crowded with a candlestick, a funny note pad in the form of a cauliflower, and 'After-Cake' mini-tissues in a box printed with a kiwi tart, a sleeping mask is slipped over the bedpost. (This mask allows those not participating in the shoot to nap in the afternoon without the bother of drawing the curtains.) The bathroom is stocked with a Porthault shower cap, a Bassetti terry robe, a fresh box of magnolia soap from Marks & Spencer, Wilberg's Pine Bath Essence, and a velvet-covered hot-water bottle tied up with ribbon. To prevent the 1870 copper tub from staining green and the guest from going mad, a hand towel is placed under the taps to catch the drips.

Here and throughout Courances, Philippine de Ganay makes the point that having the right pedigree can be more profitable than attending the best design school or hiring the most fashionable decorator. Marie-Laure de Noailles knew that a Bérard looked even better next to a Le Bernin; that the only way to take a bath was surrounded by faded bouquets; that a rare bronze looked even rarer beside a ripe green apple; and that posing a kitsch postcard of a Spanish dancer next to a little Cranach did good things for both of them. The Marquise's mother collected pictures from second-hand shops and stuck them with labels cut from the gold covers of expensive chocolate boxes. 'Given by the King,' she always wrote, without of course saying which king or to whom he had given the picture. 'This is the family recipe,' says Lauraine de Ganay, 'people are always trying to understand.'

LEFT: *Early September – an* allée *of plane trees. The château offers both the romantic atmosphere of its leafy* allées *and the cool reserve of its parterres à la française, embroidered with plumes of box.*

ABOVE: *Some guests are horrified to learn that the walls in the main kitchen (not Lauraine de Ganay's) are covered not in tiles but paper. Meals were prepared here for the Germans who occupied the château during the war, for the Americans who turned it into a prisoner of war camp after the Germans were evicted, and for Field Marshal Montgomery, who was a permanent guest at Courances between 1947 and 1954 when he headed NATO at neighbouring Fontainebleau.*

MENU
for 8

CLAFOUTI D'HADDOCK
HADDOCK FLAN

GAUFRETTES 'IMPRIMÉES', PETITS PAINS COMPLETS,
CRACKERS AU SEIGLE
'PRINTED' WAFERS, WHOLEWHEAT ROLLS, RYE CRACKERS

Chevalier de Malle   Bordeaux Blanc

SALADE DE GIBIER À PLUME SAUVAGE
À L'ESTRAGON FRAIS
FEATHERED GAME SALAD WITH FRESH TARRAGON

SALADE DE TORTELLINI TRICOLORE
TRICOLOUR TORTELLINI SALAD

VINAIGRETTE AU CIDRE
CIDER VINAIGRETTE

Les Forts de Latour 1976   Pauillac

BAVAROIS À LA RHUBARB DE COURANCES
ET SON COULIS DE CASSIS
RHUBARB BAVARIAN CREAM WITH BLACKCURRANT SAUCE

Café

CLAFOUTI D'HADDOCK

For Lauraine de Ganay, it is the smoothness of the *clafouti* contrasted with the crunchiness of watercress or alfalfa that makes this dish so successful.

400 g (14 oz) smoked haddock
300 ml (10¼ fl oz/1⅓ cups) milk
450 g (1 lb/2 cups) cottage cheese
3 eggs
1 tbs cornflour
4 tbs chopped chives, plus strands for
  decoration
freshly ground pepper
1 bunch watercress or alfalfa

1. Soak the haddock in milk overnight. Transfer to a saucepan and bring to the boil. Let cool for 5 mins. Strain and crumble the fish into small flakes, discarding the skin and any bones. Preheat oven to 180°C (350°F).
2. In a food processor, whip the cheese and eggs together until light and fluffy. Fold in the cornflour diluted in 2 tbs water, fish, chives and pepper. Generously oil a 20 cm (8 in) flan dish, add the filling and bake for approx 50 mins, or until a knife inserted in the middle comes out clean. Cool for approx 5 mins, and turn out onto a serving dish. Decorate with chive strands, surround with watercress or alfalfa, dressed with vinaigrette or not, and serve.

LEFT: *With no proper dining room, meals are served in the oak-panelled corridor with chinoiserie above the doors. Everything is wilfully mismatched: tables are round and square, covered and not. The tureen in the foreground is Compagnie des Indes.*

OPPOSITE ABOVE: *Wearing a spangled evening dress, Lauraine de Ganay came as the Princess of Wales to a fancy-dress party held at Courances to celebrate the birthdays of three members of the extended Ganay family.*

OPPOSITE BELOW: *The term 'clafouti', traditionally describing a fruit flan, is borrowed for this smoked haddock dish. Wild game salad is a good example of the kind of food that earned Lauraine de Ganay her reputation as a caterer.*

SALADE DE GIBIER À PLUME SAUVAGE À L'ESTRAGON FRAIS

The delicious broth could become its own soup course or kept to make a rich, gamy sauce for another meal.

4 stalks celery, tops trimmed
1 onion, stuck with 4 cloves
2 carrots, roughly chopped
1 leek with its pale green top, roughly chopped
1 bunch fresh tarragon, leaves and stems separated
1 bouquet garni of thyme, bay leaf and tarragon stems
1 wild duck weighing approx 1–1.5 kg (2–3 lb)
1 wild pheasant weighing approx 450 g (1 lb)
1 tbs coarse salt
1 tbs black peppercorns
2 shallots, finely chopped
salt and freshly ground pepper
vinaigrette au cidre (recipe follows)
350 g (12 oz) fresh tricolour tortellini, cooked and drained

1. Chop 1 of the celery stalks and place in a large stockpot along with the onion, carrots, leeks, bouquet garni and 2 litres (3½ pints/2 quarts) water. Simmer, covered, for 30 mins. Cool slightly.
2. Remove the 2 leg and thigh joints from the duck and cut through the ribs to separate the breast from the back. (Keep back for another use.) Place the leg–thigh pieces in the broth, followed by the breasts and whole pheasant. Add the salt and peppercorns, and water to cover. Place a plate on top of the birds to keep them submerged as they cook. Barely simmer over a very low heat, never allowing the liquid to boil, for 2 hours. Leave the game in the broth to cool completely.
3. Remove the meat from the birds, cutting it into small cubes and reserving approx 12 julienne strips sliced from the breast. Dice the remaining celery, reserve the leaves of one of the tarragon stems and chop the rest. Toss these with the cubed meat, shallots, salt, pepper and just enough viniagrette to moisten the ingredients. Mound the salad on a serving dish, drape over the julienned breast meat and sprinkle with the reserved tarragon. Toss the tortellini with the remaining vinaigrette, arrange around the salad, and serve.

VINAIGRETTE AU CIDRE

1 tsp Dijon mustard
60 ml (2 fl oz/¼ cup) cider vinegar
salt and freshly ground pepper
250 ml (9 fl oz/1 cup) vegetable oil

Whisk together the mustard, vinegar and seasoning. Trickle in the oil whilst continuing to whisk.

BAVAROIS À LA RHUBARB DE COURANCES ET SON COULIS DE CASSIS

The fruit sauce might just as well be one of redcurrants or blackberries.

2 tbs unflavoured powdered gelatin
200 g (7 oz/1 cup) sugar
800 g (1¾ lb) fresh rhubarb, trimmed and cut into small pieces
200 ml (7 fl oz/generous ¾ cup) double/heavy cream

1. In a saucepan dissolve the sugar in 350 ml (12 fl oz/1½ cups) water and bring to the boil. Skim off impurities and simmer for 2 mins. Sprinkle the gelatin over a little cold water and let stand for 5 mins. Add the rhubarb to the saucepan and cook over a medium heat until tender. Purée in a food processor.
2. While the rhubarb is still hot, add the gelatin and mix thoroughly. Chill until the mixture begins to set. Whip the cream in a chilled bowl until soft peaks form. Stir one spoonful into the purée, then carefully fold in the rest.
3. Transfer the Bavarian cream to a 1.5 litre (2½ pint/1½ quart) porcelain or glass soufflé dish and chill for 4–5 hours. To unmould, run a knife around the edge, dip the dish in a basin of hot water for a few seconds and immediately invert onto a chilled dish and serve.

COULIS DE CASSIS

150 g (5 oz/¾ cup) sugar
450 g (1 lb) blackcurrants

Dissolve the sugar in 125 ml (4½ fl oz/½ cup) water and bring to the boil. Skim off impurities and simmer for 2 mins. Add the fruit and cook over a medium heat until the blackcurrants just begin to burst. Purée in a food processor and pass the mixture through a sieve to eliminate stalks and seeds. Chill and serve.

THE GERS was the last *département* in France to be wired for electricity. Until 1957 the village of Peyrusse Massas was still without current or running water, and until 1984 one pay phone installed in a private house in Bellegrade served the entire *commune*. When the Michelin two-star chef André Daguin in Auch needed to place a rush order for two dozen pigeons or three kilos of blackcurrants with one of his suppliers, Mimi Galey, he was obliged to leave a message with her neighbours down the road.

In addition to furnishing André Daguin's Hôtel de France with game and produce and flowers, Mimi Galey has a table at the Saturday market in winter in Auch and at the Wednesday market in spring in Lannemezan.

ABOVE: *Mimi Galey began supplying flowers to the restaurant of the Hôtel de France in Auch in 1958; today, her cutting garden still brightens the place with daisies, sunflowers, zinnias, dahlias and gladioli. In addition, Mme Galey furnishes the original proprietor's son, chef André Daguin, with Swiss chard, cherry tomatoes, courgettes, aubergines, peas, green beans, mulberries, blackcurrants and raspberries.*

RIGHT: *The part of daily life at Au Perdreau that takes place indoors centres almost exclusively on the kitchen. After lunch every day Mme Galey and André Lébé take their places in chairs flanking a coal- and wood-burning stove, used only in winter for cooking and heating. The tray of redcurrants on top of it will be made into jam. The goose wings hung in the fireplace are used for dusting and sweeping crumbs from the dining table.*

ABOVE: *One school of cassoulet scholars insists that the dish was originally made with* tarbais *beans. Like all cassoulet experts, Mimi Galey admits no other recipe for this celebrated dish of the southwest than her own. She painstakingly cultivates her own famously tender* tarbais *at Au Perdreau.*

OPPOSITE: *The table in the little-used dining room, which also serves as a salon, has been laid by women in Mme Galey's family with the same handwoven linen cloth for two hundred years. The doors of the cherry-wood armoire, dated 1768, are carved with diamond facets.*

'But I'm going to tell you something: this isn't at all the life I was destined for,' she says. 'Both my parents were *beaux-arts* professors; they both painted, my mother better than my father; and I studied in Bordeaux to be a chartered accountant. But my father's father lost all his money at the baccarat table, and in 1920, when I was three years old, my parents divorced. I only got two years of studies in before World War II, and when I came home after it was all over, I found my mother and granny Lamothe living in this house in Les Adoulins where generations of Lamothes have lived since 1648. *Voilà*, that's how we found ourselves all thrown back together again, and I stayed on to work the land. Like a man.'

The Lamothe house in the south-western region of Gascony turns its back on the *route départementale*. Squat and stolid, with a *crepi*, or roughcast, façade coloured ochre from the earth, it looks immovable. The property is known in patois as Au Perdigat, or Au Perdreau, after the great number of partridges that once nested here before pesticides killed them off. Although the house has two levels, since 1984 Mimi and her companion André Lébé, a man whose gentle and accommodating nature people always remark on, have organized their lives exclusively on the ground floor, closing off the top by hanging a horse blanket halfway up the first flight of stairs. On the other side of the blanket is a mountain of broken treasures – a rich bazaar for dealers who make their living selling other people's odds and ends. They are watching Au Perdreau.

A *personnage culinaire* in the Gers, the spiritual and gastronomic soul of Gascony, Mimi Galey recites recipes for fricassee of cockscombs ('tastes like brains'), stuffed boiled hen ('Henri IV ate one every Sunday for supper'), a winter vinaigrette that substitutes goose fat for oil, and *pastis*. To make a *pastis*, apple slices marinated in Armagnac and orange blossom water are baked in flaky pastry as thin as cigarette paper, made with one part butter to four parts flour. It is one of the great specialities of Gascony, though few *pâtissiers* are prepared to observe Mimi's proportions and part with that much butter.

'*Une bonne table*' in the Gers means soup, eggs, *saucisson*, *alicuit*, cassoulet, stew, turkey, duck, chicken, partridge, hare, apple tart and *c'est tout*,' says Mimi. (*Alicuit* is a traditional ragout of poultry

giblets and wings, carrots, onions and potatoes.) 'There is also wine of course and Armagnac, but no cheese. We don't even like milk. It was the Italians who brought cheese here when they arrived in 1922. And the cheesemakers you see at the markets today are neither Gersois nor Gascon.

'Every *département* has its own way of eating and living. So what goes on in the Haute-Garonne has nothing to do with here. As for new-wave dishes like duck breast with blackcurrants, or *foie gras* with apples, they are false, silly inventions. They're like asking me to believe that the English eat cold chicken with gooseberry jam.'

Pictures of Mimi Galey show her to have been a handsome young woman with a strong, watchful gaze. Today she is enthusiastic about politics, and roots for the right. Her newspaper is *Le Figaro*. Mimi is equally informed about the latest natural disaster as the latest Rothschild fancy-dress ball, where one guest, she will tell you, was reported to have been wearing a 500,000-franc sable coat. Earth-

quakes and hurricanes have made her a big fan of the Americans because, she says, they are always on the scene first with help and money. She says what she thinks, often remarking that modern French life is deplorable. She is annoyed and disheartened by people today always buying more and bigger cars and by their feverish need to be constantly bolting away on vacation. She loves dogs and talking on the telephone; drives a camel-coloured Citroën GSA; would not mind wearing perfume but cannot, because the bees come out of their hives and chase her; and uses the same pair of secateurs in the kitchen for cutting up chickens as she does for clipping daisies in the garden. Her only regret, she says, is that she has never piloted a supersonic fighter plane.

'*Je reçois avec les ingrédients de la maison*,' says Mimi, although she is not quite sure that the word *recevoir*, or receive, describes how she entertains her friends and three children. One daughter owns the local discotheque, another is married to an Italian and lives in Italy, and her son is the watchman at the Hôtel

ABOVE: *Pigeons are raised for sale to private clients, the chef André Daguin in Auch, and market-goers in Auch and Lannemezan.*

de France. 'L'art de recevoir in France is practised by *un certain milieu très bourgeois*,' says Mimi. 'It's always the rich with the rich, and people of average means with others the same. You'll never see well-to-do French people entertaining anyone less well-off than themselves. For my part, I detest affected people. I like simple things and simple people. I can appreciate a well-dressed woman in Saint Laurent couture, but it wouldn't please me for myself. I would have to say that I am more interested in music, in painting, in how people live.'

Although Mimi says that she 'needs light' and 'hates the dark', Au Perdreau is habitually shuttered, even in summer. Inside the house the air is still, cold and heavy. The light is splintered; many of the ceiling bulbs are hidden in curious globes wound with coarse, hairy rope. If one were serious about wanting to read one of the volumes by Camus or Malraux or de Maupassant which lie on the shelves in the entrance hall, one would do better to take them and move out on to the bench in the farmyard.

Throughout the house are scattered souvenirs of Mimi's parents' *beaux-arts*

days: busts, books, objects, and their own paintings. In the dining room, beside the study of a classical discus thrower that won her mother a place at art school, a print of Boucher's *La Leçon de Musique* is pinned up. A sinister seventeenth-century Dutch-school oil of the Crucifixion in the same room is strikingly like one in the Musée de Bordeaux – 'though nobody is sure about which of us has the original.' A similar story is attached to *La Belle Inconnue* in a niche above the sink in the kitchen. 'Daguin has the same sculpture at the hotel in a room that costs 1200 francs a night, but here we know that his is the copy.' The pretty filigree sugar-bowl on the table was the bonus at the bottom of a basket of sheet music bought by Mimi's mother at an auction in Bordeaux the same day she bid successfully for the Crucifixion painting.

She loved Chopin, and at one time her playing filled Au Perdreau. But if anything can be heard today through the hissing, clucks and squawks of forty geese and three hundred chickens, ducks and pigeons, it is much more likely to be Piaf.

While André Lébé works 10 hectares (25 acres) of corn, wheat, barley and oats

for the grain to feed the birds, any surplus is sent to the cooperative in Masseube to offset the costs of cultivation. 'Looking after birds is slavery,' he says, 'and we look after them from the time they are born until they are slaughtered, plucked, prepared and delivered to the client ready to go into the oven. We have ten or twelve private customers for whom birds are killed to order, which is the only way we work. In our experience, it's the only practical and profitable way of doing it.

'Our chickens – *races gasconnes*, which are black with black feet, and white *poulets de Bresse* with blue feet – are firm and full of flavour. The flesh of industrially raised chickens is flabby and dull. You can taste the vitamins, fish flour, hormones and antibiotics in their diet. They only have a couple of centimetres to run

around in, and they're killed after a maximum of two months. Our birds really are free range; they run around for up to four months on 2 hectares.'

'That's all very well,' says Mimi, 'except that we have had clients who have gone up to Paris and got so used to commercial chicken that they don't like ours anymore. They want it so the leg just falls off. I'm going to tell you something: if people could, they would avoid eating altogether by simply buying a pill.'

Born in Auch, André drove a bulldozer for a living until 1965, when he became a farmer. 'Until recently my life as a farmer has pleased me. But now it's just got too much. I still work fourteen or fifteen hours a day in summer, following the sun, just as I did in the mid-Fifties before there were any labour laws. On

ABOVE: *Mimi Galey's mother painted the Gascon landscape that hangs above a Napoleon III clock on the desk in the entrance hall. The painting shows the Côteau de l'Arrast, with the Pyrenees in the distance.*

market days I can be loading the car until one o'clock in the morning and then be up at four to feed the birds before we leave for Auch or Lannemezan. For most farmers in France today it's thirty-five, thirty-six, thirty-seven hours a week, not more. But for me, getting up at eight o'clock on Sunday is like having the morning off.'

While Mimi describes the regional cuisine as *relativement simple mais bonne*, André Daguin, employing the same untreated produce from Au Perdreau, elevates it to the cosmos. At the Hôtel de France nectarines, *pêches de vigne* and *patissons* are all used in dishes with *foie gras*, the *patisson*, or white, flat squash-melon serving as the covered receptacle in which the fattened liver is cooked. Pigeons supplied by Mimi are prepared *en confit* (cooked and preserved in their own

fat), or bathed in truffle juice and vinegar. Daguin, the southwest's self-appointed food ambassador, often returns from his travels with seeds which he gives to Mimi to plant at Les Adoulins – exotic beans from Indonesia, new varieties of lettuce. Before Mimi started growing it, he says, broccoli did not exist in the area.

But even the well-bred pigeons and sugary broccoli of Au Perdreau are eclipsed by its *tarbais*. Named after the nearby city, it is the only dried bean that either Daguin or Mimi will consider using in that most disputatious of French dishes cassoulet. While some will shriek at the inclusion of tomatoes, for example, others will violently denounce a cook who refuses to include them. Mimi's cassoulet follows an *alicuit* to form the main course of the menu pictured here. It is composed

RIGHT: *Mimi Galey framed by wisteria.*

ABOVE: *Shutters in the bedroom are drawn against the midday heat, though the massively thick walls keep Au Perdreau efficiently cool. The portrait of Mimi Galey's maternal great-grandmother above the chair is by her father.*

OPPOSITE: *A late nineteenth-century portrait in the entrance hall.*

of duck or goose *confit*, fresh pork, fresh and garlic sausage, carrots, onions and garlic, and the precious, costly, cream-coloured *tarbais*. She insists that no other bean is as tender, and that unlike other varieties used for cassoulet, *tarbais* cook quickly. Their fine skins melt away during cooking and their texture is pleasantly floury. The parent plants like sandy soil and insist on being planted in the shade of corn so their stalks have something to wrap themselves around and climb up. And only corn will do. Mimi says you can put the bean beside a wooden stake and it will take no notice at all.

If few farmers have the courage to raise *tarbais*, it is hardly surprising. Harvested by hand, one by one, they demand an extraordinary amount of care and labour. In 1988 Mimi sold her crop for about 40 francs per kilo shelled and 15 francs per kilo unshelled. Besides being crucial to cassoulet, *tarbais* are used in *garbure*, the Béarnaise soup of pork, *confit* and cabbage, as well as in hot and cold salads dressed with vinaigrette. 'With a plateful of *tarbais* in front of you,' says a friend who often shares Mimi's table, 'it's impossible to realize the work and the incredible amount of patience that went into getting them there.'

When Mimi makes cassoulet in winter, assorted *charcuterie* is offered as hors d'oeuvres; in warm weather there are boiled green beans, sliced tomatoes, and hard-boiled eggs with mayonnaise. For dessert a small bowl of home-made raspberry jam is poised in the centre of a *tourteau*, a light breadlike ring variously flavoured with orange blossom water, lemon, orange, rum, vanilla and/or Grand Marnier. Colombar is the white apéritif wine, Côtes du Frontonnais the fruity red from north of Toulouse that is served with the meat dishes. Mimi buys the Frontonnais at discount directly from Daguin, who puts his name on a certain quantity from Château Bellevue.

'We work hard here, but we also have moments of repose,' says Mimi. '*L'argent ne fait pas le bonheur, malgré ce qu' on en fait.* We have our freedom, the pleasure of harvesting our own wheat – and we're obviously not rushing about on the *métro* all day, are we? We are responsible to no one. Don't you find that good? *Ma vie est comme ça.* In spite of everything, I've always done what pleased me.'

63

MENU
for 4

Colombar   Côtes de Gascogne
Cocktail de Fine Blanche et jus de pamplemousse
frais aux glaçons
Distilled white wine and fresh grapefruit juice cocktail,
on the rocks

———————

PRODUITS VARIÉS DE LA FERME EN HORS D'OEUVRES FROIDS

HARICOTS VERTS, SALADE DE TOMATES PERSILLEES.
OEUFS DURS MAYONNAISÉS
GREEN BEANS, TOMATO SALAD WITH PARSLEY,
HARD-BOILED EGGS WITH MAYONNAISE

Château Bellevue   Côtes du Frontonnais

———————

ALICUIT
A GERSOIS STEW OF POULTRY WINGS AND GIBLETS

———————

LE CASSOULET DE MIMI

———————

TOURTEAU À L'EAU DE FLEUR D'ORANGER
ACCOMPAGNÉ DE CONFITURE À LA FRAMBOISE
FESTIVE BREAD RING WITH ORANGE BLOSSOM WATER,
SERVED WITH RASPBERRY JAM

———————

Café
Eau-de-vie de mirabelles
Yellow plum eau-de vie

LEFT: *Pal at the window above the chicken coops.*

ALICUIT

In the spirit of not letting anything go to waste, this rural chicken dish may also include the tongue and testicles.

salt and freshly ground pepper
2 chicken wings with their tips, cut at the
  joints
1 chicken neck, cut in 4 pieces
1 'parson's nose'
4 gizzards, cleaned and halved
4 hearts
4 livers
2 tbs rendered chicken or duck fat
2 cloves garlic, peeled and halved
2 medium onions, diced into large pieces
2 medium carrots, peeled and diced into
  large pieces
2 medium waxy potatoes, peeled and cut
  into large chunks

Lightly season all the chicken pieces and brown them in the hot fat in a large pot. Add the garlic, onions, carrots and water to cover. Simmer, uncovered, for 1 hour, adding more water if necessary to keep the contents of the pot submerged. Add the potatoes and cook for 30 mins more. Correct seasoning and serve.

LE CASSOULET DE MIMI

Traditionally, this dish is prepared on top of the stove, then baked. In a move that will have the cassoulet authorities protesting, Mme Galey eliminates the baking completely. If preserved goose or duck is available, add it to the browned vegetables with the stock and cook for 20 mins before adding to the beans.

400 g (14 oz) tarbais or other dried white
  beans, soaked overnight and drained
225 g (8 oz) piece of unsmoked gammon or
  slab of streaky bacon, cut into 4 pieces
2 bay leaves
salt
2 tbs rendered duck fat or vegetable oil
2 onions, sliced
5 garlic cloves, peeled and chopped
1 carrot, peeled and cut into medium
  rounds
2 legs and 2 thighs of duck or goose, fresh
  or preserved
freshly ground pepper
home-made chicken or veal stock
8 thick slices saucisse de Toulouse
  (fresh pork sausage)
8 thick slices garlic sausage

RIGHT: *For dessert, Mme Galey offers her own raspberry jam with the traditional bread-like* tourteau. *The Lunéville service was part of her maternal grandmother's trousseau when she married in 1882.*

1. Place the beans in a large heavy pot, add cold water to cover, and simmer for 15 mins. Drain, rinse under cold water and return to the pot with the bacon, bay leaves and lightly salted water to cover. Simmer for 1 hour, or until the beans are tender.

2. Melt the fat in a second large pot large enough to hold the remaining ingredients and lightly brown the onions, garlic and carrot. Remove with a slotted spoon and brown the duck/goose. Return the vegetables to the pot, season and add stock to cover. Cook, covered, over a low heat, for 40 mins, adding more stock as needed. Add the sausages and cook for 20 mins more.

3. Arrange the contents of this pot on the beans in the other pot and pour over the stock. Cook, covered, over a low heat for 35–40 mins. Place the pork, duck/goose and vegetables in the middle of a serving dish, reducing the liquid if necessary, before pouring it over the meat. Surround with the beans and serve.

TOURTEAU PARFUMÉ À L'EAU DE FLEUR D'ORANGER, ACCOMPAGNÉ DE CONFITURE DE FRAMBOISES

There are many versions of this sweet bread, usually served on Sundays or holidays with home-made preserves. Because *tourteaux* keep well and are lovely toasted, you may want to consider doubling the recipe. An electric mixer can be used to work the dough as the hand method requires some strength.

21 g ($\frac{5}{8}$ oz) fresh compressed yeast
125 ml (4$\frac{1}{2}$ fl oz/$\frac{1}{2}$ cup) milk, warmed
500 g (18 oz/scant 3$\frac{3}{4}$ cups) flour
150 g (5 oz/$\frac{3}{4}$ cup) sugar
3 eggs, plus 1 yolk
1 tsp salt
2 tbs rum or cognac
2 tbs orange blossom water or fresh, strained orange or lemon juice
100 g (3$\frac{1}{2}$ oz/6$\frac{1}{2}$ tbs) unsalted butter, softened

1. Crumble the yeast into a large bowl, add the milk and stir to dissolve. Set aside for 5 mins. Mix in the remaining ingredients except the butter and egg yolk; the dough will be sticky. Holding the bowl firmly with one hand, aerate the dough by slapping it against the side of the bowl. Continue until smooth and elastic.

2. Incorporate the butter with the same slapping motion. Scrape down the sides of the bowl, cover with a damp tea towel, and refrigerate for 6–8 hours.

3. Turn the dough onto a floured surface and knead into a smooth ball. To form the characteristic ring shape, press your thumbs into the centre to make a hole and enlarge it evenly with your hands. Place the ring on a lightly buttered baking sheet, cover with a damp cloth and leave to rise at room temperature for approx 2 hours, or until doubled in volume.

3. Preheat oven to 205°C (400°F). Beat the egg yolk with 1 tsp water and brush the glaze over the top of the bread. Bake for 20 mins, turn the oven down to 180°C (350°F), and cook for approx 20 mins more, or until golden brown. Cool and serve.

5 The cult of the bull in the Camargue

'I AM a ranch owner first and an Arlésienne second,' says Annie Laurent, abruptly revealing what one most wants to know about her. 'If I had to choose between breeding bulls and horses and wearing the traditional dress of the Arlésienne, something very close to me that I have done spontaneously all my life, I would nevertheless choose the bulls and horses. I am a *manadière* by métier.'

ABOVE: *At Les Marquises, Annie and Henri Laurent serve* cartogène *as an apéritif, the home-made sweet wine of Provence; fleshy black olives, puffed rice cakes,* saucisson d'Arles *and* brandade de morue *are offered as accompaniments.*

LEFT: *In prehistory the sea covered what today are the marshlands of the Camargue. This natural frontier halted the passage of animals from Asia Minor across the continent, and the rude climate and meagre pastures shaped their own breed of bulls and horses –* pures races camarguaises. *The bulls – still completely wild – are muscular and sportive, capable of satisfying a people in need of distraction. The horses are small, measuring only 145 cm (14.2 hh) at the wither, but are tough enough to stand heavy work.*

Although it has been acceptable in the Camargue since the turn of the century for women to do the work Annie Laurent does, she has few peers. 'But I have no complex about it,' she says. 'I ride very well, and I know how to "select" the bull I want, driving it from the herd. I do it better than some men.'

If Annie Laurent is an anomaly charging through the salt marshes of the Camargue, it is her double life that makes her unique. After a day in regulation moleskin culottes and Souleïado print shirt, a day spent separating the calves from their mothers, it is not uncommon for her to host a dinner for friends *en Arlésienne*, meticulously coiffed and pinned into the elaborate native costume with complete historical accuracy. In both her lives, however, she is always fully and exquisitely *maquillée*.

It is always said that the women of *le pays d'Arles* owe their pure, classical features to the ancient Greeks, who colonized the city as a seaport. And over the centuries their dignified deportment and noble beauty became reasons enough to travel to Arles. 'I have an Arlésienne at last,' Van Gogh wrote to his brother Theo

in 1880, referring to his portrait of Madame Ginoux, the proprietor of the Café de la Gare where he rented a room. The artist painted her in the traditional narrow-sleeved bodice, ribbon cap and *fichu*, or small ornamental shawl.

Lying 92 kilometres (57 miles) north-west of Marseille, Arles was strategically situated and fell to the Romans during the first century BC, becoming the capital of Roman Gaul. In the fourth century AD it pleased the emperor Constantine so much that he chose it as his seat of power. Out of this presence grew one of the greatest expressions of French culture, Provençal Romanesque. Much of what one marvels at here today, and in neighbouring Aix, was built with stone stripped from Roman monuments. The architecture of Arles illustrates the unfolding of Western civilization more vividly than any other in France. Place de la République, the principal square, contains emblems from each of the city's three great epochs – an Augustan obelisk, the Romanesque cathedral of Saint-Trophîme, and the seventeenth-century Hôtel de Ville.

Arles is also the door to the Camargue, an alluvial delta of 950 square

ABOVE: *A feathery tamarisk, or tamarisso in Provençal – a tree intimately associated with the Camargue – flowers in front of the Laurents' whitewashed* mas, *or farmhouse, which was built in 1819.*

kilometres (367 square miles) regularly described as French cowboy country. While its lacy coast is lapped by the Mediterranean, the interior has a beauty that is gruff and disturbing, ruthless and unforgiving. In summer the heat is narcotic. Saltwort is one of the few shrubs courageous enough to push up through the vast clay plains known in Provençal as *sansouïro* – plains that are sometimes gorged with water and sometimes parched, cracked and crusted over with salt. Arlésiennes attending the various events organized around the bull are startlingly handsome in this setting: the contrast between their petticoated femininity and the brutishness of the weather and scenery could not be more complete.

Although no Alsatian pastry chef or Breton fisherman will admit it, the Camargue is perhaps the corner of France with the deepest sense of cultural continuity. In the same way, it is unlikely that other Provençaux will admit that it is the most sincere and in many ways the most essentially Provençal part of Provence.

At Les Marquises, the ranch Annie Laurent runs with her husband Henri and their son Patrick, guests gather in the amber light of early evening for apéritifs, a bottle of *cartogène* and its savoury accompaniments set out on the lip of the well outside the house. *Angélique*, as the local and uncommercialized sweet wine is also known, is poured into old hand-blown glasses from which it was once fashionable to drink absinthe. One recipe for *cartogène* combines four litres of the juice of freshly pressed wine grapes with one litre of 85° alcohol. The mixture is left to develop for one to two years before being filtered and served; *chez* the Laurents, it is offered with fleshy black olives cured in oil and coated with *herbes de Provence*, and small rounds of toast scraped with raw garlic and spread with *brandade de morue*. The great speciality of Nîmes, *brandade de morue* is poached salt cod into which milk and olive oil are furiously beaten by hand.

Henri Laurent's cousin and neighbour in the Camargue, Robert Bon of Le Petit Manusclat, specializes in organic long-grain brown rice with an unmistakably nutty flavour. M. Bon promotes his product as being the only naturally air-dried rice in Europe, with packaging that boasts, '*J'ai été séché par le mistral.*' He has also developed a puffed rice cake

BELOW: *The Camargue is a region of brutal contrasts. Nothing about it prepares one for the gentility of this guest room at Les Marquises.*

OPPOSITE: *Mme Laurent wears the traditional costume of the Arlésienne: velvet ribbon, originally imported to Arles from Germany, wound into a cap; an eighteenth-century hand-blocked cotton* fichu; *and a fully gathered silk skirt, which belonged to her maternal grandmother. Tradition also requires discreet jewellery and hair that is parted, back-combed, gently twisted and pinned on top of the head.*

FOLLOWING PAGE: *If the young* gardien *succeeds in winning the bouquet of rosemary and tamarisk away from Henri Laurent, he will present it to one of the pretty Arlésiennes on the sidelines. This* jeu de bouquet *was well-liked in the Middle Ages by the Popes in Avignon.*

BELOW: *After a day with the bulls. Annie Laurent rides home to Les Marquises in a Souleïado print shirt and the moleskin culottes that have been compulsory for* gardiennes, *or female bull-hands, since 1904. Annie is known for her love of the traditional* indiennes *of Provence; she, her son and her husband own 120 Souleïado shirts between them.*

served at Les Marquises alongside chewy *saucisson d'Arles*, which was first made in Roman times with a mixture that included donkey meat. Today the city's best-known *charcutier*, Pierre Milhau, prepares the air-dried salami-style sausage according to a recipe set down in 1655 by another great Arlésien pork butcher, Godart. Housed in the municipal library, the recipe combines seven parts minced pork with three parts of a combination of lightly smoked lardons and minced beef and bull meat. The whole mixture is flavoured with black peppercorns, ginger, garlic, *herbes de Provence*, salt and a splash of regional red wine. Pierre Milhau is also noted for his *caillette d'Arles*, a meat-loaf made with Camarguais rice and covered with caul fat.

There are market gardens, vineyards, rice fields and important saltworks in the Camargue, but they are all dim satellites turning distantly around the cult of the bull. 'We are all here because the bulls are,' says Annie Laurent, whose great-aunts Anna and Adèle Lescot, excellent horsewomen, proved that women could work with bulls in the Camargue. 'Everything we do is for them and with them in mind. We raise them like children. With some we are severe, with others less so. They are as distinguishable to us as human beings. When Goya died in 1986 he

was twenty-two, and I assure you it was like losing a member of our family. We knew his parents and grandparents. We cried, and people sent telegrams of condolence. When Goya was due to appear in the arena in Arles or Nîmes, all the seats were sold before the tickets were even printed. A thousand people would stand outside hoping to get in. Bulls are the kings of the Camargue.'

The divine *bïous* are not put to a catalogue of uses in the region. Too independent and uncontrollable to perform any kind of agricultural work, they are raised uniquely for sport. In *la course camarguaise*, which is also called *la course libre*, or the free race, the animal is never killed. Armed with only a *raset*, or hand rake, men enter the local arenas on foot and try to lift away the ribbon fixed to their opponent's forehead and the tassels and string wound around its murderously naked horns. Different versions of the sport have been popular in the area for ages. The joy-riding young farm boys who once pulled their wagons into a ring, and then jumped in with the angry bull in the hope of winning points with the pretty Arlésiennes on the sidelines, have been replaced today by professional or semi-professional *raseteurs*. Formerly, the *attribut* might have been a *saucisson d'Arles* instead of a tassel.

OPPOSITE: *The mounted head of Goya is set against the wall in a corner of the dining room as an expression of love and as an unavoidable reminder to the Laurents of the bull's greatness. Goya, who died in 1986, was known as the Lord of the Camargue for his performance in* la course libre.

LEFT: *Faience tureens in the form peculiar to Arles surround a dessert of fresh stewed figs and deep-fried sweet dough strips.*

The Laurents' Goya always filled the stands because he guaranteed a spectacular show. It is standard for a bull to leap over the barricade or to toss the wooden slats in the air, but Goya's uncommon intelligence and agility meant that he posed a special threat, inspiring the *raseteurs*' best moves. Mangled limbs and gouged stomachs are frequent, and although deaths are to be avoided, since 1924 nine men have been killed while playing the game.

Situated between the Grand Rhône and the *Etang de Vaccarès*, Les Marquises was built in 1819 with stone recovered from the nearby abbey of Ulmet. Founded in 1155, the abbey derived its fortune from sea salt and had holdings that included the whole of the Basse Camargue. A stopping-off point for pilgrims journeying to Santiago de Compostela, Ulmet was completely destroyed at the end of the twelfth century. The Basse Camargue passed next into the hands of the Comtes de Provence, and then into those of the kings of France until Louis XIV. It was the Sun King who awarded the Duc de Villars a number of vast properties in this part of the Camargue in recognition of his victory at Denain in 1712. On the *maréchal's* death, the fair division of these holdings among his three daughters required that one of them be shared – Les Marquises.

Henri Laurent's father Paul was a sheep farmer in Beaucaire when he purchased the ranch in 1943. The idea of becoming a *manadier* and raising bulls was suggested to him in a roundabout way by his friend the Marquis de Baroncelli-Javon, the poet and *manadier* who in 1904 set down the official dress code for *gardiens* and *gardiennes*, or bull-hands. When one of the Marquis's horses was injured by a train, Laurent sent one of his men to help. The horse was saved, and a bull was offered in thanks. Under Paul Laurent, Les Marquises developed into one of the largest and most prestigious ranches in the Camargue.

None of the family actually lived on the property until Annie and Henri undertook the renovation of the main house and moved from Beaucaire in 1975. While the stables became the salon and dining room, the hay loft was converted into four bedrooms. Filled today with an extraordinary collection of museum-quality eighteenth-century Provençal furniture, all carved in walnut and crafted in Arles, the house is an immaculate and rather sophisticated asylum from the mistral and mosquitoes. Madame Laurent's decoration attains a degree of polish that is not quite what one has in mind for the Camargue.

Against the exposed beige stone of a wall in the main room she has placed a *buffet à glissants à tabernacle*, a cabinet composed of a massive base and a narrow, recessed top with both sliding and hinged doors. In the days when an ambulant priest said Mass in farmhouses in Provence the upper portion would have provided him with a place to store the elements of the Eucharist. The buffet is sculpted with olive branches, a horn of plenty, and a flute – all motifs characteristic of the furniture of Arles. Other pieces passed down to the Laurents by their mothers and grandmothers include an *estanié*, an *étagère* designed exclusively

BELOW: *Mme Laurent lays the table at Les Marquises with vermeil cutlery and Quimper faience made in 1935 by the late Etienne Laget, a painter whose chief subject was the Camargue. A gift from the artist, the service depicts Arlésiennes dancing the Provençal* farandole. *The quilted cloth with an eighteenth-century design is from the Michel Biehn collection from Souleïado. The napkin folded into the shirt of the bull-hand, complete with neck scarf, is an innovation by Annie Laurent.*

for the presentation of pewter; a *panetière*, or bread cupboard, decorated with the tools for harvesting wheat; a *pétrin*, or dough trough; and a table and eight chairs displaying the elegant carved form of the faience soup tureen indigenous to Arles. At Christmas Annie honours Provençal custom, laying this table with three cloths to evoke the Holy Trinity.

'Is there anything special you would like to eat?' she will ask abruptly when calling with an invitation to dine at Les Marquises. If one has dined there before, one knows to ask for *tellines*, the tiny clams that form the first course of the meal pictured here. Culled from the beaches of the gypsy town of Saintes-Maries-de-la-Mer, they are simply and quickly tossed in a skillet with oil, garlic and parsley. Deep-fried aubergines and meltingly good *tomates provençales* follow with a main course of thrush, spit-roasted with their giblets and basted throughout with a *flambadou*, or steel funnel. Slightly open at its pointed end and attached to a

long pole, the funnel is heated in the coals, a chunk of lard is added, and the melted fat falls in sparks onto the miniscule birds. Grilled slices of bread placed beneath them catch all the juices and are ultimately spread with a *pommade* of the softened hearts and livers. The wine, Châteauneuf-du-Pape, is chosen for its 'size', body, warmth and spiciness. For dessert, fresh figs cooked in sugar syrup are served alongside deep-fried dough strips flavoured with citrus zest and orange blossom water.

'I always greet dinner guests *en Arlésienne*,' says Annie. 'I have thirty-two complete costumes, some from the eighteenth century. To arrange your hair, to pin the *fichu* – in all it takes two hours, providing you know what you are doing. Some take four and still end up looking wrong. When a woman of Arles says, "*Je me coiffe*," that means she is going to put on the costume. I suppose I wear it twice a week. But I do not need a special reason to dress *en Arlésienne*.'

ABOVE: *An Arlésienne pins her* fichu *into five rigid folds and carefully positions it so that it stands away from the nape of the neck.*

ABOVE LEFT: Tellines, *tiny clams, are found on the shore of the Camargue. They are dug up from under the sand with home-made* telliniers – *baskets attached to big rakes.*

OPPOSITE: *Plant life in the Camargue is tough, simple and specific to the region. Vegetation includes thistles, sand-lilies, irises, saltwort, camomile, euphorbia, narcissus, sea-panicles and aspodels.*

MENU
for 6

L'HEURE DE L'APÉRO EN CAMARGUE

Cartogène
Provençal sweet apéritif wine

POACHED SALT COD PURÉE WITH LEMON,
AIR-DRIED ARLÉSIEN SAUSAGE, PUFFED RICE CAKES,
BLACK OLIVES FROM FONTVIEILLE WITH HERBES DE PROVENCE

UN SAUTÉ DE TELLINES DE SAINTES-MARIES-DE-LA-MER
A SAUTÉ OF TINY CLAMS

Château Simone   Palette blanc

GRIVES RÔTIES SUR TOASTS TARTINÉS D'ABATTIS
ROAST THRUSH ON TOASTS SPREAD WITH GIBLETS

AUBERGINES À LA PROVENÇALE
DEEP-FRIED AUBERGINES

TOMATES À LA PROVENÇALE
PAN-FRIED TOMATOES WITH GARLIC AND PARSLEY

Château de Beaucastel 1982   Châteauneuf-du-Pape

OREILLETTES PROVENÇALES
DEEP-FRIED SWEET DOUGH STRIPS

FIGUES FRAÎCHES CONFITES
FRESH STEWED FIGS

Baron Philippe de Rothschild   Sauternes

Café

BRANDADE DE MORUE CITRONNÉE

Brandade de morue is perhaps more interesting in concept than it is on the palate. Lemon, which purists definitely do not tolerate, livens it up. Considerable strength is required for beating in the milk and oil. These quantities will make a substantial amount and will allow you to keep some for another day.

1 kg (2¼ lb) 'green' (salted only) or brine-
 packed salt cod, or 500 g (18 oz)
 salted and dried
2 bay leaves
2 cloves garlic, peeled
350 ml (12 fl oz/1½ cups) milk
350 ml (12 fl oz/1½ cups) olive oil
salt and freshly ground white pepper
lemon juice
nutmeg

1. Desalt the cod (see page 26). Place the desalted fish and bay leaves in enough cold water to cover and heat to just below simmering. Poach the cod, never allowing the surface of the water to break, for approx 10 mins. Drain. When the fish is cool enough to handle, roughly flake it between your fingers back into the poaching pot, picking out the bones and pulling away the skin with a small knife.
2. Place the garlic in a small saucepan with the milk and boil for 10 secs. Lower the heat, retrieve the garlic with a slotted spoon and purée it in a food mill. Add to the cod and turn on the heat to low. In a second pan, heat the oil to very hot and add one third to the fish, energetically beating it in with a wooden spoon. Add the milk and remaining oil about 60 ml (2 fl oz/¼ cup) at a time, alternating the liquids and beating in each addition until completely absorbed. Move the pot on and off the heat as you work to prevent the mixture scorching. Flavour to taste with the remaining ingredients and serve with rounds of grilled bread that have been scraped with garlic.

LEFT: *Miniscule thrush, in season in the Camargue from early December to late January, require only salt, pepper, strips of fresh pork fat, and a lot of kitchen string.*

OPPOSITE: *Classic* tomates à la provençales: *firm tomatoes are halved and placed face-down in hot oil.*

UN SAUTÉ DE TELLINES DE SAINTES-MARIES-DE-LA-MER

The *telline* is one of the tiniest and most tender clams in France, with a shell coloured a lovely violet on the inside. Cherrystones, littlenecks and cockles could also be cooked in the manner described here.

2 kg (4½ lb) tellines
approx 3 tbs vegetable oil
3 cloves garlic, peeled and finely chopped
3 tbs finely chopped flat-leaf parsley
freshly ground pepper

1. Soak the *tellines* in several changes of cold water for approx 4 hours, or until the water is no longer sandy. If the clams are particularly gritty, salt in the water will help flush out the sand. Drain.
2. Heat the oil in a large skillet and sauté the garlic until tender but not brown. Add the parsley and *tellines*, and cook over a high heat, tossing continuously so that the clams cook evenly. Add more oil if you see the pan is dry. As soon as the shells open, transfer to a serving platter. Spoon the liquid in the pan over the clams, leaving behind any sand, season with pepper and serve.

TOMATES À LA PROVENÇALE

All other recipes for *tomates à la provençale* are cancelled out by this one – the simplest and most authentic – supplied by Annie Laurent's cousin Olga Hugounenq.

3 tbs light olive oil
6 medium vine-ripened tomatoes, cored, cut in half horizontally and seeded
salt
3 tbs finely chopped garlic
8 tbs finely chopped flat-leaf parsley

Heat the oil in a skillet and add the tomatoes cut-side down. Cook over a medium heat for approx 5 mins, shaking the pan to prevent sticking. Turn, sprinkle with salt, and fill the cavities with the garlic and 6 tbs of the parsley. Cook for approx 5 mins more, covering the skillet with foil if the herbs do not melt into the tomatoes. Transfer to a warm serving platter, sprinkle with the remaining parsley, and serve.

GRIVES RÔTIES SUR TOASTS TARTINÉS D'ABATTIS

Tiny birds like thrush, bunting and lark are not eaten as routinely as they once were in France, but they may still be encountered, especially in the southwest. While partridge and pigeon should be dressed, woodcocks are often cooked with their innards. In this adaptation of Annie Laurent's recipe, the hearts and livers of thrush are sautéed separately so that the meat can be served medium-rare. Half the number of quail could be substituted for the thrush.

24 thrush
salt and freshly ground pepper
24 strips pork fat measuring 5 × 15 cm (2 × 6 in)
24 slices dense white bread measuring 5 × 10 cm (2 × 4 in)
30 g (1 oz/2 tbs) unsalted butter

1. Preheat oven to 205°C (400°F). Remove the innards from the thrush and discard the gizzards and gall bladders, carefully trimming the livers of any greenish stains. Roughly chop the hearts and livers and season, along with the insides and outsides of the birds. Wrap with the strips of fat and tie securely with kitchen string.
2. Arrange the game on a slotted baking sheet or rack, place in the oven, and position the bread on a shallow roasting dish beneath the birds to catch the juices. Roast for 20 mins.
3. When cool enough to handle, remove the fat strips. Melt the butter and quickly sauté the hearts and livers, which should remain a bit pink. Spread over the bread slices and arrange on a serving platter. Place a thrush on each slice and serve.

AUBERGINES À LA PROVENÇALE

When deep frying the aubergines, take care that they do not become papery.

1 kg (1¼ lb) small aubergines, cut lengthwise into 0.5 cm (¼ in) slices
salt
vegetable oil for deep frying

Line a collander with the aubergines, sprinkling salt between each layer, and set aside for 1 hour. Rinse thoroughly in cold water and vigorously wring out in a dish cloth. In a wide skillet, heat the oil until it sputters when a drop of water is added. Slip in as many aubergine slices as will fit in the pan in a single layer without crowding. Fry until golden on both sides, drain on paper towels and serve.

OREILLETTES PROVENÇALES

Recipes, forms and names for this dessert differ throughout Provence. On the Riviera they are known as *ganses* and shaped like knots and butterflies. A book on the cooking of the Lubéron north of the Camargue calls them *oreillettes-merveilles* and *bugnes de Noël*, although they are eaten during Carnival and not at Christmas.

250 g (9 oz/1¾ cups) flour
a pinch of salt
2 eggs, lightly beaten
20 g (1½ lb) sugar
35 g (1¼ oz/2½ tbs) unsalted butter, melted
grated zest of 1 orange
grated zest of 1 lemon
2 tbs rum
vegetable oil for deep frying
caster (confectioners') sugar for sprinkling

1. Sift the flour and salt into a bowl and form a well. Incorporate all the other ingredients except the oil and caster sugar and work into a ball. Cover the dough and refrigerate for 2 hours.
2. Roll the ball out into a thin rectangle, stretching the dough until you sense it is about to tear. Using a pastry wheel, cut into 15 × 5 cm (6 × 2 in) strips. Heat the oil in a wide skillet until it sputters when a drop of water is added. Place as many strips in the pan as will fit in a single layer without crowding. Fry about 10 secs per side, or until golden. Drain on paper towels. Allow to cool and dry, sprinkle with caster sugar, and serve.

E VER since the 1960s, when Mercédès-Benz tried to buy up Sivergues and transform it into a model French vacation 'village' with a man-made lake, the mayor, his eight counsellors and the hamlet's seventeen inhabitants have been on their guard. So, when the Ladu affair came up years later, they were ready.

ABOVE: *Goats, according to Chantal Ladu, are very particular: 'We have to take them on a different circuit every day in order to vary their diet. If they pass through a valley of oaks, they'll eat the youngest, tenderest leaves and branches and just walk away from the rest. When it's been raining and there's dust on the leaves, they'll leave those behind as well. They're interested in whatever's new and fresh – wild lavender, thyme, savory. Our goats choose their own menu.'*

RIGHT: *Gianni Ladu made the T-shaped outdoor dining table at Le Castelas from a fallen mulberry tree found on his 105 hectares (260 acres). He cut a low shelf into the side of the table for his small children.*

6   A *fromager*'s table in the Vaucluse

Sivergues – pitched high in the Lubéron mountains east of Avignon – became the home of Gianni and Chantal Ladu in 1982, when they were hired as the caretakers of a severely isolated vacation home on the site of a medieval pilgrim station on the route to Santiago de Compostela. When the owners decided to sell the house, they refused to consider the Ladus as buyers, seeking instead city people like themselves who would use it part-time and pay dearly for the hallucinogenic Provençal heat, the shrill chorus of the cicadas, and the crunch and fragrance of wild thyme underfoot.

The owners discovered that the biggest mistake they had made was in allowing Gianni and Chantal to keep goats and make cheese. As a result the Ladus were officially inscribed in the area as dairy farmers. With signatures from everyone in Sivergues on a hotly worded petition demanding that the local agricultural agency intercede, all they had to do to stay was prove that they could earn a living out of land that had a reputation for being too poor, too hilly.

'They said the earth was too dry, but they didn't know Gianni,' says Chantal. 'He's from Sardinia.'

'The whole thing took a year and a half,' recalls Gianni. 'But we did it, you know. We won.'

The Ladu's meet their mortgage payments today by accepting paying guests (50 beds are lined up boot-camp style on the first floor of the farmhouse); by selling oak and stone from their 105 hectares (260 acres); and by producing *tomme* and *brousse* (similar to ricotta), cheeses Gianni began making at home in Italy with his grandparents when he was eleven years old.

The dairy products from Le Castelas, as the property is called, also provide a good part of the Ladu family diet. 'In my choice of raw materials and dishes, living with an Italian has obviously influenced my cooking,' says Chantal, who is from the southwest of France near Luchon in the Pyrenees. 'But what has shaped it even more are the ingredients I have at hand. For me, cooking is not deciding to make a dish and then buying the ingredients. Whereas the woman who lives in the city says, "I am going to make grilled duck *à l'orange*", and goes out and buys her duck and oranges, I walk into the garden and into the *fromagerie* to see what is there. "Gianni has brought me

ABOVE: *At 800 metres (2,625 feet), Le Castelas is perhaps the highest farm in the Lubéron. Starting out as its caretakers, Gianni and Chantal Ladu encountered trouble when it came up for sale and they attempted to acquire it for themselves. While their employers tried to discourage them, others who wanted to buy the house offered them money to leave. In the Middle Ages the site was occupied by a pilgrim station for devout travellers on their way to Santiago de Compostela.*

OPPOSITE: *Le Castelas is also* une gite à la ferme, *the Ladus supplementing their income as dairy farmers by accepting paying guests.*

this meat," I say to myself. "I have these vegetables and this cheese, now what am I going to make?" One invents with what one has, which in our case is everything but bread. We're virtually self-sufficient. But if I lived in the Pyrenees with other *éléments de base*, my cooking would be entirely different. The only thing I would always insist on, I suppose, is a certain wholesomeness, that and harmony of colour, especially in salads. I cook a lot with colour, and I cook with the seasons.'

If the Ladus were any less shrewd or tenacious, Gianni's relations in Sardinia would probably not be sending him mail at so exalted an address as Le Castelas. Arriving in France for the first time in 1977, performing as a serenading member of an Italian folk troupe at a festival in Marseille, he met one of the event's organizers, a bright, charming, well-spoken girl named Chantal. She followed him back to Sardinia and spent two hard years in Gianni's native Desulo in Labarbagia, the highest and most remote region of the island. 'The Ladus have been shepherds and cheesemakers for generations,' she says. 'Everything was fine so long as we stayed at home among ourselves in the country. But when we went down to the village human relations were extremely difficult. It was not easy.'

If Chantal found life difficult now in the Lubéron, it would be easy to forgive her for it. The weather can be defeating. In summer even the goats cannot be seduced out-of-doors until after five o'clock when the worst of the heat is over. Sivergues proper is a small cluster of buildings five minutes away by car – if your car can take it. The road is picturesque, if excruciatingly rocky. Except for a tea salon which is theoretically open once a week, the hamlet has no commerce. The nearest towns with banks and shops are Bonnieux and Apt, 8 and 13 kilometres (5 and 8 miles) away respectively, although, as Chantal says, distance for people who live in the mountains is measured by how long it takes to go from place to place. Social contact in winter is scarce unless she and Gianni go looking for it. By then there are few if any passers-by on foot or horseback looking for a bed or a meal to eat with the family under the handsome vaulted stone ceiling in the communal room. 'But I don't feel isolated,' says Chantal. 'With the animals and trees, there is never any question of feeling alone. I am sure I would feel more isolated in a city. The postman may have

to come a long way out of his way, but the mail is still delivered to our door. And while the children go to school in Bonnieux by private taxi, we don't pay for it, the municipal government does.'

Chantal would also be forgiven for wanting a more reasonably equipped kitchen – a decent refrigerator, a decent oven, and a decent set of pans – given the number of people she serves during the high season and the quality and elaborateness of her dishes. As it is she does a lot of her actual cooking in large flat-bottomed restaurant-supply stainless-steel bowls. While she says she would not refuse a new refrigerator and oven, a more complete *batterie de cuisine* does not tempt her. 'A sophisticated kitchen would only encumber me,' she says. 'I don't know how to cook if I am not touching with my hands, feeling for consistency and texture. What would I do with a load of gadgets and devices in Sivergues?'

Sivergues was first inhabited by the tribal Ligurians; ghostly vestiges of their fortifications and *hôtel de célébration* are visible today behind the Ladus' farmhouse. But it was the Romans who carved from the powerful landscape the twisting trail up which Gianni leads his sixty goats every day. Sivergues did not earn its name, however, until the Middle Ages, when the bishop in Apt chose grottoes there as the place to hide his six daughters from the visiting Pope from Avignon. *Six vierges*, six virgins, became Sivergues. At the end of the ninth century a chapel was built at Le Castelas to serve the pilgrims on their way to Santiago de Compostela.

While overnight lodgers often pass the morning inspecting the traces of the temple built during the Wars of Religion, as well as those of a Protestant cemetery still in use a hundred years ago, Chantal and Gianni are working in the *fromagerie*. The first cheese to be made daily, with milk taken from the goats by hand, is a raw full-fat *tomme*; the same cheese made with sheep's milk in Sardinia would be *pecorino*. With the addition of rennet the milk is partially transformed into a kind of flan. Gianni then gently lowers his arms into the pail up to his elbows, and using a flicking hand motion, he breaks up the solids into tiny particles. Once the 'dry' material has fallen to the bottom and the whey has risen to the top, he takes a pointed plank of wood to cut the curd into blocks. Carefully 'accompanying' each block to the surface, he packs them into plastic moulds with holes for draining.

OPPOSITE: *Gianni and Chantal Ladu, and their son Sébastien.*

ABOVE: *An accomplished mason, Gianni Ladu built the vaulted ceiling in the dining room. Chantal's domain, the kitchen, is on the other side of the fly curtain.*

After a twelve-hour drying period the forms of cheese are either rubbed with table salt or soaked in brine. They are then placed on splintery shelves in a room at one end of the house where they are turned at least once a day and wiped clean of any emerging whey – whey that could lead to harmful mould. Twice a day in the humid spring and winter and once a day during the rest of the year fires of neutral-smelling broom or oak are lit in this room. When, after one or two months, the salt has penetrated to the core of the cheese, it is ready either to be eaten or stored in the cellar for up to five months. Further stocking requires that the wheels be smeared with thick fatty olive oil to seal in moisture. A minimum of thirteen litres of milk is needed to make one kilo of *tomme*, weighed when fresh.

The Ladus' *brousse*, which has a pronounced taste of cream, is made by boiling the whey left behind by the *tomme*. Making *brousse* is 'as delicate as making *crème anglaise*', says Chantal. 'You have to know the exact moment to extinguish the flame.' The curds that float to the top during the careful boiling operation are spooned out and only eaten fresh, often with sugar, jam, honey or fruit. 'With *brousse* you can do everything you do with *crème fraîche*,' says Chantal, who counts thirty litres of whey for every kilo of cheese. 'It's just as unctuous, and the advantage is that there's no fat.'

For *tarte à la brousse*, a recipe left behind by a tourist from Bulgaria, the cheese is combined with spinach, eggs, lemon juice, mint, nutmeg, garlic and basil. The cheese is also used at Le Castelas in gâteaux and soufflés, for grating over pasta and in the filling for the peppers in the menu shown here. At La Fenière, a fine restaurant in nearby Lourmarin, chef Reine Sammut mixes the Ladus' *brousse* with pine nuts and herbs as a stuffing for cannelloni bathed in a creamy lemon sauce. For dessert it fills crispy crêpes served with warm honey sauce and pears poached in white wine.

Lastly, Gianni and Chantal make *petites tommes*, small discs obtained from curds that have been left in whey for up to two days and that are never in any way worked or handled (a soft *pâte molle* as opposed to a denser *pâte pressée* for large *tommes*). As a result of this prolonged contact with the whey, the cheese is much more acidic. Drained and salted, *petites tommes* are traditionally turned in dried ground savory, picked in August when the herb is in blossom. After two days in the refrigerator it is eaten *frais*; stored afterwards in a humid place it develops a skin and is eaten *crémeux*; left longer in a well-aired spot it is eaten *sec*.

After thirty years of steady cheese-making in two countries, Gianni has learned that while goats that graze in the sun produce less milk than those that graze in the shade, their milk is more desirable because it is richer in fat. 'Herbs that grow in the shade are less nourishing,' he says. 'One of my goats can eat half the herbs in the sun that it does elsewhere but still produce twice the amount of cheese. We sell a lot less *brousse* when the lavender is in flower because our clients find the cheese tastes too strongly of it. When it rains a lot the texture of the cheese is less creamy and the taste fades a bit, so we are forced to feed the animals barley. I make the most authentic cheese with the most character of anyone I know. The man I used to work for in Buoux, the next village over, had machines to milk the goats. But we are artisans.'

'The others around here who make cheese aren't real country people and *fromagers* like Gianni is,' says Chantal. 'They send their animals off to be slaughtered rather than killing them themselves. And they keep goats without even knowing what the *caillette* is. Most of them, if they ever do kill a kid, just throw it out.'

Caillettes are the rennet-filled stomach sacks of kids that are less than two months old and that have been fed exclusively on their mother's milk. Rather than use them to make cheese, Gianni dries the sacks whole, hanging them from beams above the ageing *tommes*. The shrivelled leathery cases are ceremoniously split open after four or five months, and the cheese inside is stronger than anything sold in any French cheese shop. The *caillette* is passed around the table. Everyone helps himself.

The important decision of exactly where to bring cheese to maturity and cure *charcuterie* was made for the Ladus. 'The house had been shut for ten years when we arrived as caretakers,' says Chantal, 'and hanging in the room the former owner kept as a kitchen were three perfectly white, perfectly dry dish cloths.

BELOW: *The dining room at Les Castelas is also the salon, the scene of a party held once a year with friends to celebrate the slaughtering of a pig. The main dish on this occasion is* sanquette, *a kind of soufflé of onions and the animal's fresh blood, served with poached apples.*

There hadn't been a drop of moisture there in a decade.'

Most meals at Le Castelas begin with an assortment of *charcuterie* – from the Ladus' free-range pigs – handed around with tumblers of spicy sangria. Herbed fritters made with the oldest, crustiest cheese Chantal can find in the larder are a regular first course. With the *brousse*-stuffed peppers she likes to serve shoulder of fresh-killed kid, stuffed with a marinated mixture of its diced heart and liver, onions, bread, eggs, lemon juice and herbs. Alternatively, and more realistically for the city cook, she proposes shoulder of lamb stuffed with *ratatouille aux olives* and neatly tied up like a melon. Wine – a fiery and unlabelled *gros rouge* – is from the Apt cooperative which straddles the Côtes du Lubéron and Côtes du Ventoux vineyards. The children are happy when dessert is their mother's orange-flavoured chocolate cake, hidden, they will swear to you, under *inches* of powdered dark chocolate.

With Gianni and Chantal securely installed at Le Castelas, Sivergues is once again the place guidebooks never fail to describe as the end of the world. Their ninety-seven-year-old neighbour who has ventured from the hamlet only three times in her life – once to get married, once to visit a sickly cousin, and once to be operated on in Apt – does nothing to ruin her record. For her part, Chantal is perfectly happy in her remote Provençal farmhouse, among her fat bundles of herbs, dispensing wisdom. 'The woman who has sage in her garden', she says, 'never sees the doctor.'

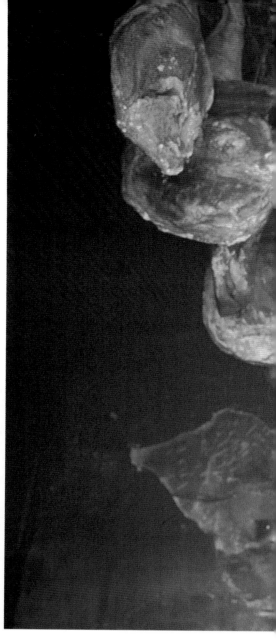

LEFT: *A candle for basting the thigh of a* marcassin, *or young wild boar is made by by inserting a wick of sulphurized paper into a slab of lard. Drops of fat fall on to the meat in sparks.*

ABOVE: *The thighs, breasts, shoulders and jaws of free-range pigs hang as* charcuterie *in the smokehouse. The high elevation, dry climate and free circulation of air all contribute to its superior quality. Fed on rich whey left over from making cheese, the animals are let loose in the mountains; they return voluntarily every two days when they are thirsty for more whey. Wheels of* tomme *are brought to maturity on shelves against the back wall.*

RIGHT: Charcuterie de la ferme *on an elm plank. The very basic dried sausage is made with small pieces of offal, cubes of fat, salt, pepper and vinegar. Chantal Ladu also makes a pâté for which the pig's head is boiled, the meat cubed and combined with parsley,* cornichons, *olive oil and vinegar. This* pâté de tête *is put aside for a year to allow the flavours to develop.*

MENU
for 8

La Sangria de Sivergues

ASSORTIMENT DE CHARCUTERIE DE LA FERME
ASSORTED CHARCUTERIE FROM THE FARM

ÉPAULE D'AGNEAU FARCIE À LA RATATOUILLE
AUX OLIVES NOIRES
SHOULDER OF LAMB STUFFED WITH
BLACK-OLIVE *RATATOUILLE*

POIVRONS FARCIS À LA BROUSSE
BELL PEPPERS STUFFED WITH RICOTTA CHEESE

Vin rouge de la Cave Coopérative d'Apt

LE PLATEAU DE FROMAGES 'LE CASTELAS'
FRESH AND AGED SMOKED *TOMME, CAILLETTE,*
TODAY'S AND LAST YEAR'S POTS OF LEFTOVER CHEESE
BLENDED WITH HERBS AND EAU-DE-VIE

GÂTEAU AU CHOCOLAT À L'ORANGE
ORANGE CHOCOLATE CAKE

Café

LEFT: La Sangria de Sivergues *is made mellow with port, spicy with cloves, and punchy with tart green apples. Ground white pepper gives it its bite.*

OPPOSITE ABOVE: *In the* fromagerie, petites tommes *are left to drain before salting. This cheese, the last of three in the production cycle at Le Castelas, is made from curds that are soaked in whey for as long as two days.*

OPPOSITE BELOW: *A chestnut serving tray was carved with corner wells for salt and pepper by an artisan in Gianni Ladu's native Sardinia. Two small shoulders of lamb enclose* ratatouille *with olives, with foil packets containing extra filling. Peppers are stuffed with a mixture of eggs, herbs and* brousse *produced on the farm, although ricotta can be used successfully in place of* brousse.

LA SANGRIA DE SIVERGUES

The wine Chantal Ladu uses for this excellent sangria measures 13% alcohol by volume. It should be prepared 24 hours before serving.

4 litres (7 pints/1 gallon) hearty red wine
250 ml (9 fl oz/1 cup) port
300 g (10½ oz/1½ cups) sugar
a pinch of ground white pepper
a pinch of ground cloves
2 lemons
2 cinnamon sticks
4 oranges, peeled, pith removed, and
  separated into sections
4 tart apples such as Granny Smiths,
  peeled, cored and cut into small cubs

1. Whisk together the wine, port, sugar, ground spices and the juice of 1 lemon. Add the cinnamon sticks, oranges and apples, and chill.
2. Thinly slice the remaining lemon, carefully stir the sangria, float the slices on top, and serve.

ÉPAULE D'AGNEAU FARCIE À LA RATATOUILLE AUX OLIVES NOIRES

The *ratatouille* that does not fit inside the lamb can fill foil packets that should be added to the oven 30 mins before the roast is done.

4 onions
175 ml (6 oz/¾ cup) olive oil
1 kg (2¼ lb) courgettes, diced
1 kg (2¼ lb) small aubergines, peeled and
  diced
2 green bell peppers, cored, seeded and
  diced
2 kg (4½ lb) tomatoes, peeled, seeded, and
  chopped
3 cloves garlic, peeled and finely chopped
4 tsp salt
freshly ground pepper
1 bouquet garni of thyme, parsley,
  rosemary and a bay leaf
100 g (7 oz/1 cup) black olives
2 small shoulders of lamb weighing
  approx 1.5 kg (3¼ lb) each, boned and
  trimmed
300 g (10 oz) pork fat in strips

1. Prepare a day in advance. Chop 2 of the onions. Heat 2 tbs oil in a large skillet, add the courgettes and cook until soft and lightly coloured. Transfer to a large

stockpot. Cook the onions, aubergines and peppers individually in the same way in the same quantity of oil, and layer in the stockpot. Add half the tomatoes, garlic, seasoning and bouquet garni. Cook, covered, over a low heat, for approx 1 hour. Pit and chop half the olives and stir them into the mixture. Let cool completely, skimming off any oil that comes to the surface. Refrigerate.

2. The following day, lay two long pieces of kitchen string crossways over a large mixing bowl that will serve as a mould for the meat. Preheat oven to 165°C (325°F). Place one shoulder in the bowl, skin-side down, season and add about one third of the filling. Cover with the other shoulder, skin-side up, tucking in the edges of the 2 pieces of lamb to form a neat, even seam. Tie the strings securely and remove carefully to a work surface. Cover the seamed area with the pork strips and, with a final melon shape for the joints of meat in mind, bind with more string.

3. Slice the 2 remaining onions, spread the remaining oil in a roasting pan and add the lamb with the knotted ends of the string facing down. Spoon the onions and remaining tomatoes around the roast, season, and cook for approx 2 hours. Allow the meat to rest for 15 mins before stirring the whole olives into the tomato sauce, heating it through, and serving.

POIVRONS FARCIS À LA BROUSSE

Choose big peppers of uniform shape that will hold the filling easily and allow it to expand as it cooks. Mix red, green and yellow peppers. As a first course 1 pepper will serve 2 people.

4 large bell peppers
450 g (1 lb) fresh brousse (ricotta)
4 large eggs, lightly beaten
1 tbs finely chopped basil
1 tbs finely chopped parsley
2 cloves garlic, peeled and finely chopped
freshly ground nutmeg
salt and freshly ground pepper
2 tbs olive oil

1. Plunge the whole peppers into salted boiling water, blanch for 1 min and then refresh under cold running water. Carefully cut out the tops and reserve. Remove the seeds and ribs and drain on paper towels. Combine the remaining ingredients except the oil. Preheat oven to 180°C (350°F).

2. Fill the peppers about three-quarters full with the cheese mixture. Oil an earthenware or glass baking dish and add the peppers, either standing up or on their sides. Bake for 35–45 mins, or until the filling is puffed and set. Garnish with the tops and serve.

GÂTEAU AU CHOCOLAT À L'ORANGE

This cake is richer than a *Génoise* and not as dense as the French Madeira cake (pound cake) known as *quatre-quarts*.

2 oranges
125 g (4½ oz) bitter chocolate, cut into small
  pieces
200 g (7 oz/1 cup) sugar
280 g (10 oz/2¼ sticks plus 2 tbs) unsalted
  butter, softened
4 eggs
210 g (7¼ oz/1½ cups) flour
50 g (2 oz/⅓ cup) unsweetened cocoa, plus
  enough to sprinkle over the finished cake
1 tsp baking powder

1. Squeeze the juice of 1 orange into a small sauce pan, add the chocolate and melt over a very low heat. Set aside to cool. Preheat oven to 180°C (350°F).

2. Grate the zest of the remaining orange directly into a bowl so as not to lose any of the flavourful oils. Add the sugar and 250 g (9 oz/2¼ sticks) of the butter, and beat until light and fluffy. Add the eggs 2 at a time, and mix until smooth. Stir in the melted chocolate.

3. Sift the flour with the cocoa and baking powder into the bowl and fold gently into the mixture. Grease a 25 cm (10 in) round cake tin with the remaining butter and dust with flour. Transfer the batter and bake for 30 mins, or until the middle is firm to the touch. Turn the cake onto a cooling rack. While still warm, squeeze the juice of the second orange over the top. When the cake has cooled, dust it with cocoa using a sieve, and serve.

OUTSIDE a circle of chefs and other food professionals, the co-author of the most authoritative and best-selling book on French cooking in the English language is unknown in her native France. Born in 1904, if she still felt up to travelling to America, she would have *foie gras* laid at her feet. In England she would be on all the breakfast chat shows explaining just why the English student who is so brilliant with *poulet en soutien-gorge* at cooking school in France goes straight back to mince pie the minute he gets home to Gloucestershire.

ABOVE: *Simone 'Simca' Beck – virtually unknown in her native France, but celebrated everywhere people read in English and follow French cuisine – at home with her friend and guardian Jeannette in Châteauneuf-de-Grasse in the hills behind the Côte d'Azur. Simca says that Jeannette, once her private cook and assistant at the cooking school run on the property, has taught her many* trucs *– like grating garlic with the prongs of a fork.*

RIGHT: *Simca's own* tarte aux agrumes, *or citrus tart, marries orange with lime in a sweet pastry shell. Sprinkled with zest and dusted with icing sugar, the tart here wears a colourful collar of twisted Provençal cotton.*

Simone 'Simca' Beck means nothing to the readers of *Paris Match* and *Madame Figaro* because her *Mastering the Art of French Cooking*, published with Louisette Bertholle and the California-born Julia Child in 1961, has never been translated into French, presumably because there has been no need for it. France has its own sacred culinary texts, its Mesdames Saint-Ange, Ali-Babs, Escoffiers, Lenôtres and Pellaprats. Simca (she will jump at you if you call her Simone) in fact studied under Henri-Paul Pellaprat, initially at the Cordon Bleu before the war, and then in her own kitchen in Neuilly in the suburbs of Paris – an extraordinary arrangement that had him working as both her private chef and private tutor. Simca's one-to-one instruction from one of the most important gastronomic figures of the first half-century is written into every page of *Mastering the Art*, a book that proved it was perfectly possible to make authentic French food without French ingredients. The goal, as Julia Child has said, was 'to take the la-de-da out of French cooking because ... a lot of it before [we came along] was a sort of one-upmanship and We Happy Few and all that.' It worked.

Simca lives today behind the Riviera in the hills near Grasse in a kind of private compound of four houses, called the Domaine de Bramafam. Her home, Le Mas Vieux, is a comfortable early eighteenth-century farmhouse of small close rooms. The décor of these rooms still retains the feeling of the late 1950s when she first moved in. La Campanette was built as a guest house and cooking school, while La Pitchoune was Julia's food lab and vacation home, though it is now rented out. The fourth house belongs to Jeannette, Simca's teaching assistant until the school closed in around 1985. Today she is her guardian and afternoon tea partner.

Having worked with Child on the second volume of *Mastering the Art*, and after writing three cookbooks on her own, the last of which is a kind of memoir with recipes, Simca insists she has said everything she has to say about beef marrow and brioche. She is on the phone with Julia, 'my American sister' in California every two or three days, and she likes nothing more than the rich company of her American neighbour from down near Toulon, the food and wine writer Richard Olney. And while she says that scrambled eggs with caviar is the only dish left that thrills her, lunch when she dines alone is usually some combination of scrambled eggs with basil and tarragon, tomato salad, a pâté of sardines and butter and mustard, *pommes de terre rissolées*, *fromage blanc*, and poached peaches.

According to Richard Olney, Simca is not one of those cooks who is willing to sacrifice a good time for a good meal if a good meal means sweating over a bowl of recalcitrant egg whites while your friends are out on the terrace under the snowy cherry blossoms knocking back raspberry

ABOVE: *Daffodils from the garden, a photograph from the early 1950s of Simca and her perfumer husband Jean Fischbacher taken at a truffle market, and a still life by Hett Kwiatkowska, the Polish painter who shared the house with M. Fischbacher's cousin Marcelle Challiol during the war.*

LEFT: *A first course of* gratin de coquilles Saint-Jacques au Muscadet.

OPPOSITE: *Simca bought the hall door second-hand in Ramatuelle near Saint-Tropez, storing it until she decided to build La Campanette as a guest house and cooking school in the early 1970s. The Directoire canapé in lemonwood formally belonged to a* notaire *in her native Normandy.*

ABOVE: *A Louis* XV *Savoyard desk carved in walnut takes up a large part of the sitting room in Le Mas Vieux. It was here, working beneath a skylight, that Simca wrote parts of* Volume II *of* Mastering the Art of French Cooking, Simca's Cuisine *and* New Menus from Simca's Cuisine, *as well as her memoirs.*

wine. Although it is not a rule easily applied to the menu she created here, Simca says, 'Whenever I have people to dine, the entire meal is finished before the first guests even arrive. There's never anything left to do but reheat.'

Simca's unshakeable ideas about entertaining reflect both her strong Norman roots and a rather terrorizing anglophile father who adhered to a complex set of late-Victorian manners. 'For a *dîner très fin*, a private dinner,' she says, 'the point is to bring together people who are intellectually compatible, on the same social rung, and who share the same way of life and religion. Perhaps religion a bit less now; that was before the war, when Protestants and Catholics didn't mix. But the same social rung I insist on. In France it's most important of all. Money doesn't count. It's breeding that does. Intellect, too, in England even more than here.'

Simca's guests also share what she calls 'the same reaction to modern life. You'll never find a communist in my house. You can mix people from the same milieu, but putting a gardener in with an artist, a *paysan* with a minister – *ça va pas du tout*. The barbecue, where everyone joins together and has a good time, that has nothing to do with France. The melting pot works in the United States but not in this country.'

Simca has been composing her table at Le Mas Vieux according to these principles since 1958; that was the year she and her late husband Jean Fischbacher, a chemist from Alsace who worked in perfumery, inherited the property from his cousin, Marcelle Challiol. An artist, Challiol had arrived twenty-nine years earlier in search of subjects to paint and good Mediterranean light in which to paint them. Living in Paris and seeing an advertisement in *Le Figaro* announcing *une vieille ferme provençale à vendre*, Challiol took the train down to Nice the same day and bought it the next – 'for pennies, needless to say,' notes Simca. 'In those days a little farm around here like Bramafam, with five hectares of olive trees and vineyards, cost nothing. But the grapes today are a sad story. In 1987 I had 2,000 kilos; but the wine cooperative is too far away, and nobody else wanted them.'

After dissolving a first marriage – an act endorsed by neither her family nor the times – Simca married Jean Fischbacher in 1937 and visited the house for the first time. (It was from Fischbacher that she acquired her nickname, when he saw how his large wife folded herself into such a small car as the Simca.) Simca was not seduced by what she saw at Bramafam: because the water from the three springs was full of lime, supplies had to be brought from Grasse; electricity had not yet found its way up from the Côte d'Azur; the place was falling to bits. 'Still much too rustic for my taste, in spite of the work that had been done,' she admits, and besides, Mlle Challiol's cat had picked a fight with Simca's poodle Vicky.

To keep her company during the war Challiol sent for Hett Kwiatkowska, an accomplished Polish artist whom she had met in Montparnasse and who had exhibited in Stockholm. Both women's work is still hung throughout Le Mas Vieux, and it is not difficult to see that Kwiatkowska was the better painter. They worked as a team hiding refugees from Israel and Yugoslavia in the buildings below Bramafam, lodgings once used by monks from the Iles de Lérins who would come for a change of air and to worship in the adjoining chapel. Simca says that the refugees did well because they could drink from one of the springs, despite the indigestibility of the water, without leaving their hiding place.

Simca, meanwhile, with both her brother and husband imprisoned in Germany – Jean in an officers' detention camp – joined the Resistance; in her dangerous new life she produced false identity papers out of her closely surveyed Neuilly apartment. She also made sure Jean and the men in his barracks ate well, sending them weekly parcels of whatever she could collect on her bicycle on wild scaring-up missions through the countryside. In exchange for a few eggs, a bar of chocolate, a ham, or a good bottle of Chinon, Simca offered her suppliers bootleg Bénédictine from the family factory. Bénédictine, the liqueur created by her maternal grandfather, was also the ingredient that preserved the chocolate truffles she posted to Germany whenever there was cream or butter.

After five years of wartime separation the Fischbachers dusted themselves off and resumed life. 'The tall woman from the north', as her former culinary collaborator Michael James has called her, finally decided to make a move professionally and do something with her knowledge of cooking. She became an author, writing a small, charming, virtually unknown book called *What's Cooking in France?* with her friend Louisette Berth-

ABOVE: *In contrast to Julia Child's professional kitchen in La Pitchoune, Simca's in Le Mas Vieux is quite humble. A skylight allows fruit to ripen on the shelf above the stove.*

olle. At the same time Bertholle was being encouraged by a friend in Grosse Pointe, Michigan, to do a French cookbook tailored to the American market. Back in France the idea was proposed to Simca, who then submitted a collection of family recipes to a publishing friend in the United States. Excellent, the woman said, but added that the recipes needed introductions which combined history with anecdotes and tips.

In 1949 Simca attended a party outside Paris; it was here, her host told her, that she would meet the person she needed to write the problematic text – an exceedingly tall American. But Simca was unable to spot her because she was sitting down. 'Yes that's me,' Julia Child said when Simca finally approached her, 'and I can do what you ask. I have my Cordon Bleu diploma, you see. I have removed the skin of an eel!'

While developing the recipes the three women launched a cooking school, the Ecole des 3 Gourmandes, in the garret kitchen of Child's apartment in an *hôtel particulier* overlooking the garden of the War Ministry on the rue de l'Université. Following their progress and correcting their mistakes was the esteemed Max Bugnard, one of Child's former professors at the Cordon Bleu and a chef who had cooked under Escoffier in London and run his own restaurant in Brussels. Because Julia's husband Paul worked at the American embassy, she and Simca were able to shop at the embassy store for the limp American flour and flaccid cream they needed to test the recipes. And when the Childs kept moving around as a result of Paul's reassignments, Simca was usually right behind them, saucepans jangling, ready to get on with the book.

The typescript they delivered in 1959 to Houghton Mifflin in Boston contained only sauces and poultry dishes, Child's attempt at reigning in their ungovernable subject. Having travelled on the *Queen Elizabeth* on that first trip to America, Simca fell in love with mint juleps while passing through New Orleans on the Greyhound bus, and learned too all about odd national customs like the sandwich at lunchtime. And she was 'surprised to see how happy and helpful you Americans are. French people are not like that!'

When the book was refused she was delighted. The one finally brought out by Alfred A. Knopf two years later kept to her original idea of an A to Z of French cooking, however selective. When Julia

appeared on the cover of *Time* magazine in 1966, because of her enormously popular television programme, sales of *Mastering the Art* exploded. Correspondence between the two women dating back to 1953, as well as manuscripts, galleys and proofs for Volume I and Volume II, published in 1970, are filed among the Julia Child Papers at Schlesinger Library, Radcliffe College, Massachusetts.

Simca did not give up the apartment in Neuilly and move to Provence full-time until 1976, by which time all the niggling hardships had been ironed out. 'To get the heating right, the bathrooms, the roof – in all it took ten years. The upper part of the salon where my desk is was added by Mlle Challiol. She used it as her atelier, which explains the skylight. She also added the kitchen, thank heaven, otherwise we might still be cooking in the fireplace in the dining room. I created two bedrooms in the attic, and when all the work was going on, I found a small leather sack buried under the stairs which contained some Louis XV silver pieces dated 1725. There wasn't a fortune ... but they did prove the age of the house.'

Raised by an English governess until the age of thirteen, Simca says she has always been happily accustomed to *la vie à l'anglaise*, a style that has insinuated itself into Le Mas Vieux with the litter of Staffordshire spaniels seated above the window seat in the salon. The provincial décor in the dining room is skewed when guests find the table has been laid not with the local green and yellow pottery, as dinner here would seem almost to guarantee, but with Spode's 'Blue Italian' earthenware. The meal itself is likely to draw on the cuisine of Simca's native Normandy: the veal pictured here is cooked in milk, bathed in a sauce infused with Calvados, and served with sparkling cider. To begin there are whole scallops cooked with shallots and Muscadet, and accompanied by the same wine. Dessert is a clever, nicely acidulous orange-and-lime tart, with lime zest worked into the crust. If anyone is still thirsty there is a cool regional rosé.

'Before I met Pellaprat I had no intention of making food my métier,' says Simca. 'All I wanted was to be able to receive my friends better. He's still the one I put above everybody else. Pellaprat was the clearest, the simplest, and most direct. I'm still making the hollandaise he taught me in 1934.'

ABOVE: *Simca and friends like Richard Olney, the American authority on French food and wine, spend a lot of time around the table in the salon. The television also draws her here; one of her favourite programmes is the American soap opera Santa Barbara.*

OPPOSITE: *Many of the recipes for* Volume II *of* Mastering the Art of French Cooking *were developed and tested in Julia Child's kitchen in La Pitchoune, the house she built next to Simca's in the early 1960s. There are outlines of the utensils on the pegboard so that they can be rehung quickly. The construction of the house was supervised by Simca, who stocked it with everything 'my American sister' could need.*

MENU
for 6

Vin de framboises
Raspberry wine

GRATIN DE COQUILLES SAINT-JACQUES AU MUSCADET
GRATIN OF SCALLOPS WITH MUSCADET

Domaine des Dorices   Muscadet de Sèvre-et-Maine

FRICANDEAU DE VEAU DE LA FERME AUX CHAMPIGNONS,
FAÇON NORMANDE
FARMHOUSE VEAL WITH MUSHROOMS IN THE NORMAN MANNER

COURGETTES 'BRAMAFAM'

PURÉE DE FENOUIL AUX PETITS POIS
FENNEL AND PEA PURÉE

Cidre Brut Normand
Brut cider from Normandy

TARTE AUX AGRUMES BIEN ACIDULÉS
VERY TART CITRUS TART

Château Réal Martin   Côtes de Provence rosé

Café

GRATIN DE COQUILLES SAINT-JACQUES AU MUSCADET

Buy the meatiest scallops your fishmonger has to offer. A single dish – enamelled cast iron is best – can be used for both cooling and serving.

18 fresh scallops, weighing a total of
  approx 650 g (approx 1½ lb), corals
  attached
120 ml (4½ fl oz/½ cup) scallop juice, clam
  juice or home-made fumet de poisson
5 shallots, finely chopped
60 g (2 oz/4 tbs) unsalted butter
3½ tbs finely chopped flat-leaf parsley
1 bay leaf
1 tsp thyme
salt and freshly ground pepper
250 ml (9 fl oz/1 cup) Muscadet wine
250 ml (9 fl oz/1 cup) crème fraîche *or*
  double/heavy cream
45 g (1½ oz/⅓ cup) plain home-made
  breadcrumbs

1. If using unshelled scallops, open them over a strainer lined with cheesecloth and set inside a bowl. If you do not recoup 125 ml (4½ fl oz/½ cup) liquid, make up the difference with clam juice or *fumet de poisson*. (If using shelled scallops, use all clam juice or *fumet de poisson*.)

2. In an enamelled pan large enough to hold the scallops in a single layer, sauté the shallots in 40 g (1½ oz/2½ tbs) of the butter until softened. Add 2 tbs of the parsley, the bay leaf, thyme, pepper but no salt, scallop juice or wine. Simmer for a few minutes to cook off the alcohol and then extinguish the heat. Add the scallops, which should be barely covered by liquid. Cover, and leave for 5 mins. Remove and set aside the scallops, and reduce the liquid to 250 ml (9 fl oz/1 cup). Correct the seasoning and whisk in the cream. Simmer, stirring occasionally, until the mixture lightly coats the back of a spoon. Light the grill (broiler).

3. Spoon the sauce over the scallops and cover with the breadcrumbs. Dot with the remaining butter and grill until lightly browned. Sprinkle with the remaining parsley and serve.

LEFT: *Veal marinated overnight in milk is served with a purée of fennel and peas, mushrooms, and grated courgettes. The sauce is flavoured with Calvados.*

FAR LEFT: *Cypresses framing le Mas Vieux in mid-March.*

FRICANDEAU DE VEAU DE LA FERME AUX CHAMPIGNONS, FAÇON NORMANDE

'Motts' is Simca's acryonym for a mixture of dried herbs composed of 1 part marjoram, 1 part oregano, 2 parts thyme and 1 part savory. To make Motts, process the correct quantities of herbs in a food processor until powdery, and then push through a fine strainer.

700 ml (25 fl oz/3 cups) milk
2½ tbs olive oil
5 garlic cloves, peeled
salt and freshly ground pepper
1 bay leaf
1 boneless veal roast weighing approx 1.5 kg (3¼ lb), the tender top round of the leg, tied
2 tbs flour
45 g (1½ oz/3 tbs) unsalted butter
250 g (9 oz) firm white mushrooms, sliced
juice of 1 lemon
2 tsp Motts or thyme
1½ tbs Calvados or Bourbon

1. Boil the milk, cool to room temperature, and combine with the olive oil, garlic, salt, pepper and bay leaf. Place the roast in a snug-fitting loaf tin, pour over the liquid, and marinate in the refrigerator for 6–8 hours, turning occasionally.
2. Place the veal in a cold oven and heat to 160°C (325°F). Cook for 1 hour, rolling it over 2 or 3 times, then test by inserting an instant meat thermometer. The veal is done when it reads 80°C (175°F).
3. Blend the flour and all but 15 g (½ oz/1 tbs) of the butter to make a *beurre manié*. Dab the impurities off the meat with paper towels, remove to a warm place and cover. Strain the marinade through a collander lined with damp cheesecloth and measure out 475 ml (16 fl oz/2 cups). Pick out the garlic cloves and pass them through a food mill.
4. Toss the mushrooms in the lemon juice, salt, pepper and herbs. Cook, covered, in the remaining butter over a high heat for 2–3 mins whilst shaking the pan. Transfer to the veal platter. Add the marinade and garlic purée to the pan, bring to a simmer, and whisk in the *beurre manié*. Simmer for 5 mins, stirring until the sauce thickens, and adding the Calvados towards the end of the cooking time. Correct seasoning. Slice the veal, spoon over the sauce, garnish with the mushrooms and serve.

COURGETTES 'BRAMAFAM'

Simca proposes two very different dishes using one courgette preparation.

900 g (2 lb) small tender courgettes, trimmed and grated
3 tbs finely chopped shallots
1 garlic clove, peeled and crushed
60 g (2 oz/4 tbs) unsalted butter
2 tbs vegetable oil
salt and freshly ground pepper
2 tbs finely chopped flat-leaf parsley
2 tbs finely chopped chervil
130 ml (4½ fl oz/½ cup) crème fraîche *or double/heavy cream*
1 tbs Dijon mustard

For version 1:
1. Squeeze the water from the courgettes. Transfer to a collander, cover with paper towels and press hard.
2. Sauté the shallots and garlic in the butter and oil until soft. Add the courgettes and seasoning. Mix well. Cook slowly, uncovered, for 10–15 mins. Sprinkle with 1 tbs of each herb and serve.

For version 2:
Proceed as above up to the addition of the courgettes to the pan in step 2. While they are cooking, combine the cream, mustard, salt, pepper and 1 tbs each of the parsley and chervil. Add to the pan after 10–15 mins when the courgettes are done, and simmer until most of the cream has been absorbed. Correct seasoning, sprinkle with the remaining herbs, and serve.

PURÉE DE FENOUIL AUX PETITS POIS

4 tbs best-quality olive oil
1 kg (2¼ lb) fennel, trimmed and sliced
3 garlic cloves, peeled crushed
250 ml (9 fl oz/1 cup) home-made chicken stock
salt and freshly ground pepper
1 tsp Motts (see veal recipe above)
350 g (12 oz) freshly shelled peas
15 g (½ oz/1 tbs) unsalted butter

1. Heat the oil in a heavy skillet, add the fennel and garlic and cook, turning often, for approx 10–15 mins, until soft and lightly coloured. Add the stock, seasoning and Motts, and slowly braise for 25–30 mins more, or until tender. Simmer the peas in salted water until tender.
2. Transfer the fennel to a food processor and purée with the peas and butter. Correct seasoning and serve.

TARTE AUX AGRUMES BIEN ACIDULÉS

Simca's inventive orange and lime tart.

For the pastry:
1 tbs sugar
grated zest of 1 lime
180 g (6½ oz/1⅓ cups) flour
110 g (4 oz/7½ tbs) unsalted butter, chilled and cut into large pieces
a pinch of salt
2 tbs crème fraîche *or double/heavy cream*
2 egg yolks
For the filling:
1 tbs arrowroot
175 ml (6 fl oz/¾ cup) freshly strained lime juice, plus grated zest of 3 limes
125 ml (4½ fl oz/½ cup) freshly strained orange juice, plus grated zest of 1 orange
3 eggs, plus 1 yolk
125 g (4½ oz/⅔ cup) sugar
100 g (3½ oz/6½ tbs) unsalted butter, cut into large pieces
icing sugar for sprinkling

For the pastry:
1. In a food processor pulse the sugar, zest, flour, butter and salt 4 or 5 times, or until the mixture resembles tiny pebbles. Beat the cream into the yolks, add to the ingredients in the machine and process quickly. Flatten the dough into a disc, cover with cling film and chill for 1 hour.
2. Preheat oven to 205°C (400°F). Line at 24 cm (9½ in) false-bottomed tart tin with the pastry, either rolling it out or pushing it into place with your fingers. The dough should be twice as thick on the sides as it is on the bottom. Prick with a fork and line with foil or greaseproof paper. Fill with pie weights, rice or dried beans and bake for approx 15 mins, or until pale gold. Leave the oven on to finish the tart. Allow the shell to cool before.

For the filling and to assemble:
3. While the pastry is baking, dissolve the arrowroot in the citrus juices, and then beat into the eggs and sugar. Transfer to a heavy-bottomed saucepan and cook for approx 7–10 mins, stirring continously with a wooden spoon. Make sure that the mixture stays below simmering point. Remove from the heat and whisk in the butter. Cool slightly, continuing to stir.
4. Fill the shell and bake for 18–20 mins, or until set. Wait until the last minute to sprinkle one half with the lime zest, one half with the orange zest, and the whole tart with icing sugar.

8 Drama and dinner
in the sixteenth

*D*IX-*huitième* purists may sniff at the turn-of-the-century *hôtel particulier* that houses Jean-Louis Riccardi's Paris apartment, but for the Monaco-born decorator it has always offered the perfect stage for his brooding interiors layered with atmosphere and piled deep with objects. Redoing the flat four times in eight years (this is version three), whipping up ambience like a magician, each of his schemes has been more romantic, more theatrical, and pitched at a higher emotional level than the one before it.

ABOVE: *A sprigged cotton* indienne *from Braquenié was used to cover the late nineteenth-century chaise longue in the dining room.*

LEFT: *Jean-Louis Riccardi pours coffee from twin lustreware jugs at a Napoleon III table skirted with fringe and covered in Renaissance-motif petit point. If, as he supposes, it was designed as a games table, then the modern cups and saucers with his favourite playing card imagery are well-matched. Kings and queens, diamonds and spades turn up on the* bobèches, *or glass collars, of the candle-powered lamp, and M. Riccardi will even scatter cards on a table laid for a dinner party.*

103

The second-floor apartment on a hushed street off clattering Trocadéro has splendid bones – classical structural columns, fourteen-foot ceilings, an enormous skylight, elaborately carved mouldings, and intricately worked parquet. Designed as a one-family residence for the Comte and Comtesse de Leusse, the house was built at a time when this part of Paris, now the sixteenth *arrondissement*, was still countryside. The Leusses and other aristrocrats who made homes for themselves in the quarter are considered its settlers.

In a city where space is often savagely subdivided, it is reassuring to know that Jean-Louis's rooms are used in the way the architect of the building intended them, the salon as the salon, the dining room as the dining room. A decorator known for his powerful nineteenth-century interiors, Jean-Louis has stamped his flat with the influences of Emilio Terry, whom he considers to have been the greatest interior designer in Europe in the late 1940s and 1950s, and his former employer, Madeleine Castaing. Mme Castaing, the *antiquaire* and high priestess of French decorating, is noted for bringing English mahogany furniture across the Channel after World War II, and for preferring the look of nineteenth-century England, Russia and Italy to that of eighteenth-century France.

Given Jean-Louis's horror of fashionable society, it is just as well he has the melodrama of his rue Vineuse apartment to entertain him. When he is at home alone, he says, carefully contrived shadows and other stagy effects conspire to make him feel deliriously *dépaysé*, or uprooted. 'I don't feel at all like I'm in Paris here. I dream. Depending on the light, it can be Naples or central Europe. I am often bored when I go out socially, but I am never bored here alone. At my house it's either me by myself, or me and my friends. I do not give "Parisian" parties, meaning parties where all the guests automatically know each other; they're the people one is *supposed* to see, though they're not always happy to see each other. A Parisian party is also one where the food is not very important.'

Jean-Louis entertains in the same way that he decorates, offering one diversion and following up quickly with another. While guests fold and tuck themselves into richly upholstered and trimmed furniture set out in small groupings that encourage secret conversation,

champagne is popped and poured into etched ruby glass tumblers; coffee scented with cloves and cinnamon is served in cups patterned with playing cards; and chocolate-covered orange peel is dispensed from a giant crystal clog. Whenever someone even thinks of sitting down there are piles of ornamental cushions to fill in the hollows.

The person who ensures that the food is important *chez* Jean-Louis is Georgette Galien, his cook-for-hire since 1983. Georgette's livelihood has been linked to food since the 1940s when, still a couple of years shy of her teens, she began working as a *bonne à tout faire*. She made the leap from serving meals to cooking them the minute she saw that she could earn better money, and that her hollandaise was silkier than the ones she was being paid to pass around.

'It's simply that I decided I could do better,' says Georgette, who is old enough today to be a grandmother but fit enough to do her clients' shopping on a bicycle. 'While I was working in the early days for the director of the Comédie-Française, the cook once arrived late with the *canard à l'orange* – late and with the bird roasted beyond recognition. As a result of that disaster, *canard à l'orange* became the first real dish I ever made for my children and, well, I don't know... All that seems like ages ago.'

Georgette and Jean-Louis were brought together by his former housekeeper, who moonlighted down the street in a building where Georgette has another client. Menus are composed over the phone, with Georgette consulting a diary that tells her when and what she has cooked for Jean-Louis in the past, thus avoiding any undesirable repetition of recipes. For him the marriage is a success, 'because Georgette's is a classic *cuisine bourgeoise française*. Her dishes are well presented, with a familial quality that I love. It's not three piles of mysterious food surrounded by an even more mysterious sauce. I don't like complicated food or food that is all packaged up, and I would never serve tripe or liver or kidneys or anything like that. A lot of the people Georgette works for are bachelors or people with Moroccan or Portuguese or Spanish housekeepers who don't live in. Even those with housekeepers who cook need someone who can make good French food for a formal dinner. Georgette does the shopping herself in her own neighbourhood in the fifteenth *arrondissement*

OPPOSITE: *Plaster* commedia dell'arte *characters – Pierrot, Columbine and Harlequin – sculpted by a Swiss artist in the 1930s, and bought by Jean-Louis Riccardi at the Saint-Ouen flea market just outside Paris.*

ABOVE: *Jean-Louis Riccardi commissioned the screen from Dominique Derive, a decorative painter who works in Paris. The French* petit point *chest, designed to store wood, holds a straw basket with* verre de Venise *decanters that contain pear, prune, strawberry and raspberry eaux-de-vie. To bring good luck, M. Riccardi adds to the sheaf of wheat every year.*

where she knows the butcher, the fishmonger, the *fromager*, everyone.'

For friends who dine frequently *chez* Jean-Louis, the first sign that Georgette is in the kitchen is a bunch of radishes carved into crisp-petalled tulips and posed on the bar. Across the salon, French windows hung with white lace and ice-blue taffetta give on to a pretty, shallow terrace smothered in ivy and dotted with pots of honeysuckle that fill the flat with fragrance in spring and summer. Deliberately crowded with French, Russian, English, Italian and Austrian furniture, much of it Biedermeier and Directoire, the rooms are the opposite of academic reconstructions. Instead, they are the products of Jean-Louis's memory and imagination, so there is nothing strained or stilted or reheated about them. The only notes of artificiality are intentional ones.

Each of Jean-Louis's storms of redecoration has hurled more objects into the apartment: another pair of Eiffel Tower candlesticks on the Eiffel Tower table, another plaster *commedia dell'arte* character standing frozen next to Harlequin and Columbine, so many footed wrought-iron sunflowers that there is now a field. '*Je suis un conservateur horrible.* Look, it's just like the flea market,' says Jean-Louis, throwing open the doors of a massive 1850s Gothic Revival bookcase brought up from an *hôtel particulier* in Toulouse. Inside, more irresistible curios: an electrified brazier made by Guerlain in the 1960s; a jungle hut of woven metal strips stuck with jewelled insects and used as a sugar-bowl; mountains of Bohemian glass, Longwy and Rubelles faience, Habitat ashtrays, Vieux Paris porcelain, Monoprix baskets and heaps of Cardeilhac silver.

After years of hoarding antique *passementerie* bought at Paris flea markets, Jean-Louis has been able to use old trimmings to provide the lush flourishes in his own flat. The mirrored French doors that divide the salon from the building's public hall are hung with nineteenth-century wool draperies, held back with minutely detailed braid that finishes in bushy tassels. The twisted cord on the sleigh bed in the same room reappears in the dining room where the top of the wall meets the moulding. Some of the *passementerie* in the apartment is threadbare, like some of the furniture. But Jean-Louis is definitely not insulted when one of his dinner guests asks him if that leopard-covered slipper chair over there is safe to sit on.

Born to a French father and an Italian mother – 'I wish he'd been Italian too; they have more charm, and I feel more Italian than French anyway' – Jean-Louis moved with his family from Monaco when he was ten, settling in a typical late eighteenth-century Provençal house in the hills behind Nice. He enrolled at seventeen in the Ecole Boulle, an applied arts school in Paris, and, when he was twenty-four, he began working for Mme Castaing and Jacques Grange simultaneously. Later he assisted Alberto Pinto.

After years of training with these rather demanding personalities, Jean-Louis recognized in Georgette Galien someone with a fastidiousness akin to his own. Characteristically, when serving Camembert she insists that the *croûte* must first be removed, the cheese rolled in home-made toasted breadcrumbs, and a wedge cut out of it as a way of inviting people to sample it. The decorative breadcrumbs, the missing wedge – both, she says, may be small formalities that distinguish dining in *maisons bourgeoises*, but they are important ones.

Georgette is so conscientious that, if it happens to be convenient for her to buy the ingredients at the Marché de Malakoff the day before she has a job, but she does not like the look of what is available, she will wait until the next day hoping it will be better. Recipes, no matter how long she has been doing them, are always being revised – the cut of meat changed, cooking times adjusted. If Georgette really likes you she will even use produce from her own garden patch at Clamart in the Paris suburbs. Potatoes, carrots, cabbage, spinach, peas and raspberries are harvested there and hauled home by bicycle. As a lot of her fruit and vegetables are deep-frozen, it is possible to ask her to prepare a steaming bowl of buttered peas, for example, even when they are out of season. But again, she does have to like you.

Except for big parties – lamb curry for fifty, for instance, which would be prepared in Georgette's own kitchen – all the cooking is done in the client's home, with eight hours of shopping, cooking and travelling calculated for every meal. At

BELOW RIGHT: A bouquet of radishes is passed around before dinner with drinks – brut *champagne unless someone asks for something else. The fact that the host himself is perfectly abstemious does not intrude on the pleasure of his guests.*

BELOW: An electrified bronze brazier, made by Guerlain in the 1960s, was inspired by brûle-parfums *popular in France in the eighteenth century.*

Jean-Louis's apartment Rachida, his Moroccan housekeeper, is Georgette's smiling assistant, washing pots and pans, running out for a forgotten tub of *crème fraîche*. Georgette gives the orders; Rachida takes them. The efficient little ground-floor kitchen and pantry where they work as a boisterous, often comical team is connected with the dining room by a narrow flight of stairs carpeted in a Madeleine Castaing dog-rose design.

The menu shown here is typical of the traditional, un-showy French food that is Georgette's speciality. The first course, a rich, slightly sharp mushroom *croustade*, is part of the tart–quiche family. But whereas quiche contains both cream and eggs, a *croustade*, according to the cook, has only cream – in this case floods of it. The main course, topside of veal cooked slowly with vermouth on top of the stove, is served with orange sauce and Cairanne, a Côtes du Rhône-Villages with the power and 'generosity' to moderate the thickness and sweetness of the caramelized sauce. Cairanne's high percentage of Grenache grapes, which have a note of caramel, also make it especially suited to this dish. Among the four individually braised vegetables are tender fresh peas *à la française*, which requires that they are cooked with lettuce and pearl onions. Jean-Louis says that only one kind of cheese makes up the cheese course, to underline the fact that this is a private home where most of the decisions have been made for you, not a restaurant with a trolley of possibilities. A simple salad of lamb's lettuce dressed with tarragon–chervil vinaigrette is followed by an unexpected black cherry 'soup'.

Over the years two other of Georgette's menus have been especially successful at Jean-Louis's. One includes crab soufflé with shrimp sauce, *canard à l'orange*, *haricots verts* and *pommes de terre dauphines*, and *oeufs à la neige*. The second menu begins with a *tourte* filled with spinach, watercress and béchamel, followed by sea trout with hollandaise sauce, and julienned carrots and leeks poached in *fumet de poisson*. This time the dessert is either a raspberry charlotte, *tarte Tatin* or *crêpes Suzette*.

For a quick supper for friends in the warm and lazy months Jean-Louis will himself prepare cantaloupe and fresh figs, and pasta with a raw sauce of olive oil, torn basil leaves, and peeled and seeded tomatoes. For a more formal dinner Rachida's brother Zin may be hired to open the door for arriving guests. (In his navy blue Chinese worker's uniform Zin was once mistaken by one of Jean-Louis's friends for a fellow guest; she gave him her hand instead of her coat.) And it is Rachida who installs herself at the stove for an all-Moroccan menu: couscous; a salad of grilled peppers dressed in olive and peanut oil, cumin, lemon juice, hot red pepper and parsley; and *pastilla*, the traditional, broad and thin flaky pastry pie filled with pigeon, eggs and fried almonds. For dessert Jean-Louis requests his favourite *kaab el ghzal*, or gazelle horns – crescent-shaped almond cakes scented with orange blossom water and dusted with icing sugar.

No matter who is in the kitchen the service is never *à la française*, with guests serving themselves from platters held before them. Instead it is *à l'anglaise*, which is considered less formal and less elegant, with guests having their food served to them.

'To do it the French way you need a *maître d'hôtel* with white gloves and a proper uniform,' says Jean-Louis. 'I have neither a *femme de chambre* or a valet. Rachida is like a member of the family. It would be pretentious for me to do it any other way. Remember the long beautiful dinner scene in *The Dubliners*? It's that feeling I like.'

The fact that Jean-Louis has no butler fits in perfectly with Georgette's view of her job; as the one who cooks the food she thinks she should also be the one to serve it. 'I don't like it when clients hire a *maître d'hôtel* and I am obliged to stay in the kitchen. When I serve I always say a word to the person I'm serving: "Let me give you this piece, *madame*," or, "I haven't given you enough, *monsieur*." One of the ladies I work for told me, "Georgette, you make my meals come alive." But whereas I'll answer the door at a dinner in my own house, I would never do it for a client – and I am asked to. I'm willing to let things go in the kitchen at home and suffer the results, but not when I'm working.'

There are definitely nights when Jean-Louis could do with Georgette, or Zin or someone, at the door. 'Sorry we're early,' a couple of guests once apologized as Jean-Louis greeted them, still fumbling with his laces.

'But it's not you who are early,' he insisted, the couple having arrived at ten to eight for dinner at eight o'clock. 'I'm the one who's late.'

ABOVE: *Lattice-rimmed faience from the French factory Rubelles is mixed with contemporary glass plates and goblets from Venice, modern Bohemian tumblers and a vintage Baccarat carafe.*

OPPOSITE: *Dinner in the sixteenth. Jean-Louis Riccardi shipped the 1850s Neo-Gothic bookcase, which also serves as a clothes-press, from an* hôtel particulier *in Toulouse. The French candelabra were fashioned in the same way as stalagmites in a grotto in the late nineteenth century, while two engravings, part of a series entitled* Heures de nuit *and inspired by Pompeii, were produced during the reign of Louis XVI.*

MENU
for 6

UN BOUQUET DE RADIS 'EN TULIPES'
AMANDES GRILLÉES ET SALÉES
A BOUQUET OF RADISHES, ROASTED AND SALTED ALMONDS

Taittinger Brut Champagne 1979

CROUSTADE DE CHAMPIGNONS AU PORTO
MUSHROOMS CROUSTADE WITH PORT

Domaine Richaud   Cairanne

RÔTI DE VEAU À LA COCOTTE ET À L'ORANGE
CASSEROLE-ROASTED VEAL WITH ORANGE SAUCE

PETITS PAQUETS DE LÉGUMES BRAISÉS
BRAISED VEGETABLE BUNDLES

SALADE PURE MÂCHE À LA SAUCE VINAIGRETTE
À L'ESTRAGON ET AU CERFEUIL FRAIS
LAMB'S LETTUCE SALAD
WITH FRESH TARRAGON AND CHERVIL VINAIGRETTE

CAMEMBERT PELÉ ET ENROBÉ DE CHAPELURE GRILLÉE
BOULETTES DE PAIN AU LEVAIN 'LE MOULIN DE LA VIERGE'
PEELED CAMEMBERT ROLLED IN TOASTED BREADCRUMBS
WITH SOURDOUGH ROLLS

SOUPE DE CERISES FLAMBÉE AU KIRSCH
CHERRY SOUP FLAMED WITH KIRSCH

Café parfumé à la canelle et aux clous de girofle
Coffee scented with cinnamon and cloves

CROUSTADE DE CHAMPIGNONS AU PORTO

Georgette Galien was inspired to work out this recipe having tried some *amuse-gueules* from her fifteenth *arrondissement* Paris *pâtisserie*. It was Georgette's idea to transform what she first knew as an hors d'oeuvre into a *croustade* serving many. Try it for Sunday supper with a simple green salad.

pâte brisée *(see page 185 for recipe) lining a 25 cm (10 in) false-bottomed flan dish, chilled*
2 shallots, finely chopped
50 g (2 oz/3½ tbs) unsalted butter
750 g (1 lb 10 oz) white mushrooms, thinly sliced
100 ml (3½ fl oz/6½ tbs) port or dry white vermouth
juice of 1 lemon
salt and freshly ground pepper
1 tbs cornflour
475 ml (17 fl oz/2 cups) crème fraîche or double/heavy cream
150 g (5 oz/1½ cups) grated Gruyère cheese

1. Place a baking sheet in the oven and preheat to 190°C (375°F). Line the pastry with foil or parchment paper, and weight with pie weights, rice or dried beans. Bake for 15 mins, remove the weights, and cook for approx 10 mins more, or until golden brown. Repair any cracks with the reserved trimmings and leave the oven on to finish the *croustade*.
2. Sauté the shallots in the butter until soft but not brown. Add the mushrooms, port, lemon juice and seasoning, and cook over a high heat until all the liquid evaporates.
3. Stir the cornflour into the cream, add the mixture to the pan, and cook for 5–10 mins more, or until thick. Let cool.
4. Fill the partially baked pastry shell with the custard, sprinkle on the cheese, and bake for approx 30 mins, or until the *croustade* takes on a rich brown colour. Cool slightly before serving.

LEFT: *For dessert, cherry soup in an antique* cristal de Bohème *bowl. Both the* Vieux Paris *porcelain and Cardeilhac silver are mid-nineteenth century.*

OPPOSITE: *An eccentric standard candelabrum was created by placing bronze branches of waste metal on a tripod designed to hold a flower pot.*

PETITS PAQUETS DE LÉGUMES BRAISÉS

A lot of juggling on top of the stove, but worth it.

6 large artichokes
3 lemons, halved
450 g (1 lb) peas, shelled
8 baby white onions, peeled
½ small head of lettuce, halved and each
  wedge tied with string
½ tbs sugar
60 g (2 oz/4 tbs) unsalted butter
salt and freshly ground pepper
350 g (12 oz) carrots, cut into strips
300 g (10 oz) French green beans, trimmed
1½ tbs chopped parsley

For the artichokes and peas:

1. Snap the stems off the artichokes and cut off the tops approx 4 cm (1½ in) from the bottom. Tear off the leaves as near to the base as possible until you reach the tender fleshy ones that turn inwards. Rub the cut surfaces with 4 of the lemon halves to prevent discolouring. Using a non-reactive pot, bring a generous quantity of salted water to the boil, add the juice of the remaining lemon, and cook the artichokes, covered, for approx 35 mins, or until tender. Drain cut-side down and cool. Slice away remaining stems, peel away the leaves until you come to the hairy choke, and pick out the choke with your fingers. Cover the artichoke bottoms with cling film (plastic wrap) and reserve.
2. Combine the peas, onions, and lettuce wedges in a pan with the sugar, 30 g (1 oz/2 tbs) of the butter, salt, and approx 3 tbs water. Cover and cook, slowly, until almost all the water has evaporated and the peas are tender. Discard lettuce, drain if necessary, and correct seasoning.
3. Five minutes or so before the peas are ready, steam the artichoke bottoms, and brush with 1 tbs melted butter. Fill with the peas and arrange on a platter.

For the carrots:

4. Bring to the boil enough salted water to barely cover the carrots, add the remaining butter, and cook slowly, covered, until tender. Drain, toss with butter, season, and arrange in 6 bundles on the vegetable platter.

For the beans:

5. Cook the beans, uncovered, in a generous amount of boiling salted water until tender. Drain, toss with butter and the parsley, season, and arrange in 6 bundles on the vegetable platter.

RÔTI DE VEAU À LA COCOTTE ET À L'ORANGE

The challenge is to produce a succulent roast that could stand on its own, if it had to, without the piquant sauce. Although encasing the veal in pork fat is best, a few pieces of blanched bacon lard across the meat will baste the roast while it cooks.

75 ml (2½ fl oz/⅓ cup) vegetable oil
1 boneless veal roast weighing approx
  1.5 kg (3¼ lb), topside or silverside,
  covered with fresh pork fat and tied
2 or 3 veal bones, cracked
1 onion, quartered
200 ml (7 fl oz/generous ¾ cup) dry white
  vermouth
salt and freshly ground pepper
8 medium oranges, the zest of 2 cut into
  julienne strips
25 g (1 oz/2 tbs) sugar
150 ml (5½ fl oz/⅔ cup) Cointreau or Grand
  Marnier
100 g (3½ oz/6½ tbs) unsalted butter
250 ml (9 fl oz/1 cup) home-made veal or
  chicken stock
1 tbs cornflour

1. Heat 3 tbs of the oil in a heavy casserole and brown the veal on all sides. Remove and brown the bones and onion. Discard the fat and return the meat to the casserole with the remaining oil, vermouth, 200 ml (7 fl oz/generous ¾ cup) water and seasoning. Cook over a low heat, covered, for 20 mins. Baste and turn the roast often. Add the juice of one of the peeled oranges and cook, covered, for 65 mins more, basting and turning often.
2. Meanwhile, add the zest to a pan filled with 250 ml (9 fl oz/1 cup) cold water and boil for 2 mins. Strain the zest, run under cold water, and return to the pan, adding the sugar, 100 ml (3 fl oz/6½ tbs) of the Cointreau and the juice of the other peeled orange. Cook until reduced to a thick, syrupy caramel and reserve. Peel the remaining oranges. Carefully remove the membrane, separate the sections, and arrange in a (preferably non-stick) pan with the butter. Reserve.
3. When the veal is done, cover loosely with foil and remove to a warm place. Strain the juices. Deglaze the casserole with the remaining Cointreau, add the strained juices and stock, and boil vigorously to reduce by as much as half.
4. Carve the veal thinly, arrange on a serving platter and cover. Dissolve the cornflour in a little water. Reheat the sauce, beat a little into the cornflour, and combine this with the sauce in the casserole. Reheat the candied zest and add to the sauce. Heat the reserved orange sections through. Arrange around the veal slices and pour the sauce over the meat but not the fruit and serve.

SOUPE DE CERISES FLAMBÉE AU KIRSCH

Serve with vanilla ice cream and traditional biscuits such as *tuiles aux amandes* shaped like curved roof tiles, or *crêpes dentelle*.

50 g (2 oz/3½ tbs) unsalted butter
1 kg (2¼ lb) fresh black cherries, stoned
  (pitted)
2 pinches ground cinnamon
½ bottle good Côtes-du-Rhone
150 g (5 oz/¾ cup) sugar
3 tbs kirsch
1 tbs cornflour
fresh mint leaves for decoration

1. Melt the butter in a saucepan, add the cherries, coating them with the butter, and cook for 5 mins. In a second saucepan, stir the cinnamon into the wine, boil briefly and set aside. Add the sugar to the fruit and cook for 5 mins more. Add the kirsch and flame.
2. Combine the cherries and wine, and cook for 5 mins more. Strain, place the fruit in a serving tureen, and return the liquid to the saucepan. Dissolve the cornflour in 1 tbs water, add to the soup, and thicken over a low heat. Pour over the cherries in the tureen, and serve the soup hot or warm, decorated with mint.

BEHIND a dull and neglected façade in leafy Boulogne in the immediate suburbs of Paris a young architect and his antique-dealer wife pursue beauty – or do they police beauty? Nad Laroche's antennae are never down and never stop receiving signals; even as the strawberry and passion fruit bombe comes out of the kitchen on an old piece of green Apt faience, she exclaims: 'Such harsh colours!'

ABOVE: *Where once there was a garage, there is now a greenhouse. Eugénie, the housekeeper, gets dinner started.*

LEFT: *Nad Laroche's basement dining room was inspired by the kitchen at Brighton Pavillion; the decorative panel attached to the ceiling originated in a turn-of-the-century charcuterie. Flasks on the uppermost shelf contain sand Mme Laroche has collected from beaches all over the world. The table is laid with engraved crystal and a dinner service painted with a variety of birds, both dating from the mid-nineteenth century. The vintage terrine is used to prepare* lapin en gelée *and* boeuf mode.

Knowledgeable about wines, her husband Christian likes the Côtes du Rhône-Villages made by the Vacqueyras co-operative, but he does not like the label. So, he buys it in bulk, bottles it himself, seals each magnum with a big decorative blob of yellow wax, and before sticking on the label, he chops off the offending half.

Such feverish concern for what is beautiful and what is not has given the couple's mid-nineteenth-century house an atmosphere of hothouse aestheticism. 'A home is a skin, a carapace for what goes on in one's head,' says Nad, a nickname derived from Marie-Bernadette. 'In my bedroom there are photographs, books, favourite pieces of glass, my collection of stones, and the whole point is that they do not add up to what is thought of as a décor. Everything, rather, is there for a purpose. Living with things that have personal meaning, there is always the pleasure of coming back to them after you have been away. The two things I don't resist are books and objects. Everything else I don't really mind about. Clothes ... every day in Paris I am dressed as if for the country. Houses reflect an intellectual outlook, and the whole charm of ours relies on its being not a suburban house but instead a real *maison de campagne* a few minutes from the centre of Paris.'

After earning her *baccalauréat* Nad Laroche hoped to become a decorator, enrolling at the age of eighteen at the Ecole Camondo, the noted design school attached to the Musée Nissim de Camondo in Paris. But the early death of her father forced her to withdraw and obliged her mother Monique Petit to work. In 1967 Madame Petit opened an antique shop in the sixteenth *arrondissement* that expressed her love of England, her huffy impatience with anything 'mundane, conventional or bourgeois', and her amorous preference for 'earthenware to porcelain, quilted cotton to velvet, and bamboo to mahogany'. Nad is an unofficial partner in La Pastorale, as the shop is called, and she has been a terrifically attentive student, learning the tricky ABCs of Monique's tender vision of a provincial style which ranges from 'a peasant's cottage to Marie Antoinette's hamlet at Versailles'.

When Nad arranges some lacy cow parsley and trailing branches of blackberry in a jar in that hasty way she has of getting most things done, she is eloquently quoting her mother. And surely it was her mother who introduced her to the

ABOVE: *Tea is ritually taken en plein air. The table is laid with a Sarreguemines teapot, wooden sugar box, English 'Anemone'-patterned cups and saucers from the last century, eighteenth-century glass jam pots with horn spoons, and vintage Apt faience from the atelier Bonnet.*

OPPOSITE: *Viewed from the first-floor laundry and music room on the first of May, the north-facing garden is lorded over by a huge acacia. Though it is too early in the season to tell, the garden is planted exclusively with white-flowering plants – meadow sweet, asters, azaleas, rhododendrons, hydrangea – a modest reference to the famous white garden at Sissinghurst.*

sensible idea that good food carefully prepared with first-rate ingredients is no luxury but a realistic daily priority. And yet the two women are divided – by the nineteenth century of all things. While *barbotine* vases encrusted with leaves and carefully coiffed dolls in their best *habillement* are part of the décor *chez la mère*, they are regarded by *la fille* with something not unlike disgust – 'Not my thing,' she says with finality.

After years in an apartment in Saint-Cloud and 'without a centime', the Laroches became the thrilled proprietors of the house in Boulogne in 1980. (The flaking façade turns out to be intentional; they do not want people taking too much notice.) An old and sickly man had owned

the house previously and Nad says to describe it as derelict would be journalistically irresponsible: 'It was *dégoûtant.*' Eight days after she had first visited it she was in there pulling up the orange carpet on the staircase, scraping off the wallpaper, hideous even by French standards, and masking the bright turquoise walls.

Faced with ordinary proportions and interiors of no architectural distinction, Nad was determined that her new rooms should relate to each other with a kind of fluency. The effect of passing from one space to another should be liquid, she thought – the opposite of the clobbering impression one has in a house where all the energy has gone into delineating the Red Room from the Green Room from the

ABOVE: *In the salon, which backs onto the garden, the walls are a pale, pale shade of coffee mixed by Mme Laroche. The huge sofa is upholstered in thin, supple dusty pink calico – rather difficult in the daylight, she says, but all right at night when, under lamp- and candlelight, the sofa takes on the burnished look of an antique shawl.*

Blue Room. Consequently, all real colour was ruled out, and the entire place was painted in whisperingly subtle shades of *blanc cassé* and sienna, mixed herself and then applied painstakingly with a brush. The scheme in the salon, for example, was to hang the windows with plain pale-coffee silk from Rubelli, paint the mouldings and architraves an even paler version of the same colour, and paint the walls a still paler version of the woodwork. The only colour with any force that was admitted was 'the mottled green of a watermelon rind' used on the panels above all the doors.

The other linking element is books: poetry in the laundry and music room, children's books in the girls' rooms, cookbooks in the dining room, novels in the bedroom, and forty-five vintage volumes of Voltaire as well as works on art and gardening in the salon.

Once this thread was established Nad felt confident enough to unravel it a bit, treating each room independently. Curiously, the salon, filled with her poetically composed tableaux of objects, has ended up with a 'transparent' and *faux* baroque quality that is almost Italian. It is to this room and to its voluptuous eight-foot George Sherlock sofa from London that guests repair after dinner for tisane – *verveine* or *tilleul* from the open market at L'Isle-sur-la-Sourge in the Lubéron where the Laroches have a country house.

While the boring conventions observed in the houses of the French middle class produce shrieks from Nad's mother – shrieks perfectly duplicated by Nad herself – 'bourgeois' is nevertheless the de-

RIGHT: *Rather Flemish in style, this dining room still life, which includes a fan of silver-gilt knives, is one of many composed by Nad Laroche throughout the Boulogne house to communicate complicated and mysterious emotion.*

ABOVE: *A velouté of celery with Stilton is served from a* faience d'Apt *tureen dating from about 1800. Cream, cheese and egg yolks are folded into a mixture of chicken stock, vermouth, milk and vegetables stewed in butter. The Creil plates are Directoire.*

OPPOSITE: *Nad Laroche was determined to have this late eighteenth-century English convent cupboard – despite the fact that it was made in six pieces and had to be shipped at enormous expense from England, and despite the fact that it was too tall for the downstairs dining room and had to be cut down. Good quantities of powerful, spicy Vacqueyras from Christian Laroche's cellar accompany the cheese course.*

scription Nad volunteers for her own dining room, 'a room that makes you want to sit down and eat'. A rich chocolate-coloured toile de Jouy from Braquenié was used for the simple tied-back draperies and to cover the walls, and part of Nad's extraordinary collection of Apt faience, Creil, Sarreguemines, Uzès, Pont-aux-Choux and her favourite creamware is displayed on a pair of *étagères* she designed with her husband. First manufactured around 1760 by Josiah Wedgwood, creamware is earthenware with a clear lead glaze. It is decorated by piercing, moulding, transfer-printing and under- and over-glaze painting. Though developed as a substitute for porcelain, it was originally popular as a replacement for delftware. In France, where production began sometime before 1775, creamware became known as *faïence fine*, *faïence anglaise*, *terre de pipe anglaise* (literally, English pipe clay), *cailloutages* and Pont-aux-Choux ware.

Meals for more than nine are served in the basement in a second dining room equipped with cooking elements but with no oven, and modelled on that most famous of kitchens in the Brighton Pavillion – for Nad the apogee of '*le style champêtre*'. A massive late eighteenth-century English convent cupboard in six pieces was cut down imperceptibly to be squeezed under the low ceiling, which is itself covered in colourful glass panels that originally adorned the ceiling of a turn-of-the-century *charcuterie* – Nad's one concession to an epoch she otherwise dreads. Bought in Montreuil before she was married and before she even had any use for them, these panels are decorated with a boar, a hare and a fox, painted on toile and fixed to glass.

'The kitchen at Brighton is the perfect embodiment of that rural style that the English have and that the French generally miss – rustic and at the same time sophisticated,' says Nad. 'The only big country kitchen I can think of in France that doesn't lack that element of refinement is the one at Vaux-le-Vicomte.'

Throughout the house Nad sought to create another harmony, another accord between furniture and objects never destined to live under the same roof. Her model in this difficult decorating psychology is Sissinghurst, where, in Vita Sackville-West's tower room, old Persian rugs cover the floor while collections of beads, pebbles, shells, shards and pots line the windowsill. On the mantelpiece in the same room are set out a pair of Chinese crystal rabbits, Persian blue ceramics, and illuminated prayers and poems on vellum. Family photographs are arranged on the worm-eaten oak writing table, notes Nad, and of course there are books everywhere.

What she admires in the famous tower room in Kent and what she strives for herself is a certain orderliness and rigour. 'Every object in the house has its place *bien précise*. If I put something *there* it means it doesn't belong anywhere else. Equally, every room has its possessions. I cannot imagine my marble things anywhere except in the salon.'

Nad could not claim Sissinghurst as her spiritual home if she had created anything but an all-white garden in Boulogne. Dominated by a huge acacia, the 150-square-metre plot is informally but lushly planted with asters, azaleas, rhododendrons, meadow sweet, hydrangeas, ferns and bamboo. The stone paths are lined with potted jasmine, and honeysuckle climbs up the trellis behind a white garden bench on which two handsome forcing bells take their seats. Below the bench, pansies and dead nettle make pretty ground cover, and where a really nasty garage once stood, there is now a small and inviting greenhouse. Breakfast is taken out-of-doors until late September and if homework has to be done, the north-facing garden provides the three Laroche girls with a good venue. Forty-two square metres is given over to the bricked terrace in front of the house and eighty to the house itself. 'One of the things I love best,' says Nad, 'is the way it all turns away from the outside world.'

The Laroches' soulfully cultivated domestic idyll is the strict preserve of the family and a small number of dear friends. It is difficult to penetrate their circle, one of them says, and difficult to get them to leave the hearth. The social wilderness on the other side of the *périphérique* is definitely not their idea of heaven. '*L'art de recevoir* means only friends, *en principe*,' says Nad. 'It's good conversation in good chairs and with good things on the palate. My way of entertaining is refined rather than sophisticated, and simple – simple inasmuch as it's me in the kitchen, the meal is never served by personnel, and one big table is dressed rather than several small ones. Nothing would change if I were rich, and when I'm seventy I'll still be doing it the same way. I guess it's simply the naturalness of this

ABOVE: *Preferable to mediocre champagne, good sparkling Vouvray is served as an apéritif with courgette fritters in the back garden.*

ABOVE RIGHT: *To finish, a modest orange sponge, decorated with shredded candied peel.*

OPPOSITE: *A simple salad topped with crisp bacon and hard-boiled egg crumbs.*

approach that appeals to me so much.

'My cooking is *capiteux*,' says Nad, meaning that no apologies are given for strong, assertive dishes that command the palate rather than woo it. For the menu prepared here, celery is stewed with leeks and passed through a Moulinette with Stilton cheese for a *velouté* no Frenchman will remember from his childhood. A main course of wild goose, shot by Christian Laroche, is filled with an aromatic stuffing, slow-cooked so the flesh attains the melting texture of a *confit*, and served with baked pear halves that arrive at the table cradling cranberries – or are they rubies? Dessert is a simple orange sponge; the recipe is from a book by the Michelin three-star chef Georges Blanc, who learned it from his paternal grandmother. It is luscious.

'Returning from a shoot in Holland with twelve geese and ten ducks, I freeze the birds with their feathers on,' says Christian. 'I do it this way not just out of láziness but by choice. Every time I pluck a bird later in the year, I relive the shoot.'

The wine, too, is *capiteux* – the

mighty, heavily spiced red from the Vacqueyras cooperative in the Vaucluse. Among Côtes du Rhône-Villages wines none is more highly rated. A good Vacqueyras can be ranked just below a Gigondas or a Châteauneuf-du-Pape, and while it will keep ten years or longer, it should not be drunk younger than three or four.

Like all Nad's meals for which there is even a suggestion of an occasion, this one went into her special book that records what she served, what went right and what went wrong. The entry for 1 January 1983 is typical: '*Toast au saumon frais* (M. Guérard); *Foie gras de canard maison* (needed more salt and pepper); Stuffed goose (mushrooms, liver, breadcrumbs, sausage meat, spices, egg, Armagnac; roasted the 5 kg goose for 3 hours – a little too long); Celery mousse (M. Guérard; followed Pierre's advice – *délicieuse*); Potatoes sautéed in goose fat; Domaine de Beaurenard (Châteauneuf-du-Pape '83); Salad; Cheese (Epoisses, vieux Cantal, Brie, *chèvre*); Raspberry liqueur ice cream (*c'était divine*); Café à l'orange.'

MENU
for 6

FRITURE DE COURGETTES EN LAMELLES
THIN-SLICED COURGETTE FRITTERS

Domaine du Clos Naudin   Vouvray Mousseux

VELOUTÉ DE CÉLÉRI AU STILTON
CREAM OF CELERY SOUP WITH STILTON

Vacqueyras 1984   Cave Coopérative

OIE SAUVAGE, RICHE ET MOELLEUSE, FARCIE
RICH AND TENDER STUFFED WILD GOOSE

DEMI-POIRES BEURRÉES AU FOUR ET AUX CANNEBERGES
BUTTERY BAKED PEAR HALVES WITH CRANBERRIES

FROMAGES
ÉPOISSES, VIEUX CANTAL, BRIE DE MELUN,
CHÈVRE (POIVRE D'ÂNE, RAMEQUIN DE BUGEY, BOSSON MACÉRÉ)

SALADE VERTE
GREEN SALAD

GÂTEAU À L'ORANGE 'GRAND-MÈRE BLANC'
AU ZESTE D'ORANGES CONFIT
GRANDMOTHER BLANC'S ORANGE CAKE WITH CANDIED
ORANGE PEEL

Café
Verveine menthe de L'Isle-sur-la Sorgue

VELOUTÉ DE CÉLÉRI AU STILTON

Nad Laroche first tasted a version of this soup at a restaurant in London. While working out the recipe for herself, she discovered that French Roquefort works just as well as English Stilton. Bleu d'Auvergne is a third possibility.

50 g (2 oz/3¼ tbs) unsalted butter
1 bunch celery, leaves removed, trimmed and roughly chopped
4 small leeks, trimmed, washed and roughly chopped
4 medium onions, roughly chopped
1.25 litres (2¼ pints/5¼ cups) home-made chicken stock
250 ml (9 fl oz/1 cup) milk
125 ml (4½ fl oz/½ cup) dry white wine or vermouth
75 ml (2½ fl oz/⅓ cup) double/heavy cream or crème fraîche
200 g (7 oz) Stilton, crumbled
salt and freshly ground pepper
3 egg yolks, lightly beaten

1. Melt the butter and sauté all the vegetables until tender and translucent. Add the stock and milk, and simmer for 10 mins. Stir in the wine and cook for 10 mins more. Cool slightly, combine with the cream and 50 g (2 oz) of the cheese, and season.
2. Purée the mixture in batches in a food processor. The soup may be prepared in advance up to this point and completed just before serving.
3. Gently reheat the soup. Place the egg yolks in a serving tureen and mix in approx 250 ml (9 oz/1 cup) of the warm liquid. Stir in the rest of the soup, sprinkle with the remaining cheese, and serve.

FRITURE DE COURGETTES EN LAMELLES

Tempura-style fritters are well matched by sparkling Vouvray.

3 medium courgettes, seeded and sliced thinly into short strips
125 ml (4½ fl oz/½ cup) milk
1 egg, separated, the white beaten stiff
2 tbs vegetable oil, plus enough for deep frying
125 g (4 oz/1 scant cup) flour
salt

1. Whisk the milk, egg yolk and measured oil into the flour and salt lightly. Gently fold in the beaten egg white.
2. Heat the deep-frying oil until it sputters when a drop of water is added. Sprinkle the courgettes with salt and dip each strip in the batter, before carefully dropping as many into the pot as will fit in a single layer without crowding. Fry until golden on both sides, turning down the heat if you see they are browning too quickly. Drain on paper towels and serve immediately.

OIE SAUVAGE, RICHE ET MOELLEUSE, FARCIE

This stuffing is so rich that you will not need more to serve than one can fit in the cavity of the goose. Nad Laroche's recipe includes a pinch of sugar that she says will eliminate any unpleasant gaminess. The bird is freely seasoned inside and out with her indispensable *Mélange Special Concassé*, a heavily perfumed mixture of black and white peppercorns and Jamaican allspice from the *épicerie* Hédiard in Paris. It would be easy enough to make your own mixture by buying the spices individually, combining them in equal quantities, and filling the pepper mill.

1 wild goose weighing approx 3–4 kg
  (6½–9 lb), dressed
6 juniper berries, crushed
2 tbs Hédiard Mélange Special Concassé,
  plus enough to season the stuffing
juice and grated zest of 2 oranges
350 g (12 oz) minced pork shoulder
1 egg
100 g (3½ oz/1½ cups) unflavoured home-
  made breadcrumbs, dried
2 tbs finely chopped flat-leaf parsley
a pinch of dried thyme
2 tbs cognac
a pinch of sugar
½ tsp salt
2 bay leaves

1. Rub the goose inside and out with the pepper mixture and place the juniper berries in the cavity. Cover and refrigerate for several hours.
2. Thoroughly combine the orange zest with the remaining ingredients except the bay leaves. Poach or pan-fry a spoonful of the stuffing and correct seasoning. Pre-heat oven to 235°C (450°F).
3. Squeeze half an orange into the cavity to freshen it. Fill with the stuffing and truss or skewer closed if the mixture needs to be held in. Squeeze a second orange half over the top of the bird, drape the bay leaves over the breast, and roast for 15 mins. Turn the oven down to 150°C (300°F) and cook for 2 hours more, basting often with the pan juices and the juice of the remaining orange. Transfer to a serving platter and let rest for 10 mins under a loose tent of foil before carving.

DEMI-POIRES BEURRÉES AU FOUR ET AUX CANNEBERGES

An uncommon pairing of fruits.

3 medium pears, peeled, halved and cored
40 g (1½ oz/3 tbs) unsalted butter
juice of 2 oranges, plus the grated zest of 1
100 g (3½ oz) fresh cranberries
25 g (1 oz/2 tbs) sugar

1. If the pears will not sit flat even when crowded into a baking dish, take a small slice from the roundest part of each half. Arrange flat-side up in the dish, placing ½ tbs butter in each cavity. Squeeze over the juice of 1½ oranges and bake for approx 30 mins, or until tender.
3. While the fruit is baking, combine in a non-reactive saucepan the remaining orange juice with the zest, cranberries and sugar. Cook over a medium heat until the cranberries burst. Turn down the heat and continue cooking, stirring, until the liquid reduces and thickens a little. Spoon into the pear halves, arrange around the goose, and serve.

OPPOSITE: *The English teapot is an example of marbled ware, made using coloured slips or tinted clays that are 'wedged'. Josiah Wedgwood made glazed ware in the eighteenth century to look like marble, malachite, onyx and porphyry.*

BELOW: *Crushed juniper berries inside the wild goose perfume the meat before it is stuffed. The pear halves are baked separately and then filled with cranberries cooked in orange juice.*

GÂTEAU À L'ORANGE 'GRAND-MÈRE BLANC' AU ZESTE D'ORANGES CONFIT

A cake so more-ish and easy to make that you may want to anticipate its success and bake two.

For the cake:
150 g (5 oz/⅔ cup) unsalted butter, softened
150 g (5 oz/¾ cup) sugar
grated zest of 2 medium oranges, plus the
  strained juice of 1
2 eggs
115 g (4 oz/generous ¾ cup) flour
½ tsp baking powder
shredded orange peel for decoration
For the glaze (optional):
115 g (4 oz/generous ⅔ cup) icing sugar,
  sifted
1 tbs kirsch
strained juice of the remaining orange
  from the cake recipe

For the cake:
1. Preheat oven to 205°C (400°F). Cream the butter and sugar. Incorporate the orange juice and the eggs, one at a time. Add the flour, baking powder and all but 1 tsp of the zest, and mix vigorously.
2. Generously butter a 23 cm (9 in) false-bottomed cake tin, dust with flour and pour in the batter. Bake for 20 mins, or until the centre is set and springs back. Cool slightly and turn out onto a serving dish. Glaze if desired, sprinkle with the remaining zest, decorate with the peel and serve.
For the glaze:
3. While the cake is baking, dissolve the sugar in the kirsch and orange juice. Pour evenly over the warm cake.

10 An ancestral vineyard in the Beaujolais

AT EIGHT o'clock on a Saturday evening when she is giving a *placé* dinner for twenty, the Marquise de Roussy de Sales is in the *potager*, harvesting the tenderest *cardons* from under jute blanching sacks. Ten minutes later she races over the rigid parterre laid out by Le Nôtre, gives her Brouilly vineyards an inspecting look, and enters Château de La Chaize, built by Mansart. And by half-past eight she is among her guests in the salon, sensibly coiffed, reasonably dressed in a simple silk blouse by Valentino, and pouring out a Pimm's, a Kir, or a highly seasoned château-issue tomato juice.

Since 1676 ancestors of Nicole de Roussy de Sales have been quaffing cocktails of one sort or another at La Chaize, which lies cradled in the hills just north of Lyon, in the core of the Beaujolais wine-growing district.

ABOVE: *An exuberant* potager, *perfectly maintained, furnishes La Chaize with both comestible and ornamental vegetables.*

LEFT: *Jules Mansart, the architect of Versailles, and André Le Nôtre, who designed the palace gardens, were also responsible for La Chaize. Completed in 1676, the château was built for and named after the military commander in Lyon under Louis XIV. Grapes grown directly behind the house in a plot still referred to as 'la réserve du château' were once used to make wine designated uniquely for the château table.*

Built to Mansart's sober (save for the enchanting double colonnade) plans in just two years – a fact that accounts for its exceptional architectural balance and purity – the château was constructed for François de La Chaize, head of the military regiment in Lyon under Louis XIV and known as 'captain of the king's door'. Finding himself tragically without a male successor, François passed the estate on to his niece Anne and her husband the Comte de Montaigu. (The French ambassador to Venice, the Comte had as his secretary the writer and philosopher Jean-Jacques Rousseau.) The last Montaigu to occupy the château was a turn-of-the-century beauty who hated children and loved bridge in equal measure, Nicole de Roussy de Sales's famously difficult great-aunt. When she died in 1967 among her parures, and among her Paquins, Worths and Schiaparellis, the ninety-four-year-old Marquise left La Chaize to Nicole.

Did François de La Chaize dine on *cardons* from Le Nôtre's splendid kitchen garden? Unfortunately no records exist of what was originally planted. *Cardons*, or cardoons, are thistle-like perennials re-lated to the artichoke; those grown by Nicole are served with poached beef marrow, a popular regional dish and a speciality of Christian Mabeau, a young chef whose *restaurant gastronomique* is found in the nearby village of Odenas. Filling in for the château's vacationing staff cook during the month of August, Mabeau is accustomed to delivering the odd last-minute *coq au vin*. More rarely, as in the menu shown here, he is called in to build a lavish meal around a whole fresh pike caught in the Dommbes, the neighbouring region of lakes also known for carp and frogs. On these occasions Mabeau arrives at the house with his own battery of whisks, piles of immaculate plastic boxes containing decorative garnishes, and a huge microwave oven that made the Marquise go white the first time she saw it. Confidence was restored when the chef assured her that it was strictly for reheating.

Nicole's close friend and collaborator on the garden at La Chaize, landscape designer Jérome Vital-Durand, describes how entertaining at the château – orangery dinners, poolside lunches, grand soirées and tented marriage receptions on

ABOVE: *A suite of Restoration mahogany* canapés *covered in rare hand-painted velvet are placed against a wall in what was formerly a private theatre at La Chaize. Masked balls were also held in the room, which retains much of its original stuccowork.*

OPPOSITE: *A blazing jumble of styles makes the* chambre du Roi *the most amusing room in the house. Originally it was decorated in the hope that the Sun King would pay a visit; he never did. While the mantelpiece ensemble is Louis XIV, the* bergère *and half of a* duchesse-brisée *are Louis XV. Fashionable hairstyles of the period were accommodated by the* bergère's *slightly scooped back. The cornices, medallions and swags of the Restoration wallpaper are* trompe l'oeil *devices.*

ABOVE: Caisses de Versailles *flank a tall iron gate leading into the courtyard. The gate is painted blue in the seventeenth-century manner.*

OPPOSITE: *Fresh linen, grosgrain ribbons and lavender bags – La Chaize still maintains a vast laundry.*

PREVIOUS PAGE: *Lyon-based landscape designer Jérome Vital-Durand planted flowerbeds on the bank as a bridge connecting the parterre with the cutting garden and* potager, *giving the effect of* gros point *needlework. Outsized topiary suggesting a giant chess piece seems about to advance across the parterre.*

the lawn – are all characterized by 'an awareness of how life is lived today, coupled with tremendous rigour'. While it is perfectly okay, for example, to appear for summer lunch in the dining room dressed in tennis shorts and a T-shirt, the rule that places the most senior guest beside Nicole is never relaxed, despite all the laughing that sometimes goes on about it. 'La Chaize is no museum,' Vital-Durand says. 'The same lively spirit that animates the château animates the wine production. And always there is this rather formidable sense of *savoir-faire*, of great conviviality.'

Nicole works with Christian Mabeau in the same telepathic way as she does with Vital-Durand. Both she and the chef are quick, precise, and knowing. Nicole has had to be. When her husband François died of cancer in 1985, the management of the estate, which includes 140 hectares (360 acres) of Ganay-planted vineyards and 60 inhabitants, fell completely to her. Having inherited the desperately down-at-heel domain, she and François had set out to transform it. Until 1968 the property produced a relatively indifferent wine, with only 13,000 bottles a year marketed as La Chaize. The bulk was handled by *négociants*, or middlemen, who blend and sell under their own names. The Roussy de Sales reversed that tradition by doing all their own vinification and bottling, and by commercializing the vintages under the stylish black-and-red Château de La Chaize label.

Their strategy was to emphasize the wine's château provenance, giving it more room on the label than its Brouilly *appellation*. In this way it was handled more like a Bordeaux, and the strategy worked. While not the most prestigious of the ten Beaujolais *grands crus*, or noble growths (Fleurie and Moulin-à-Vent are generally more highly regarded), Brouilly is the largest; it stretches over 1,075 hectares (2,655 acres) and produces more than 8 million bottles a year. No one would argue that the 600,000 from La Chaize are not the best. Light, soft and redolent of raspberries, its luminous colour a pretty violet–red, La Chaize, as with practically all Beaujolais, relies on freshness for its essential charm. It is drunk young, one and no more than three years after bottling, and slightly chilled – 'Not *glacial*,' says Nicole. 'Cellar temperature, or twelve degrees, is ideal. People frequently make the mistake of serving it too cold.' Her Brouilly also represents an

excellent quality–price rapport and is known for the way it easily accompanies a great variety of foods, from hors d'oeuvres to fish and meat. It is a good choice for meals at which a single wine will be served.

Nicole and François – born in Canada and a graduate of Harvard Business School – were simultaneously faced with the same task of rehabilitation at the château as they were at the vineyards. When the Marquise de Montaigu was asked in the 1960s if she thought La Chaize needed anything doing to it, she was grossly insulted. The place was, in fact, falling apart. Plumbing to the formidable old lady meant two domestics dousing her with water from huge pitchers while she stood in her tub on the ground floor, the only part of the house she occupied. Every inch the iron-corseted Marquise, she would install herself at La Chaize each May, setting off again each November for her Paris apartment on the avenue Victor Hugo and for rounds of amusing *mondanités*. Even after she chose François to succeed her (and Nicole says that her great-aunt never really liked her and that it was François she chose because she believed that he

was capable of running the estate), she forbade him to observe the *vendange* or enter the *chai*. Whenever he tried to raise the subject of the wine she pretended not to hear him.

Nicole's 'sleeping beauty' was gently nudged into consciousness with the help of Jean-Paul Faye who, early in his career, worked with the old-guard French interior designer Victor Grandpierre. Faye's decoration for La Chaize is the kind that does not show. He worked only with what was already in the house, including vast attics of graceful furniture that would have been disdained by Nicole's nineteenth-century ancestors as unfashionable. The *fauteuils* and *bergères* at La Chaize, signed Georges Jacob – the foremost craftsman specializing in chair-making in France in the eighteenth century – demonstrate his shaping influence on the Louis XVI style.

Exploring the greater, uninhabited part of the château, Nicole also discovered mahogany Empire beds and a huge stock of very useful clocks, vases and candlesticks. These replaced the layers of anonymous curios and trinkets which had accumulated over the centuries, and which combined to make the

BELOW: *In the late 1940s, the sprawling kitchen in the basement of the château fell out of use and this more accessible one on the ground floor was created. The table is set for a children's supper. The room's earlier function as a* salle de musique *is betrayed by the lyres below the railing on the mezzanine where the musicians performed.*

ABOVE: *Guest rooms offer comfort if not company: alcoves added during the Restoration sleep only one. Part of the bed-making procedure involves entering the closet on the right and working through a hatch in the wall above the foot of the bed. To discourage mosquitoes in summer, guests can rub themselves with citronella placed in a glass of water on the bedside table.*

ABOVE RIGHT: *The marble columns in the entrance hall are topped by the masks of eight hounds, each wearing a different expression. Incorporated in the coat of arms of La Chaize, the dog appears as a motif throughout the château, on the fireback in the* chambre du Roi, *for example. The bouquets include plum and apple branches as well as hortensia, delphiniums, cabbage, lettuce, rhubarb, thistles, zinnias, cosmos and hydrangea.*

house forlorn and unwelcoming. In the guest rooms Faye kept the charming Restoration single sleeping alcoves, but transformed the cabinets which were built into the *boiseries* on each side into closets and bathrooms. The small chambers at the entrances, where a servant would have slept, were treated as the tiniest salons. The privacy is delicious.

If La Chaize could not guarantee absolute privacy, Nicole would rethink her policy of keeping the house filled with guests. 'The most important thing to me is that I'm able to offer people breakfast in bed. The idea of serving breakfast as a meal with everyone walking in and out ... no one on time ... everything always needing to be reheated – never, not in this house. If I'm staying with friends and they tell me to be down at nine for breakfast, I don't go. I always try to find someone to bring me coffee in my room.'

A naïve painting of La Chaize, dating from the construction of the house and hanging now in the salon, suggests that

the occupants of the guest rooms today enjoy many of the same perspectives enjoyed by those in François de La Chaize's day. The plots in the *potager* have kept their original shape; the parterre retains the same fierce balance and proportions; a wide path leading to the front gate still pierces a cluster of trees (oak, chestnut, pine, ash and lime); and a handsome double ramp embraces an oval basin. The arabesques of box in the painting have disappeared, however, and there are no jets in the canal at the bottom of the staircase leading up to the château.

With the painting always in mind Nicole and Jérome Vital-Durand continue to develop the garden in a way that respects Le Nôtre's bold, stark outline. In 1988 she had the idea to plant the entire border on the *potager* side of the pavillion with nothing but box, lavender and roses, including Madame Meilland, Mahina, Romantica, Landora, the tea-pink Jardin de Bagatelle, and Princess Stéphanie, which does a good job of snubbing

ABOVE: *The table, laid with eighteenth-century Meissen porcelain, displays the Montaigu monogram or coat of arms, which appears on the linen damask tablecloth, silver and carafe, all dating from the last century.*

Catherine Deneuve. Vital-Durand's most dramatic gesture has been the addition of an embroidered bank of grey and green plants that serves as a graphic junction between the kitchen garden and parterre. Rhubarb is encased in exuberant garlands of calamint and sedum, and santolina, packed in huge precise circles, is surrounded by nepeta. Each section of the *potager* itself is neatly enclosed in box, and a bower was erected to further delineate the purely decorative part of the garden from the one giving the château all its flowers, and virtually all its herbs, fruit and vegetables. Favourite family dishes and preserves are made from this produce, including cream of sorrel soup, *ratatouille*, raspberry soufflé, tomato *coulis* with basil, pea consommé with mint, stuffed courgettes and cabbage, greengage jam and redcurrant jelly.

Christian Mabeau relies on the *potager* for the herbs in the salmon *tartare* that fills his salmon 'pancakes', a first course matched by Nicole with Saint-Véran, a dry white wine from the Mâconnais made only from the Chardonnay grape, and similar in style to the Pouillys from the same area. The pike, served with an elegant crayfish sauce, courgette flan and La Chaize Brouilly, is followed by *fromage au gène*, a pungent local cheese made from a combination of cow's and sheep's milk. Dipped in *marc*, the eau-de-vie obtained by macerating spirit with the cake of grape-skins and stalks remaining after the grapes are pressed, the cheese is finished by pressing some of this cake into the surface. For dessert, a jellied loaf of fresh white peaches is prepared with Brouilly, orange and lemon juice and redcurrant jelly.

'Everyone comes together for meals at La Chaize,' says Nicole, 'but otherwise there's no schedule. You spend the days as you like. I can spend two months here in the summer without going to Lyon. I drive the 12 kilometres to Villefranche once every two weeks for whatever I don't find in the grocery shop in Odenas. We live a bit removed from real time. Days go by and we don't even see a paper.

'People who impose schedules on their guests are anti-*l'art de recevoir*. The charm after all of a big country house like La Chaize is that you can spend half the day without seeing anyone. Everyone feels relaxed, independent. There's none of this sitting on the edge of your bed in the morning wondering if it's five minutes too early to come down.'

ABOVE: *The late afternoon light of late August in the Lyonnais. The crystal chandelier and mahogany dining chairs, their velvet cushions handpainted with a variety of birds, are Empire. Several small, informal bouquets, composed of santolina, Madame Meilland and geranium roses, vervain and honeysuckle, are scattered on the table.*

RIGHT: *In the time of the Marquise's great-aunt, bowls of cobalt glass arrived at the table between the salad and dessert courses cradling a small glass of water. Having rinsed their mouths, guests would spit the water into the bowls. Today, with sprigs of santolina floating in them, they are used as finger bowls.*

MENU
for 8

Pimm's, Kir au Sauvignon de Saint-Bris,
Jus de tomate du potager

'PANNEQUETS' DE SAUMON FUMÉ AU TARTARE
DE SAUMON FRAIS, CRÈME AUX HERBES FRAÎCHES
SMOKED SALMON 'PANCAKES' WITH FRESH SALMON TARTARE,
FRESH HERB CREAM

Domaine Duperron 1986   Saint-Véran

ESCALOPES DE BROCHET AUX ÉCREVISSES
ESCALOPES OF PIKE WITH CRAYFISH

FLANS INDIVIDUELS AUX COURGETTES

Château de La Chaize   Brouilly

FROMAGE À LA GÈNE
CHEESE PRESSED WITH GRAPE SKINS AND STEMS

PÊCHES BLANCHES EN GELÉE
AU BROUILLY 'CHÂTEAU DE LA CHAIZE'
WHITE PEACHES IN BROUILLY JELLY

Café

'PANNEQUETS' DE SAUMON FUMÉ AU TARTARE DE SAUMON FRAIS, CRÈME AUX HERBES FRAÎCHES

These refreshing salmon rolls could be tied with a 'bow' of chive or blanched leek green as a final decorative flourish.

8 slices smoked salmon
450 g (1 lb) fresh salmon, diced into large
  pieces
juice of 1 lemon
2 tbs home-made mayonnaise
4 shallots, finely chopped
4 tbs finely chopped flat-leaf parsley
4 tbs finely chopped chives
2 tbs finely chopped gherkins (tart pickles)
2 tbs finely chopped capers
salt and freshly ground pepper
250 ml (9 fl oz/1 cup) sour cream or
  fromage blanc
1 head lettuce, washed

1. Chill a stainless-steel mixing bowl and the bowl and steel blade of a food processor. Cut the smoked salmon slices into squares by cutting them in half.
2. Coarsely chop the fresh salmon in the food processor by turning the machine on and off several times. Transfer to the mixing bowl and combine with all but 1 tsp of the lemon juice. Mix in the mayonnaise, shallots and 2 tbs each of the parsley, chives, gherkins and capers, and season. Place a spoonful of filling in the middle of each smoked salmon slice. Fold in the ends, roll into tubes, and chill, seam-side down, until ready to serve.
3. Combine the sour cream with the remaining herbs and lemon juice, and season. Line a serving platter with the lettuce leaves, arrange the 'pancakes' seam-side down, and bring to the table with the sauce, which is served separately.

LEFT: *Christian Mabeau's elaborate dinner for the Marquise and her family. The canvases in the dining room by Lacroix de Marseille depict an eighteenth-century scene at the city's port. Before they arrived at La Chaize, the paintings decorated a bastide outside Marseille and a house in the Berry.*

ESCALOPES DE BROCHET AUX ÉCREVISSES

An extremely elegant dish with a lovely salmon-coloured sauce. Well worth the work.

For the stock, crayfish and pike:
2 pike weighing approx 1 kg (2¼ lb) each,
  scaled, eviscerated and filleted, head and
  bones reserved
2 carrots, peeled and thinly sliced
2 onions, chopped
4 shallots, sliced
60 ml (2 fl oz/¼ cup) olive oil
2 stalks celery
2 bay leaves
4 cloves garlic, peeled
1 bottle dry white wine
juice of 2 lemons
salt and freshly ground pepper
80 crayfish weighing approx 1 kg (2¼ lb),
  de-veined
30 g (1 oz/2 tbs) unsalted butter

For the sauce:
2 tbs olive oil
2 carrots, peeled and finely chopped
2 onions, finely chopped
4 shallots, sliced
4 medium tomatoes, cored and chopped
2 tbs tomato paste
1 bottle dry white wine
40 g (1⅓ oz/4 tbs) flour
150 g (5⅓ oz/⅔ cup) unsalted butter
100 ml (3½ fl oz/6⅓ tbs) crème fraîche
salt and freshly ground pepper

For the stock:
1. Wash the heads and bones in several changes of cold water and break up the bones with a heavy knife. In a large casserole, sauté the carrots, onions and shallots in 2 tbs oil until softened. Add the celery, bay leaves, garlic, wine, lemon juice, seasoning, bones and 1 litre (1¾ pints/4 cups) water and bring to the boil. Reduce heat, skim, and simmer for 30 mins. Strain without pressing on the solids and reserve.

For the crayfish:
2. Heat the remaining oil in a frying pan until very hot, add the crayfish (in batches if necessary) and cook over a moderately high heat for approx 5 mins, stirring continuously. Leaving the tail meat attached, shell 16 of the crayfish and reserve the shells. Remove the tail meat from the remaining crayfish, reserving the shells and bodies.

For the sauce:
3. Using the pan in which the crayfish were cooked, heat the oil and sauté the carrots, onions and shallots until very soft. Add the crayfish shells and bodies, tomatoes, tomato paste, wine and stock, and simmer for 20 mins. Strain into a saucepan, pressing firmly to extract as much juice as possible.

For the pike:
4. Using tweezers, remove the small bones from the pike fillets. Wash and dry the fillets, cut each into 4 escalopes and season. Melt the butter in a frying pan and cook for 3 mins on each side. Remove to a buttered and warmed serving dish, and cover.

To finish and assemble:
5. Make a beurre manié by blending the flour with 60 g (2 oz/4 tbs) of the sauce butter. Reduce the sauce by half over a high heat and add the cream. Reduce the heat and whisk in the beurre manié. Whisk in the remaining butter and correct seasoning. Add the crayfish meat to the sauce, heat through and pour carefully over the pike. Decorate with the whole crayfish, one on each piece of pike, and serve.

FLANS INDIVIDUELS AUX COURGETTES

Delicious warm or chilled, as a first course or side dish.

4 shallots, finely chopped
6 cloves garlic, peeled and finely chopped
70 g (2½ oz/5 tbs) unsalted butter
1 kg (2¼ lb) courgetttes, trimmed and cut
  into large pieces
salt and freshly ground pepper
4 tbs finely chopped flat-leaf parsley
4 tbs finely chopped chives
4 eggs, plus 4 yolks
75 ml (2½ fl oz/⅓ cup) double/heavy cream
  or crème fraîche
a pinch of nutmeg

1. Sauté the shallots and garlic in 60 g (2 oz/4 tbs) of the butter until soft and translucent. Add the courgettes, season lightly with salt, and cook, uncovered, over a medium heat until very tender and any liquid released by the vegetables has evaporated.
2. Purée the mixture in a food processor, then process with the herbs, eggs, yolks, cream and seasoning. Preheat oven to 180°C (350°F) and heat water for a bain-marie.
3. Grease 8 individual 250 ml (9 fl oz/1 cup) ramekins or a 2 litre (3½ pint/2 quart) soufflé dish with the remaining butter. Pour in the mixture and bake in the bain-marie for approx 15 mins for the ramekins and approx 30 mins for the soufflé dish. The flan is done when the middle is set. Let sit for 5 mins before running a sharp knife around the edge of the mould(s) and turning onto a serving platter.

PÊCHES BLANCHES EN GELÉE AU BROUILLY 'CHÂTEAU DE LA CHAIZE'

In addition to this cooling dessert, Brouilly from La Chaize is used in recipes for oeufs en meurette, matelote, coq au vin and tarte aux poires, all of which are served at the château.

8 ripe white peaches
1 bottle Château de La Chaize
425 g (15 oz/1⅓ cups) redcurrant jelly
juice and grated zest of 1 orange
juice and grated zest of 1 lemon
2 tbs (2 envelopes) unflavoured powdered
  gelatin
fresh mint for decoration

1. Plunge the peaches in boiling water for 30 secs, and remove their skins. Over a bowl, so that you can recoup any juice, remove the stones and any tough or fibrous parts around them. Cut the peaches in quarters.
2. Combine the wine, jelly, zest, and orange and lemon juice in a saucepan, and boil for 8 mins. Sprinkle the gelatin over a little cold water and let stand for approx 5 mins before stirring it into the wine mixture. Reheat for a few minutes until the gelatin has completely dissolved. Add the peach juice.
3. Pour enough liquid into a 1.5 litre (3 pint/6 cup) terrine to cover the bottom. Refrigerate. Just as the jelly begins to take, add a single layer of peaches, cover with more of the wine and refrigerate. Repeat this procedure, each time waiting for the jelly to set, until all the peaches have been used. Refrigerate for 3 hours or so after the last addition of the liquid. Float the terrine in warm water for a few seconds, turn out, decorate with the mint leaves, and serve.

137

'IT IS THE MAN who wins the bread but the woman who butters it', according to an unsentimental Ouessantin adage. As merchant seamen the men of Ile d'Ouessant hired carpenters and masons to build their compact and astonishingly efficient houses, but even in this century it was their wives and their wives' sisterly neighbours who spared the domestic kitty by hauling the granite stones used for the façades and shovelling earth for mortar. Until the Second World War the same women laid the roads with macadam, drove their own wagons, and gathered and dried their own *taouarc'h*, the clods of sod or heather used as cooking fuel. They also coaxed barley for bread and potatoes for *fars* out of tiny parcels of land with just a hoe and a spade.

On a storm-rocked island of murderous shipwrecks, cruel folk tales, and a mystic Catholicism that conspired with the cult of the dead, the woman was the central and tragic figure.

ABOVE: *Ouessant lies 25 kilometres (15 miles) from le Conquet, making it the furthest from the Continent of all Brittany's islands. Ouessantins insist that it is the beginning of the world, not the end.*

RIGHT: *A morning catch of squid will appear on the lunch table as* calmar à l'Américaine, *served with rice pilaf. 'A l'Américaine' describes a sauce of cognac, shallots, garlic, white wine,* fumet de poisson *and fresh chopped tomatoes. The basket made from willows grown on Ouessant was woven by Victor Guermeur.*

11 Seafood and *taouarc'h* on a Brittany island

ABOVE: *Interiors on the island were designed with great sensitivity to space. In the* penn louz, *the body of the table was used as a dough trough, while bread would have been stored on the rack above the window, hopefully out of the reach of rodents. The entrance to one of the box beds is glimpsed just above the bench, the top of which could be lifted off to create an extra place for a child to sleep.*

Victor Guermeur was born on Ouessant in 1935 before women were sent to the mainland to give birth. He was engaged by the Airborne Division of the French Navy between 1954 and 1977, and has bounced around the globe enough to be considered a kind of career cousin of the island's footloose merchant sailors. As the owner of one of their immaculate and ingenious mid-nineteenth-century cottages, he certainly lives like one.

Because there are so few trees on Ouessant her people once prayed: 'Holy Mary, my good Virgin, please bring a fine wreck to our island.' For they fished splintered fragments from the sea with special grapnels and went straight to work, fitting out their tiny pristine houses as if they were ship's cabins and every centimetre counted. Starting with one long oblong room with fireplaces halfway along both ends, they furnished each of the four corners with a table and two benches. One bench was placed against the wall beside the fireplace while the one facing it across the table was built into a floor-to-ceiling unit comprising an armoire and *lit clos*, or box bed. Hugging the exterior walls and extending almost to the middle of the room, these units acted as partitions, leaving two intersecting passageways to run between them, cutting the space like a cross. Two identical rooms were thus formed at each end of the house, taken up almost entirely by the ensembles of tables and benches. One, the *penn louz*, was used for cooking and eating, and the other, the more carefully appointed *penn brao*, was reserved for receiving. Elements of the *penn brao* had been haphazardly dispersed throughout the ground floor before 1963 when M. Guermeur moved into his cottage.

Typically, a merchant seaman would have set sail from Ouessant – at 25 kilometres (15 miles) from the coast, the most remote of all Brittany's islands – for the first time when he was only eleven. Two or three or more years later he would return home from China or Japan, Valparaiso or Cape Horn with his salary spent long ago on drink, but with exotically decorated plates packed carefully into his kitbag. Slipped into the plate rack in the spruce end of the house, they were cherished souvenirs announcing to special guests like the curate the far-flung places the owner had visited.

Having husbands who might or might not turn up for dinner this year or next, or the year after, did not make romantic visionaries of the women of Ouessant. And of course sometimes the husbands never turned up at all, though news was communicated so slowly that wives often did not learn that they had been widowed until their men had been months dead. When they did find out it was through strict observance of an agonizing Ouessantin ritual known as *proëlla*, which is derived from the Latin *pro illa*, meaning 'in place of'. *Proëlla* took the place of a funeral. The uncle or grandparent first told of the sailor's disappearance went to church to collect two crosses, one crafted in silver and one made of wax. When night fell he made his way with the crosses to the dead man's house and recited the dreadful words that every island woman prayed she would get through life without hearing: '*Il y a proëlla chez toi ce soir.*'

The emotional torture of *proëlla*, the unbelievable burden of agricultural self-sufficiency and the vulnerability they felt in the wide-open landscape combined to create a society of fiercely capable women. In the middle of the afternoon they would look up from their work in the fields, limp but not defeated, hoping to see a ribbon of smoke from the chimney, the sign that ferns had been lit, and that hot coffee and buttered bread or *biscuits de mer* would be carried out to them by a sympathetic daughter or sister. Men were at such a premium on the island that the women even initiated marriage. A woman chose her young man and brought him cakes (some say a piece of lard) that he ate while sitting up in bed to signal acceptance. But what if he refused the touching proposal? How was the poor Ouessantine to know if it was she herself who displeased him or merely her cake?

The crisis in merchant shipping in France in the second half of this century did not, of course, spare Ouessant. Tourism now brings more money to the island than the handful of men who still work on oil rigs or process cargo. But tourism is modest. Ouessant measures only 4 by 8 kilometres ($2\frac{1}{2}$ by 5 miles), and in winter the inhabitants number just 900 (locals always add that there are again as many sheep). During the summer the boat that leaves from Brest and stops off at le Conquet discharges 1,200 people a day, but as there are only 80 beds available, most cannot stay the night. In the high season the number of people on the island, including those who lease or own vacation houses, is said to reach 4,000.

Brittany is noted for its potatoes, and

ABOVE: *A narrow passageway formed by cupboards and* lits clos *leads to the* penn louz, *one of the two identical rooms in the traditional Ouessantin house. The mercury balls hanging from the mantelpiece represent men at large at sea as well as buoys; they also helped to brighten the tiny room by reflecting light.*

LEFT: *The island's merchant seamen always acquired a statue of the Virgin when passing through Marseille. They also returned home from every voyage with a souvenir plate for the plate rack.*

those from Ouessant – *desirées*, *danys*, *fin de siècle* and the island's own *pommes de terre d'Ouessant* – have so much flavour that people are even drawn from the mainland to buy their winter reserves. In recent years an effort was made to capitalize on these vegetables by exporting them, but the attempt failed, due to the old and predictable problems of insularity. 'You don't realize you're on an island until you have to get off,' says mayor Michelle Malgorn, who also owns Ouessant's only off-licence (liquor store). 'All problems can be traced to trying to leave.'

Since the 1980s, however, mussels and comestible seaweed have been cultivated with humble success by the *coopérative agricole*, which has Victor Guermeur as its president. The seaweed, called *wakame*, came to France by accident as spores attached to oysters imported to the Midi from Korea. On Ouessant it is raised from a culture in salt-water labs to a length of two to three centimetres, then transferred to sea farms where it is strung out on lines and left to grow for kilometres before being harvested. Dried in hangars in the same way as tobacco leaves, it is crumbled into bark and sold back to the Far East as well as to the four island chefs. But beyond describing it as vaguely suggestive of the sea, nobody seems to be very good at evaluating how *wakame* actually tastes. Salty, musty and acrid seems a fair description.

The island's tenacious *mytilus gallo provincialis* mussels, the variety that is also raised in Spain, are noted for their size, fleshiness and vivacious red colour, and for their saline and slightly wild flavour – all qualities heightened by the conscientious way in which they are cultivated. Mussels grown on pillars are lifted out of the water, unhappy and hungry, at low tide. In addition, the sea bed with

which they may come into contact may be dirty. On Ouessant they are cultivated on ropes and nets hung from buoyed cables, which means they remain immersed in water at all times and never touch the bottom. And as a result of filtering up to 160 litres (40 gallons) of water every 24 hours, they fatten twice as quickly. There is a *marché aux moules* in town once a week in winter and three times a week in summer.

The island's unsheltered port has tended to discourage the men of Ouessant from trying to earn a living as fishermen. Families fished, but normally for their own tables. In a traditional dwelling like Victor Guermeur's, these were the four pine tables that allowed thirty-two people to sit down to a meal at a time, albeit at different ends of the house and without a great deal of elbow room. Once a week they were scrubbed with fresh water. Three or four children slept in the *lits clos* directly above the benches on beds of chaff or barley straw. Infants were placed in cradles on the benches, conveniently positioned to be rocked by their mothers from just inside the box beds. For the poorest families there were no sheets, only old worn clothes, and never enough of the colourfully painted faience bowls they used every day. With space at a premium, the classic interiors of Ouessant may have given some a reassuring sense of intimacy and others a threatening sense of being jailed in, the only perspectives being those offered by the two narrow gangways.

With precious wood reserved for furnishing the house first and fashioning farm tools second, the annual supply of clods – used to feed the cooking fire – was collected from along the coast in early summer when they were driest. *Taouarc'h* in the Celtic tongue of the Breton people and *mottes* in French, clods smoke but do not flame, and they give off a sharp animal smell. Even today some women of Ouessant use them to lend an earthy smokiness both to rice pudding and to a rustic ragout of mutton, onions, carrots and potatoes flavoured with a bouquet garni and moistened with water, wine being an excess that still occurs to no one. *Taouarc'h* are lighted outside against the wall of the house one hour before they are packed around and over a cast-iron casserole containing the browned meat and vegetables carried out from the kitchen. *Le ragoût dans les mottes* then cooks for three hours. Timing is tricky because there is no way of surveying its progress, and because once it has been removed from the cinders there is never any question of putting it back. But this method was ideally suited to *les femmes cultivatrices*, for they could easily set the pot to simmer and devote themselves to their land, pigs and sheep.

When a more concentrated heat and lively flame was required to boil water or milk, dried ferns or mixed *galettes* were burned. A mixture of animal dung and hay, *galettes* were slapped against the garden wall and left exposed to the sun and wind to dry. When no longer needed in the fireplace they were wrapped and placed instead of bricks among the bedclothes to warm them. Apparently, because the dung was dried, there was no foul smell.

The sheep looked after by the women graze throughout the year on the island's *prés salés*, or salt pastures. They are the reason for an annual fair that is one of Ouessant's oldest customs. From the first Wednesday in February to the *fête de Saint-Michel* (29 September), the period of lambing and slaughtering, the animals are tethered in pairs and moved twice a day to guarantee adequate grazing. The rest of the year they roam the island, untethered and earmarked, in two flocks – one in the north and one in the south. During this period the sheep are allowed to breed naturally, a 'system' that does not oblige every farmer to keep a ram. On the designated Wednesday of the fair, beaters are employed to round up the animals. In 1988 they earned twelve francs for every animal they captured. Whereas formerly the sheep were too prized as suppliers of wool to be done away with for the table – such definitive extravagance – today they are a gastronomic attraction, often ending up as

BELOW: *Ingenious carpenters, Ouessantins built the furniture and* boiseries *in their homes with the wood of shipwrecks. At the turn of the century a box bed might have slept as many as four children.*

143

ABOVE: *The plate racks, benches and table in what is now the kitchen* chez Victor Guermeur *at one time furnished the* penn brao. *This, however, is how M. Guermeur found the cottage when he purchased it in 1963.*

LEFT: *A few women on Ouessant still observe the island custom of cooking with clods,* taouarc'h *in Celtic.*

chops grilled in the fireplace.

Victor Guermeur eats mutton ragout cooked in clods as often as he likes: the women of the village have turned out to be perilously susceptible to his kindly, shuffling manner and big bachelor's heart. Now that he has retired from the navy, M. Guermeur heads the island's rescue team, and fishes every day the sea allows. He also makes his own sturdy, beautifully finished willow baskets in which to carry away the catch, distributed between his friends and his freezer. Victor learned the craft of basket-making, all but abandoned on Ouessant, from his father.

As head of the cooperative there is always shellfish on his table – there are eleven kinds for the dinner pictured here. Mussels make a course of their own stuffed with a pastis-flavoured mixture of salted Breton butter, shallots, garlic and parsley. Next, there are thick slices of pollack on beds of *wakame*, baked in foil packets shaped like gondolas, and served with plain boiled *desirée* potatoes. Muscadet may be the prototypical dry white wine but Victor chooses one that is yet drier and greener, a Gros Plant du Pays Nantais. Made from the Folle Blanche grape and bottled quickly to preserve its freshness, Gros Plant is a classic shellfish wine. Vineyards planted along the Atlantic coast on the mainland ensure a bracing, lemony bouquet.

While a *far* in other parts of Brittany is a polite flan, at the home of a true Ouessantin like Victor Guermeur it is a crusty English-style pudding made with grated potatoes, flour (barley flour in the old days), big worrying chunks of lard, raisins and prunes. The laughing friends around his table agree that there is something in the stubborn texture of a good *far oaled* that seems to spell their island.

RIGHT: Only dishes that do not require surveillance, such as this very basic mutton stew, lend themselves to cooking in clods. The brightly painted plates are characteristic of those once used every day.

FOLLOWING PAGE: *A* planche de fruits de mer *for nine.*

MENU
for 8

PLANCHE DE FRUITS DE MER
LOBSTER, MUSSELS, CRABS, PERIWINKLES, *AMANDES*,
COCKLES, *PRAIRES*, CLAMS, *CREUSES* OYSTERS,
LANGOUSTINES, SPIDER CRABS

SAUCE PÊCHEUR
FISHERMAN'S SAUCE

VINAIGRETTE AUX ÉCHALOTES, MAYONNAISE NATURE
SHALLOT VINAIGRETTE, PLAIN MAYONNAISE

PAIN COMPLET, PAIN DE SEIGLE
WHOLEWHEAT AND RYE BREAD

Les Jalousies   Gros-Plant du Pays Nantais

———————

MOULES OUESSANTINES REMPLIES AU BEURRE DEMI-SEL
PARFUMÉ AU PASTIS
OUESSANTIN MUSSELS FILLED WITH LIGHTLY SALTED,
ANISEED-FLAVOURED BUTTER

———————

STEAKS DE LIEU EN PAPILLOTTE
AUX ALGUES SÉCHÉES DE L'ÎLE
POLLACK STEAKS *EN PAPILLOTTE* WITH DRIED ISLAND SEAWEED

SAUCE SABAYON
POMMES DE TERRE DÉSIRÉE DU COIN À L'EAU
LOCAL BOILED *DÉSIRÉE* POTATOES

———————

FAR OALED
CRUSTY BRETON PUDDING WITH PRUNES

———————

Café

(The mussels, pollack, potatoes and *far* make a complete meal for 8 people)

SAUCE PÊCHEUR

This rich and colourful sauce can only be made in the coldest months when female crabs are filled with eggs. Ideally, at least two varieties should be combined, although if those given here are not available, it would also be worth experimenting with the roe of the male and the eggs from such fish as salmon, cod and lumpfish. Buy the quantity of shellfish you plan to serve and make the sauce with whatever this yields, according to the proportions detailed here.

*8 tbs crab eggs (large British crabs,
  Dungeness, king, spider or blue)
100 ml (3¼ fl oz/6⅔ tbs) white wine vinegar
6 large shallots, finely chopped*

Blend all the ingredients in a food processor by quickly turning the machine on and off. The eggs should be broken but not completely mashed. If preparing the sauce by hand, combine all the ingredients in a bowl with a fork, crushing the eggs. Chill until ready to serve.

STEAKS DE LIEU EN PAPILLOTTE AUX ALGUES SÉCHÉES DE L'ÎLE

Wakame is one of the finest tasting seaweeds. If it is not available, fresh seaweed may be substituted, but only to flavour. Coarsely chopped parsley could also be used at a pinch.

*20 g (¾ oz) wakame or other dried and
  crumbled comestible seaweed
8 pollack steaks, each 5 cm (2 in) thick
freshly ground pepper
175 ml (6 fl oz/¾ cup) clam juice or fumet de
  poisson*

1. Place a baking sheet in the middle of the oven and preheat to 205°C (400°F). Cut 8 pieces of aluminium foil, each large enough to enclose a pollack steak. Place an equal quantity of seaweed on each as a bed for the fish, reserving a little to sprinkle on the top, place the pollack on their beds and season with pepper. Distribute the remaining seaweed on top, spoon over the clam juice or stock, and roll the edges tightly together.
2. Transfer the parcels to the baking sheet and cook for 20 mins. Serve in the foil cases.

MOULES OUESSANTINES REMPLIES AU BEURRE DEMI-SEL PARFUMÉ AU PASTIS

If one were living in Brittany and preparing this dish, the local *demi-sel*, or lightly-salted butter, would be the only one acceptable. Its fresh, clear taste can be approximated outside the region by mixing a little sea salt into top-quality unsalted butter. The great amount of salt in commercial butter – much more than in *demi-sel* – guarantees its long shelf life and is responsible for its stale taste.

50 large mussels
115 g (4 oz) shallots, finely chopped
450 g (1 lb) unsalted butter
1 cup parsley, finely chopped
1 tbs pastis (aniseed-flavoured apéritif)
sea salt
freshly ground pepper
8 cloves garlic, peeled and finely chopped
50 g (2 oz/1 cup) home-made unflavoured
  breadcrumbs, dried

1. Scrub the mussels with a stiff brush under cold running water, then scrape off the beards with a small knife. Soak for at least 1 hour, changing the water several times. Discard any mussels that float to the surface or do not close shut when squeezed. Drain and rinse.
2. Transfer the mussels to a large pot and cook, covered, over a high heat just until they open. Drain immediately and reserve the liquid, passing it through a coffee filter if it is sandy. Shell the mussels, pulling off the dark rims and returning them to the deeper of their two shells.
3. Quickly poach the shallots in the mussel juice. Strain and reserve the liquid for the sabayon. Combine the shallots, butter, pastis, parsley, garlic and seasoning. Spread the mixture over each mussel, filling the shell. Press the breadcrumbs on top and arrange in a baking dish. As the pollack comes out of the oven, turn it off and put in the mussels – they will only need a few minutes. Serve immediately.

RIGHT: *Equal parts of grated potatoes and flour are used in the rather sinister-looking* far oaled, *Ouessant's version of the batter pudding native to Brittany.*

ABOVE: Wakame *seaweed, grown on sea farms off the island and then dried, makes a bed for pollack steaks. Mussels, another product of Ouessant, are filled with a mashed mixture of shallots, lightly salted Breton butter and pastis.*

SAUCE SABAYON

Light, *mousseuse*, and quick

4 egg yolks
75 ml (2 fl oz/⅓ cup) mussel juice, reserved
  from the recipe above
a pinch of wakame

Combine all the ingredients in a heavy saucepan or bain-marie and whisk continuously over a low heat, never allowing the mixture to simmer, for approx 5 mins, or until thick and lemon-coloured. Pass around with the fish.

FAR OALED

A recipe out of another century and another world. The people of Ouessant are proof that you can eat *far oaled* and still live to tell the tale.

250 g (9 oz/1¾ cups) flour
250 g (9 oz) potatoes, peeled and finely
  grated
125 g (4 oz/¾ cup) dark raisins
125 g (4 oz) unstoned prunes
150 g (5 oz) back fat (fatback), cut into
  chunks

Preheat oven to 205°C (400°F). Mix the flour and 600 ml (approx 1 pint/2½ cups) water in a large bowl, add the potatoes and mix again thoroughly. Fold in the raisins, prunes and fat. Generously butter a 25 cm (10 in) loaf tin, pour in the batter and bake for 1 hour. Lower the heat to 150°C (300°F) and bake for 2 hours more. Cool, turn out, and serve.

'IT HAD the wisdom to remain on a human and familial scale. It is an aristocratic home, a dwelling of people of quality, without pompousness, and without vain ostentation . . . I point it out therefore to our readers. If they know a man of taste – and, thank God, they still exist! – who wishes to acquire a thoroughbred house, a place charged with beauty and history, one in which he could realize wonders, don't hesitate to call his attention to Querville.'

ABOVE: *A curate's chair from the sacristy of a country church now stands in the hall at Querville.*

RIGHT: *Cider orchards occupy nearly 20 per cent of Querville's 80 hectares (200 acres). Dating from the sixteenth century, the manor was a ruin when the Courtemanches rescued it in 1959. The almost completely enclosed interior courtyard is formed in part by farm buildings where cider is fermented and Calvados distilled. Rather than lay their entire roofs in plain matt tiles, Norman builders liked to include a few glazed ones.*

12 La pomme et sa transformation

ABOVE: *The massive oak staircase with vase-shaped balusters and extremely wide steps with shallow risers was added when Querville was enlarged during the reign of Henri IV . The technique by which the half-timbered walls are constructed is known as* colombage *or* pan de bois.

OPPOSITE: *The seventeenth-century* lit à baldequin *in the* chambre de jeune fille, *or young girl's room, originally furnished a hospital; here it has been wrapped with Pierre Frey woven cotton.*

Reading the November 1958 issue of *Le Pays d'Auge*, a small magazine published in this gently rolling and most Norman corner of Normandy, the *notaire* quickly called Querville to the attention of Régis and Françoise Courtemanche. Madame Courtemanche was being fastidious, rejecting property after property, and always pressing for what she called an 'ensemble' – not just good grazing land for the cows and sheep they would raise, but a house and setting whose rare beauty and layered past would give her the morale to fill her post as farmer's wife. 'A farm without a woman – *ça va pas*,' says Françoise today. 'She's implicated in the life of the property, and if the house lives it's because she's in it. And she's in it all the time. I couldn't work in a place that didn't please me, that I did not find beautiful. I need to feel there is a soul. The man in that little journal wrote, "Who would like to buy a pretty manor that's destined to die?" Well, we did.'

Querville has been radiating its powerful soulfulness since the early sixteenth century. One hundred or so years later a second house was backed on to the original; the noble ground-floor façade, made of white limestone and rosy brick to discourage humidity, dates from this latter epoch, as does an upper façade in sturdy and rustic *colombage*, or *pan de bois*, terms that describe the graphic half-timbered mode of construction native to Normandy. While throughout the region the spaces between the ribs of wood are generally plugged with plaster, at Querville they are filled with an intricate herringbone pattern of thin terra-cotta tiles held in place with mortar. The beams at the back of the seigneurial manor are decorated with the heads of *vieillards*, their eyes, brows and cheeks carved in the form of oak leaves. Cracks have disfigured the faces of these poor old men in odd and cruel ways, but otherwise they have been wearing the same gloomy expressions for almost five centuries.

When the Courtemanches purchased Querville they had no idea that they would one day be fermenting apple juice for cider and distilling cider for Calvados. But as keen and susceptible career farmers living in the Pays d'Auge, the *département* noted for producing the finest cider and Calvados in Normandy, they arrived without any difficulty at the decision to centre their activities on *la pomme et sa transformation*. In 1976 Régis Courtemanche planted his first apple trees – 'It was

ABOVE: *A modern copy of a seventeenth-century* verdure *from Artis Flora, Paris, hangs above an eighteenth-century fruitwood farm bureau in the* salle. Verdure *designates a tapestry composed of fruits, flowers and birds.*

the reasonable thing to do,' he says.

Because the quantity of the apples that may be picked from a cider tree is inversely proportional to their quality, most cider is bland and unmemorable. Cider factories favour the varieties with the greatest yields and to hell with flavour. But Régis's idea was to make cider and Calvados of distinction, Querville products in which he hoped people would detect a degree of originality and a stamp of real Courtemanche character. They do. His cider is made like a vintage Bordeaux and his Calvados like a blue-chip brandy. Both, along with the apples themselves, are fundamental to the Norman concept of cooking.

'Sauté some apples in butter and you have your vegetable,' says Françoise. 'Add a bit of Calvados and cream and you have a good little sauce. Anything you flame with cognac you can flame with Calvados.' In her chapter on Normandy in *French Regional Cooking,* Anne Willan names fourteen recipes that employ these three primary ingredients alone or in combination: *turbot Vallée d'Auge* (baked turbot with apple and cider sauce), *les demoiselles de Cherbourg* (baby lobsters served with a sauce of reduced *court bouillon* spiked with Calvados), *filets de sole normande* (sole with shrimp and mussels cooked in cider), *filet mignon de porc normande* (pork tenderloin with Calvados and caramelized apples), *tripes à la mode de Caen* (tripe with cider and Calvados), *boudin blanc aux pommes en l'air* (white chicken and veal sausages with sautéed apples), *sauce normande* (cider and cream sauce), *côtes de veau Vallée d'Auge* (veal chops with baby onions, mushrooms, Calvados and cream), *cailles en douillons à la normande* (apples stuffed with quail and baked in pastry), *jambon au cidre* (ham baked with cider), *salade normande* (apples, shellfish and fresh cheese with herbs), *tarte aux pommes grillagée* (latticed apple tart), *sucre de pommes de Rouen* (apple sugar sticks), and *couronne de pommes à la normande* (Calvados-flavoured custard ring filled with poached apples).

Although the Courtemanches acquired Querville and its 50 hectares (125 acres) of pasture in 1959, they had to wait until 1962 to move in with their four children, aged between four and eleven. Three years were needed to introduce bathrooms and heating, though of all the things the manor can be said to be, toasty is still not one of them. When Françoise makes announcements like 'Autumn in Normandy begins on the fifteenth of August', people feel almost obliged to ask about the problems of heating so huge a house. But the Courtemanches insist that there is no problem; the thermostat is simply adjusted according to their most recent bank statement.

For eight years before moving in to the manor at Prêtreville, 38 kilometres (25 miles) southeast of Deauville, Françoise and Régis were tenant farmers on a livestock farm 96 kilometres (60 miles) away in the Seine-et-Maritime in the Vallée de l'Héronchelles. (Before that they had a similar arrangement in the Sologne.) During the years that the house was being refurbished they travelled once a fortnight to survey the work. Albums filled with snapshots of the manor during this period, its dazzling façade seen through a curtain of dust and a tangle of scaffolding, testify to the sorry and crumbling condition in which the couple bought it. The man writing in *Le Pays d'Auge* prayed that Querville would not fall into the hands of 'barbarians'. He hoped 'that no one would degrade it, that no one would debase it, by transforming it into chicken coops, or a suburban villa. Having money doesn't always signify having taste!' he warned his readers. He could not have hoped for more compassionate buyers.

Françoise remembers the *salle* – 'this is the country so it's a *salle* not a *salon*; *salon* is a city word' – as being the only space that was vaguely habitable when Querville was first proposed to them. The farmer renting the estate then had divided up the room so that all his activities, even the drying of the cheese he made, could be confined to one place. Originally, Querville comprised only this *salle basse*, the *salle haute* directly above it, and an attic. Because the first lords of the manor did most of their living and all of their receiving upstairs, the *salle haute* (now the Courtemanches' bedroom) was the cleaner and more elaborately furnished of the two. Linking the levels is a narrow spiral staircase; encased in a box of *colombage*, it has been overshadowed and overlooked ever since the time of Henri IV, who ruled from 1589 to 1610, when the manor was substantially enlarged. A second, more sumptuous staircase of sculpted oak dates from this period.

The expansion of Querville was so thorough and so successful that it is difficult to discern where the old house ends and the new begins. The face it shows

BELOW: *One of Régis Courtemanche's ancestors, painted at the time of the Revolution, looks down on the seventeenth-century oak farm table laid for a family dinner.*

RIGHT: *The terra-cotta crockery on the dining table was handed down to Régis Courtemanche from his mother; the modern napkins were made in* le pays Basque *following the traditional linen designs of that region; and the* pain brié *(nothing to do with the cheese) is a type native to Normandy.*

OPPOSITE: *The ingredients for Mme Courtemanche's* daube au cidre *are pictured with a nineteenth-century* carafe à cidre. *Before World War II this sort of carafe was used on cider farms throughout Normandy to transport fermented apple juice directly from the keg to the table.* Cidre bouché, *or bottled cider, was at that time drunk only on special occasions. The marbled stewing beef is from the ambulant butcher who installs himself in Prêtreville every Wednesday and Saturday.*

to the almost completely enclosed interior courtyard of farm buildings and a checked *porte cochère* demonstrates the importance placed by Norman builders on decoration. Set into the façade are vertically crenellated red-brick columns; within these columns darkly glazed bricks were inserted on end to give the effect of a woven chain of diamonds. And to relieve the monotony of a long stretch of plain mat terra-cotta roof tiles, colourfully glazed ones were interspersed at random. By the time the Courtemanches became the proprietors of Querville, however, the *pavés*, or floor tiles, of fired earth native to the region, had mostly left the house with one of its previous owners. Patterned with flowers, arabesques or a coat of arms that incorporates blackbirds, the handful that do remain are displayed as part of the manor's heritage on an eighteenth-century fruitwood farm bureau in the *salle*.

Although now bottles of pure cider are daily popped open with absolutely no ceremony in the *salles* of cider-making properties all over Normandy, before the last war they were reserved strictly for *fêtes*. For everyday use cider was drawn directly from the cask into a carafe or pitcher and diluted with water to make it lighter and more digestible. Labourers carried round stoneware flasks of the stuff out to the fields with them, and beer and wine were unheard of. As recently as 1913, amazingly, three glasses of cider were drunk for every one glass of beer in France. More shocking still is that in the same year the consumption of wine was only double that of cider. Today, except in

Normandy and Brittany where it is taken seriously as a drink, cider in France is considered quaint, and is ignored.

Régis Courtemanche grows thirteen varieties of cider apples and, depending on the recipe, he can make ciders that range from very sweet to very dry. 'A good cider depends on balancing three elements: alcohol, tannin and acidity. But as there isn't, in my opinion, a variety of apple so complete that it offers everything we need to attain this balance, making good cider is extremely difficult. We also look for body, which generally comes from using bittersweet and therefore tannic apples like the *Saint-Martin*, the *mettais*, and the *argile rouge bruyère*.'

Régis compares his apples to wine grapes – 'You don't see them on the table, and variety is as important in making cider and Calvados as it is in wine; a lot of bittersweet apples would go into making dry cider, for instance. Whether a cider is *sec*, *demi-sec* or *brut* depends on its density when it is bottled, because it's the density that determines the amount of sugar that remains in suspension. Finally, the slower the fermentation – slowness that allows the release of fermentary flavours – the better the cider. As with wine, the ideal is to have a combination of these flavours and those of the fruit itself.'

Following tradition, the Calvados at Querville is made with completely fermented cider. It is sent twice through an *alambic charentais*, the same type of still used in the Charente to make brandy. The first distillation produces what is called a 'petite-eau' in the Pays d'Auge and a 'brouillis' in the Cognaçais of between 28°

and 30° The second and much more delicate distillation, 'la bonne chauffe', separates the 'heart' of the alcohol at 69° or 70° from the unwanted 'head' and 'tail'. The level of alcohol is lowered over the years through evaporation, initially in new and then in older, broken-in casks of Limousin oak. How many years? The Courtemanches first distilled in 1984 but will only start selling in 1991. It should be noted, however, that unlike wine, Calvados and cognac do not improve once in the bottle.

The cuisine practised by Françoise at Querville is rich in Calvados and all the other archetypally Norman foodstuffs: milk, butter, cream, cheese (Livarot, Pont-l'Evêque, Neufchatel, Camembert), cider and first-quality meat. Another speciality, *truite d'eau vive fumée*, smoked freshwater trout, is served with horse-radish sauce as a first course, as it is here. Buttered corkscrew pasta goes with a lightly caramelized *daube* that requires $1\frac{1}{2}$ bottles of cider for every 1.5 kilograms of braising beef. Cider replaces red wine on the table as it does in the stew, and more apples – fritters dusted with icing sugar – appear for dessert.

'People come to Querville for the relaxed atmosphere of a big country house when we entertain, not luxury,' says Françoise. 'No one comes for the heat or the furniture. A long walk with a tour of the property is automatic after we've eaten. Everyone is in big sweaters and gumboots, and the dogs follow behind... What draws our friends to Querville is everything that is impossible in a Paris studio of thirty square metres – a big *salle*, a big fire, and a big table.'

LEFT: *The classic* trou normand *is a plain glass of Calvados taken between courses to create a* trou, *or hole, for the food to come; dousing apple sorbet with the alcohol is considered a refinement of this tradition. A* trou *is offered between the two meat courses or between the meat and fish. 'The absorption of a glass of eau-de-vie in the middle of a meal procures a kind of dilation that makes everything go down,' says M. Courtemanche. 'It's more aesthetic than the Roman method for achieving the same effect.'*

ABOVE: *Apple fritters on an eighteenth-century* faïence de Rouen *platter.*

RIGHT: La pomme et sa transformation. *Cider distilled into Calvados in 1984 is patiently sampled; the Courtemanches will not begin selling it until 1991. During this period the alcohol level is reduced through evaporation.*

MENU
for 6

TRUITES D'EAU VIVE FUMÉES À LA SAUCE RAIFORT
SMOKED FRESHWATER TROUT WITH HORSERADISH SAUCE

Cidre Brut 'Manoir de Querville'

TROUS NORMANDS AVEC SES BOULES DE SORBET AUX POMMES
APPLE SORBET DOUSED WITH CALVADOS

BOEUF EN DAUBE AU CIDRE BRUT DE LA MAISON
BEEF *DAUBE* WITH *BRUT* HOUSE CIDER

TORTIGLIONI AU BEURRE DE MAÎTRE D'HÔTEL
TORTIGLIONI WITH PARSLEY BUTTER

BEIGNETS DE POMMES
APPLE FRITTERS

Café
Calvados   Cuvée spéciale du Manoir de Querville

TRUITES D'EAU VIVE FUMÉES À LA SAUCE RAIFORT

If fresh horseradish is unavailable and you are obliged to use prepared, reduce the amount of lemon juice here to compensate for the vinegar that is usually added to the ready-made product.

6 whole smoked trout weighing approx 170 g (6 oz) each, body skin removed
125 g (4½ oz/½ cup) freshly grated horseradish
juice and zest of 1 small lemon
125 ml (4½ fl oz/½ cup) home-made mayonnaise
60 ml (2 fl oz/¼ cup) sour cream or crème fraîche
salt
Tabasco sauce to taste

Combine the horseradish with the lemon juice and zest. Mix in the mayonnaise and sour cream. Season with salt and tabasco sauce and chill. Arrange the fish on a serving platter and serve, passing the sauce separately.

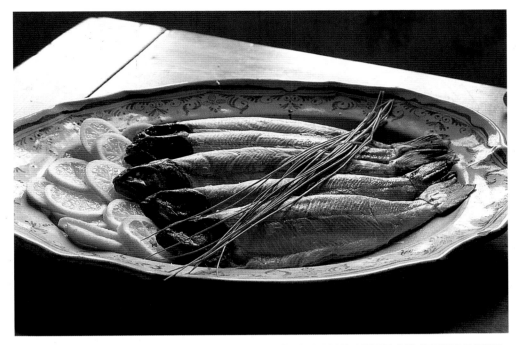

OPPOSITE: *Butter pressed into a vintage butter mould is from M. Julien in Le Mesnil-Germain near Querville. M. Julien's butter contains so little whey that clarifying is unnecessary. And because it refuses to melt even in a hot kitchen, it makes difficult puff pastry easy.*

LEFT: Truit d'eau vive fumée, *smoked freshwater trout, is a little-known Norman speciality. Françoise Courtemanche is supplied with his fish by M. Daufrèsne in Ouilly-le-Vicomte near Lisieux.*

TROUS NORMANDS AVEC SES BOULES DE SORBET AUX POMMES

Tart apples such as McIntosh or Granny Smith are recommended.

200 g (7 oz/1 cup) sugar
approx 450 g (1 lb) tart apples, peeled, cored and cut into pieces
juice of ½ lemon
6 measures (shots) Calvados

1. Stir the sugar into 125 ml (4½ fl oz/½ cup) water and bring to the boil. Reduce the heat, skim off the impurities, and simmer for 2 mins. Add the apples, poach until tender and allow to cool in the syrup. Using a slotted spoon, transfer the apples to a food processor and purée with the lemon juice. Return the mixture to the pan containing the poaching liquid and mix.
2. If you are using a commercial ice-cream maker, add the mixture to the machine and proceed according to the manufacturer's instructions. If you are using the freezer method, which will pro-duce more of a *granité* than a sorbet, pour the mixture into a shallow metal dish and freeze.
3. Cut the frozen purée into small pieces and blend them in a food processor. Quickly turn the machine on and off to achieve a smooth texture. Alternatively, allow the cut purée to soften slightly and stir by hand until smooth. Serve in scoops, alongside individual measures of Calvados.

BOEUF EN DAUBE AU CIDRE BRUT 'MANOIR DE QUERVILLE'

When cooking with cider, always use the driest available.

1.5 kg (3¼ lb) stewing beef, cut into 6 cm (2½ in) squares, 2 cm (¾ in) thick
125 ml (4½ fl oz/½ cup) vegetable oil
4 onions sliced
1 kg (2¼ lb) carrots, peeled and sliced into thick rounds
3 tbs flour
2 cloves garlic, peeled and crushed
1 bouquet garni
salt and freshly ground pepper
1½ bottles sparkling brut *cider*
3 tbs chopped flat-leaf parsley
450 g (1 lb) tortiglioni pasta, cooked and drained
parsley butter

1. Without crowding and in several batches if necessary, brown the meat on all sides in 2 tbs oil in a heavy-bottomed casserole big enough to hold the entire *daube*. Remove the meat, discard the fat, and wipe out the bottom of the casserole if necessary. Cook the onions in 4 tbs oil until softened and lightly browned. Re-move and repeat with the carrots in the remaining oil.
2. Return the meat and onions to the casserole, sprinkle with the flour and combine well. Add the garlic, bouquet garni, seasoning and cider. Mix again and cover. Gently simmer for 2 hours and then taste for tenderness – depending on the exact cut of meat, you may want to cont-inue cooking the *daube* for 15–30 mins more. For a thicker sauce, remove the solids and reduce the liquid. Sprinkle with the parsley and serve with the corkscrew pasta tossed with parsley butter.

BEIGNETS DE POMMES

The success of these meltingly delicious fritters depends on beating the egg whites separately. You might also try bathing the apples in Calvados before frying.

100 g (3½ oz/¾ cup) flour
2 eggs, separated
2 tbs vegetable oil, plus enough for deep frying
900 g (2 lb) Golden Delicious apples, peeled, cored and cut horizontally into 6 mm (¼ in) slices
caster (confectioners') sugar for sprinkling

1. Blend the flour, egg yolks, 2 tbs oil and 125 ml (4½ fl oz/½ cup) water in a food processor. Beat the egg whites until stiff and fold into the batter.
2. Heat the frying oil in a deep pot until it sputters when a drop of water is added. Turn the apple slices in the batter in batches, and fry in a single layer without crowding until golden on both sides. Drain on paper towels, sprinkle with sugar and serve immediately.

13 A new life for a *maison de famille*

FOUR generations of Rohan-Chabots had tried unsuccessfully to build a second salon on to Château de Duègne before Jean de Rohan-Chabot's grandfather finally walled in their attempts. Each endeavour had been thwarted by war or revolution. But how could that possibly mean anything to Jean's fearless wife Joy? 'You must understand,' says this wilfully enthusiastic DIY decorator and decorative painter. 'I cannot stop myself. I am dangerous. I could paint anyone who walks by.' The people of Joy de Rohan-Chabot's village in the Auvergne warned her that there would be trouble if she re-opened the business of the salon again. 'So don't,' they said.

ABOVE: *The shepherd from the Rohan-Chabots' village in the Auvergne in front of Château de Duègne, which was built in the late fifteenth century by the Chancellor Giac and remodelled for better or worse by the architect Duban in around 1840. The castle has a tortured history; all was not really well until the present owner's grandfather discovered and expelled a corpse which had been secreted in a wall of the castle.*

LEFT: *A refectory table in the kitchen bears the produce of the kitchen garden: strawberries, apricots, rhubarb, greengages and redcurrants are made into jam, while peas, green beans and asparagus are stored in preserving jars for consumption in the winter. A semi-professional Rosières stove designed by Paul Bocuse stands in the corner to the left, and the Chinese baskets ranged on the right of the fireplace were collected by Mme de Rohan-Chabot from the refuse outside a Chinese supermarket in the thirteenth* arrondissement, *the Chinese quarter of Paris.*

Joy built her salon and there was no war. Razing the wall, she created a kind of loggia by placing three tall arched windows at the end of the room, waking the place up with natural light. House guests who play chess and write letters here all summer have their eyes drawn straight across to the Puy de Dôme. Joy decorated the salon itself in the rich and overstuffed style of the Second Empire, copying the swirling Napoleon III design of the carpet from a document and changing the colours. In front of the fireplace two long rounded ottomans, *turqueries* first popular in France with Louis XV, face each other across a gold-trimmed *indiscret* upholstered in emerald paisley silk.

Having realized her salon and having therefore triumphed over history Joy, née de Rouvre, retired her tool box. 'When Duègne passed to us in the late 1970s it was really falling to pieces, which I loved. It was like something out of a fairy tale,' she says, 'and apart from making it a little more sophisticated, I mean trying to make everything less sort of broken-looking, it was this fairy-tale quality I wanted to keep. With this kind of house you add but

never destroy. As the French say, and they are very sticky about it, "You don't touch the stones." The château had belonged to the Comtesse Catherine de Chabrol-Tournoël, my husband's maternal grandmother; she was eighty-something and at eighty-something, you don't worry about things like changing the curtains. Unless my son keeps an eye on me, I promise you Duègne will be falling to pieces when I'm eighty too.'

Built on the site of a royal fortress in the late fifteenth century by Giac, Chancellor to the Duc de Berry, Duègne was enlarged in the sixteenth century and remodelled, for better or worse, in the nineteenth. Jean de Rohan-Chabot says that Giac was a *personnage diabolique*, a sorcerer who performed human sacrifices and whose victims were bundled in sacks and dumped in the Loire or Cher. The really ghoulish chapter in the château's history, however – the one which still worries the villagers – was written after the chancellor, when three brothers with the family name Rochefort-d'Ailly moved in. Two of them ganged up on the third and murdered him, stuffing his corpse into

ABOVE: *Topiary in the formal garden at Duègne stands up to the frozen blue light of winter. The Rohan-Chabots host informal buffets here throughout the summer.*

OPPOSITE: *A guest room on a mid-December morning.*

164

an interior wall in the château. The murdered brother became the house ghost, viciously taunting Jean's ancestors from the late eighteenth century, when Duègne came into his mother's family. Furniture was rumbled and bottles and dishes thrown around, before the skeleton was discovered by Jean's grandfather while central heating was being installed in half the house. The old man, sleeping directly below the spot inhabited by the ghost, had the worst of it. Finally, on the advice of the village priest, he changed his bedroom. The skeleton has since been removed to the town cemetery.

While the architect Duban did not fiddle with the exterior walls at Duègne, he did dismantle the quadrangle in around 1840, breaking down two ramparts. On to the narrow face of the wing where Joy would later add the loggia he stuck a *faux*-Renaissance façade, mimicking those of the authentic Renaissance houses of the Loire Valley to the north. Duban, who came to be overshadowed by his notorious student Viollet-le-Duc, also remodelled the Palais des Beaux Arts in Paris and Château de Blois.

As Jean's very distant cousin – 'I think we sort of share the same eighteenth-century grandmother' – Joy visited him at Duègne for the first time as a girl of fifteen. She had an even grander family castle in which to lose herself: Château de Busset in the Bourbonnais, near Vichy. But while Busset was bigger,

BELOW: *Joy de Rohan-Chabot decorated the salon in the voluptuous style of the Second Empire, placing an* indiscret *between two long rounded ottomans,* turqueries *first favoured in France by Louis XV. The Napoleon III carpet design was copied from a document and made up in new colours.*

the starched code of conduct made it less fun. She preferred Duègne, where no one remarked on the trouble you got into, and where you did not have to dress for lunch and dinner every day. Then, as now, the feeling was that of a circus.

Joy remembers that 'Whereas my parents' house was very strict and formal, with butlers and a first cook and a second cook and generally just a very boring kind of atmosphere, at Jean's there was always something crazy going on. The first time I went to Duègne it was full of lots of old ladies – aunts and a cousin of his grandmother's – who were all totally nuts. There was also a little boy who kept jumping out of the window with an umbrella, and a pianola played alone in a

dark room. It was very magical. In my husband's family the children ruled everything. They threw darts at the family portraits and his grandmother said, "How nice." We were all allowed to run in and out of the kitchen, which I would have never done at home. There was a great teenage atmosphere, with everyone flirting with everyone – boys chased after girls, girls chased after boys, and Jean chased after me. We were more or less engaged when I was seventeen and married before I turned twenty.'

The Rouvres and Chabrol-Tournoëls also had very different ideas about food. 'My parents are remembered as being the only people who ever went to Troisgros and ordered boiled eggs and spinach, a

167

dish we always had at home and which drove the chef mad – he thought he was there to do something else. But the cooking at home was healthy, whereas at Duègne there were always lots of different dishes and one always ate far too much. You spent hours at the table because there were so many old people and they took so long to chew. And as I've already said everyone was crazy. I am sure, quite sure, the cook was crazy, too.'

Joy's half-Scottish mother, who was born a Balfour and whose society portrait by Adriene Drian is one of the great twentieth-century treasures at Duègne, always imagined that her daughter would employ, if not a chef, then at least a cook. While Joy does take one and sometimes two students from the Cordon Bleu school in Paris down to the château with her for the summer, she is also often on her own. But just how she has come to be known for her cooking is not clear. In Paris she has helped award an important cookery book prize; she is invited everywhere; and she can have anyone she likes at her table, Rothschilds included. The Rohan-Chabots are extremely social.

'People come for Jean's wit,' says Joy.

'People come because Joy is so beautiful,' says Jean.

'They certainly don't come to us for the food,' says Joy, 'at least I hope they don't. And I don't think I'd like it if they did. I would want people to come even if there was only some *saucisson* and a scrap of bread, and the wine was bad. I think the company rather than the food should be the reason one goes to a private house. No matter how good the meal, if the people aren't thrilling, it's just not worth being bored for the whole evening. I have great friends whose food I know will be perfectly disgusting and I don't care. I have soup at home before I go and something when I get back.

'People really do love Jean's way of being both funny and nasty, and I suppose I don't mind if food is one of the reasons they come to see us. Perhaps some people really *wouldn't* come if the food were terrible, but I would never spend two days perfecting a dish to keep them. If I ruin a meal, I think, "So what". I am as capable as ever of roasting a chicken that is black on the outside and raw in the middle.'

To the people who share her table and who are more reverent about food than she is, Joy's so-what, make-do philosophy is perversely appealing. That she is such a good cook in spite of – or is it because of? – this carelessness both exasperates and titillates them. They want to scold her for not slowing down and taking more care, but as they cannot get her to recognize the seriousness of having reached for the sugar for a cheese soufflé when she really wanted the salt, how can they make her see the importance of white and not black pepper in a *chaud-froid*?

The celebrations surrounding Bastille Day at Duègne every year make such minute considerations seem positively infantile; the shuddering reality of the holiday means serving 296 individual meals. 'The château has 37 beds,' Joy calculates, 'They are all full; there are 2 meals a day; and the party goes on for 4 days.' It is a long weekend of Rohan-Chabots, one of the oldest families in France, and one that

RIGHT: *The studio is requisitioned for young guests in summer when all the château's thirty-seven beds are full. Mme de Rohan-Chabot says that she can easily envisage a time when her son will manage the château and she will move into the orangery that contains this iron bedstead.*

OPPOSITE: *An orangery standing in the shadow of the village church in the middle of the kitchen garden acts as Joy de Rohan-Chabot's studio. Trompe l'oeil is her speciality – trays made in* tôle *and decorated with feathers or shells, and lacquer screens draped with cashmere shawls or mounted with porcelain.*

since 960 has furnished the church with cardinals and kings with *femmes légères*.

Lunch is customarily a cold buffet around the pool, and dinner is a warm buffet set up in a different outdoor location every night, whether in the topiary garden at the back of the house or in the courtyard near the romantic crumbling tower. Joy had special wooden trolleys made to transport everything, and at the early meal, typically, they are piled with home-made pizzas, curried chicken salad, local ham, a salad of green beans and crisp lardons dressed with vinaigrette, cases of Saint-Pourçain, and a platter of regional cheeses – young and old Cantal, the conical Gaperon, farmhouse Saint-Nectaire, Fourme d'Ambert and Bleu d'Auvergne,

the cow's-milk version of the more highly rated sheep's-milk Roquefort made in the Languedoc. Fruit for a salad and strawberries for sorbet are grown at the château.

In the dining room when the weather is less favourable, Joy frequently offers sorrel soup or stewed sorrel in cups with poached eggs, and then a leg of lamb roasted for seven hours with brandy and aromatic vegetables in a casserole in the slowest oven. Called *gigot à la cuillère*, because the meat is so tender it can be eaten with a spoon, it is served with redcurrant jam as venison would be, and with one green and one orange purée (pea and carrot respectively). Dessert is an *île flottante*, *crème brûlée*, apple or peach

LEFT: *Breakfast things spread out in the kitchen at Duègne. Tea, coffee, breads, butter, jams and fruit are placed beneath a collection of antique copper charlotte moulds on the massive oak dresser, and guests help themselves at whatever hour suits them. 'If anyone wants an egg,' says the chatelaine, 'they boil it themselves.'*

ABOVE: *In the years when Jean de Rohan-Chabot's grandmother, the Comtesse Catherine de Chabrol-Tournoël, was chatelaine, the panelled laundry with a planked floor would have been charged with activity; even now château-issue napkins, big as kites, are starched, meticulously folded and stored here.*

crumble or, as for the meal pictured here, a novel *tarte Tatin*, made with brown sugar. Satiny pumpkin soup opens the same dinner, followed by a main course built around that sustaining emblem of Auvergnat mountain cooking, cabbage. Also crucial in the local *potée*, or soup, cabbage is here boiled whole and then a herbed sausage-meat gingerly stuffed between its leaves. Draped with strips of fat, tied and baked, it is served with wild rice and Château du Petit Thouars, a red Touraine made in the Indre-et-Loire by Jean's cousin, wine authority Marguerite du Petit Thouars. Touraines like this, made with the Cabernet Franc grape, are serious wines with a substantial bouquet and a definite fruit flavour.

'Cooking was never something I thought I had to do; I could always make do with a baguette and a slice of ham,' says Joy. 'But then it began to seem more and more like painting to me. I saw that I could mix colours and invent. I think about food more at Duègne than I do in Paris, and I make a bigger effort. The fact that everyone is always doing something, including our house guests, is what gives the château its special atmosphere. They see I'm busy and they want to be busy too; so they help make jam, or rake the courtyard, or potter around in the garden. When you are invited to stay in a perfect house you eat, you sleep, and you read. But I have no feeling for houses that are perfect.'

MENU
for 8

SOUPE AU POTIRON DANS SA COQUE
PUMPKIN SOUP IN A PUMPKIN TUREEN

Château du Petit Thouars   Touraine rouge

———

CHOU FARCI ENTIER
WHOLE STUFFED CABBAGE

RIZ SAUVAGE
WILD RICE

———

*TARTE DE DEMOISELLES TATIN AU SUCRE BRUN
ET À LA PÂTE FEUILLETÉE*
UPSIDE-DOWN APPLE TART
WITH BROWN SUGAR AND PUFF PASTRY

Château Bastor-Lamontagne 1980   Sauternes

———

Café

BELOW: *Displayed on a sideboard, the ingredients for a* tarte Tatin *are simple and few: apples, brandy, brown sugar, flour and butter, and* crème fraîche *to top the warm* tarte.

SOUPE AU POTIRON DANS SA COQUE

This traditional French dish was originally a whole baked pumpkin filled with onions, breadcrumbs and meat stock. If a religious holiday dictated that cooking be meatless, milk would replace the meat stock. The flesh of the pumpkin was scooped out with the stuffing and made thick or thin with more liquid depending on whether it was to be served as a vegetable or as a soup. Here the shell of the pumpkin makes a sturdy, colourful tureen, complete with lid, for the creamy soup.

1 pumpkin weighing 4–5 kg (8–10 lb)
1 onion, stuck with 4 cloves
1 litre (1¾ pt/1 quart) milk
salt and freshly ground white pepper
a pinch of sugar
60 g (2 oz/4 tbs) unsalted butter, cut into
 pieces
2 tbs finely chopped flat-leaf parsley

1. With a short, stiff-bladed knife, cut a large lid out of the top of the pumpkin. Carefully trim 1.5 kg (3¼ lb) flesh from the underside of the lid and pumpkin interior, leaving a thick shell in which to serve the soup. Cut the flesh into even pieces.
2. Simmer the pumpkin pieces and onion in lightly salted water to cover until the pumpkin is tender. Strain, recouping approx 250 ml (9 fl oz/1 cup) of the cooking

water to thin the soup if necessary. Remove the cloves from the onion and discard. Purée the onion with the pumpkin in a food processor.

3. Combine the purée and milk and heat through without boiling. Stir in the salt, pepper and sugar. Just before serving, swirl in the butter. Transfer the soup to the pumpkin shell, sprinkle with the parsley, and serve.

CHOU FARCI ENTIER

The cabbage used here is the bright green variety known as 'wrinkle-leafed Savoy'. The loose leaves allow it to be stuffed easily, and the vibrant colour makes the final presentation pretty.

1 green cabbage weighing approx 1 kg
  (2¼ lb), washed
3 medium onions
2 stalks celery, trimmed, leaves removed,
  and finely chopped
15 g (½ oz/1 tbs) unsalted butter
salt and freshly ground pepper
1 slice of bread, crumbled
60 ml (2 fl oz/¼ cup) milk
1 egg
450 g (1 lb) minced shoulder of pork
a pinch of nutmeg
6–8 strips of pork fat or unsmoked bacon
1 carrot, peeled and cut into large pieces
2 cloves garlic, peeled and halved
475 ml (17 fl oz/2 cups) home-made chicken
  or veal stock
450 g (1 lb) wild rice

1. Remove and discard the outer cabbage leaves that are discoloured or damaged, then remove and reserve 4 or so more. Trim the stem so that the cabbage sits flat, and cut a deep cross in the base to ensure even cooking. Plunge the cabbage and detached leaves into boiling salted water to cover and blanch for 10 mins. Stop the cooking under cold running water, then drain the cabbage upside-down on a clean tea towel. Reserve the leaves.

2. Finely chop 2 of the onions and sauté with the celery in the butter until soft. Season with salt and cool. Soak the bread in the milk and combine with the egg, onion mixture, pork and seasoning. Poach or pan-fry a little of the stuffing; taste and correct seasoning.

3. Spread open the leaves of the cabbage and, starting from the inside, spoon the stuffing between the leaves. Drape with the fat or bacon, then tie into a neat balloon, making a loop of string at the top to use as a handle. Preheat oven to 175°C (350°F).

4. If you are using a meat thermometer, insert it in the centre of the cabbage. Place in a heavy ovenproof, high-sided casserole, cut the remaining onion into large pieces and scatter, with the carrot and garlic, around the cabbage. Pour over 125 ml (4½ fl oz/½ cup) of the stock, sprinkle with salt and bake for 2½ hours, basting from time to time with the remaining stock. (There should always be a little liquid in the bottom of the casserole.) The cabbage is done when the thermometer reads 80°C (170°F).

5. Remove the string and fat and allow the cabbage to rest for at least 5 mins before serving. Transfer to a platter, cover with the reserved leaves, which are strictly for presentation, and surround with the rice. 'Carve' into wedges and spoon over the cooking juices.

TARTE DE DEMOISELLES TATIN AU SUCRE BRUN ET À LA PÂTE FEUILLETÉE

The brown sugar in France is not the 'packable' kind found elsewhere, and though white granulated sugar tastes less of caramel, it may be used here instead of brown.

250 g (8 oz) puff pastry
caster (confectioners') sugar for sprinkling
100 g (3½ oz/6½ tbs) unsalted butter
200 g (7 oz/1 cup) granulated brown or
  white sugar
2 kg (4¼ lb) Golden Delicious apples,
  peeled, cored and halved

1. Roll out the pastry to 3 mm (⅛ in) thick, line a 24 cm (9½ in) tart tin and chill thoroughly. Preheat oven to 190°C (375°F). Prick the pastry with a fork and bake until golden, leaving the oven on to finish the tart. Light the grill (broiler). To ensure a crispy crust that will not absorb the apple juices, sprinkle with caster sugar and pass under the grill until the sugar melts and caramelizes.

2. Melt the butter and granulated sugar in an ovenproof skillet until it bubbles and smells like caramel. (When using white sugar, the mixture will turn golden.) Remove from heat and arrange the apple halves standing up in neat, snug concentric circles, their cut sides facing towards the centre. If they do not all fit, cut the apples into smaller pieces and wedge them into the free spaces. Bake in the bottom third of the oven for 45–60 mins, or until the apple juices have thickened. If the apples have released too much juice and thickening is minimal, return the skillet to the top of the stove and cook over a medium–high heat to reduce the liquid.

3. While the apple-sugar mixture is still warm, place the cooked pastry on top, and invert onto a serving dish. If the top is not sufficiently browned, sprinkle with a little granulated sugar and caramelize under the grill. Serve with *crème fraîche*.

R ETIRED now and living in Germany, Fritz Mittelstaedt planned a special trip to Alsace to visit the eighteenth-century house in which he had spent so much of his childhood. But when he finally stood in the rue des Barons-de-Fleckenstein in Soultz-sous-Forêts, on the corner he knew to be right, he discovered that the building had been wiped away and replaced by a woeful new medical centre. M. Mittelstaedt returned to Germany shocked, saddened and chagrined.

ABOVE: Kelsch, *the traditional checked cottons and linens of Alsace, are most often sewn into pillow slips and duvet covers.*

LEFT: *A dessert buffet* chez *the Maurices includes* a kougelhopf, meringues, butter biscuits, apple tart with almond streusel, dark chocolate cake with raisins, lemon meringue pie, pear and almond tart, and cottage cheese and raspberry tart. *The inscription embroidered in Alsatian on the cloth below the window translates as 'Work and application justify the price.'*

WINTER SUPPER IN AN ALSATIAN *STUBE*

'A year later he read by chance in a German magazine that I had in fact dismantled the building and put it back together in a village just outside Strasbourg as a home for my young family,' says Dominique Maurice. 'Shortly afterwards there was a charming old man knocking on our door and explaining how he had known the house in another place in another time, and would we mind if he looked in quickly. Of course his head was full of memories. He caressed the banisters and cried.'

For Richter more remembrances were triggered by the gracefully arching *porte cochère*, stone window jambs, Louis XIV oak doors, and mansard roof. Determined to build a home with an Alsatian soul, Dominique Maurice and his wife Marie-Noëlle energetically recovered all these elements from a house of many different lives. Before World War II the building in Soultz was a textile and man's shirt shop, and for some twenty years afterwards it was a chemist. What the Maurices bought was an empty shell.

'The horrible aluminium machine-made houses financed by the French credit agencies in Alsace today go up in three months – and that's with the last picture hung on the wall,' says Dominique. 'We wanted something that demonstrated our sympathy for vernacular architecture and decoration. After three years' work we were still living, quite happily, with bare brick walls.'

LEFT: *The* stube, *the combined living and dining room in an Alsatian home, is fitted with a working antique wood-burning* kachelofen, *faced with faience tiles.*

ABOVE: *In its other life the house was a man's shirt shop and then a chemist's shop.*

RIGHT: *Monday, wash day, was* baeckeoffe *day, in old Alsace. In the morning, women on their way to the wash house would leave a stew with the baker, whose oven was still warm from baking bread. Returning home at midday, they would pay the baker and collect their casserole – containing pork, beef, lamb and a pig's foot and tail – which they then served for lunch. The custom lives on, if only in the name of the dish, for* baecke *means baker and* offe *means oven in Alsatian.*

Dominique, a vet by profession, says he would never have realized his plan without the fearless and patient André Brenner. A specialist builder, Brenner is celebrated in the area for inviting himself into houses he considers promising to see if there is anything he can persuade the owners to part with for his next job. 'Unlike André, a conventional building firm would never have waited for me to find and buy everything I needed,' says Dominique. 'For although the basic structure came from the house in Soultz, the seventeenth-century *boiseries* in the library are from Saint-Pierre-le-Vieux, the church in Strasbourg, and those in the dining room are from an eighteenth-century village house in Kuttolsheim. They all needed cutting and adapting, and often there were three or four coats of paint to be scoured off with caustic soda.'

The terra-cotta floor tiles throughout the house are from a *maison bourgeoise* in the Saône-et-Loire, and the double-glazed windows were made especially for the Maurices in the Vosges using old casement bolts. 'We are well known locally for our love of old things – so well known that a man in town gave us one of the wooden poles that hangs in front of the *kachelofen* [heating stove] to dry clothes,' says Dominique. 'And although I think of Alsace as a region of tradition, unimaginable incidents still occur – like the cutting down of the 200-year-old chestnut tree, around which the village *fêtes* took place. The man living beside it insisted it was dying, which of course it wasn't. It was just that he didn't like the shadow it cast.'

If the people of Alsace can be blasé about their heritage and traditions, their neighbours on the other side of the Rhine are rather more interested. 'The Germans are buying up and transporting many of our beautiful old farmhouses,' says Dominique. Germany has a long history of coveting Alsace – annexing it from 1870 to 1919 during the Franco-Prussian War and again from 1940 to 1944. And yet since the Treaty of Westphalia awarded it to Louis XIV in 1648, Alsace has always insisted on its Frenchness. The people will tolerate being identified with German rigour and punctuality, but that is as far as it goes, even if, as Waverley Root has observed, their ties go much deeper. 'Germany… has given Alsace its customs, its domestic architecture, its eating habits [sausage, sauerkraut, the cult of the pig] and its language,' Root wrote in *The Food of France*, published in 1958. 'Perhaps the Alsatians would not care to be spoken of as French Germans, but that is unquestionably what they are….'

French schoolchildren still study the text and illustrations in *Mon Village*, which first appeared in 1913, in order to learn what folk life was like under the despised Prussian gendarmes. 'The dreadful war and cruel annexation has turned our old life upside down; the old customs have disappeared with the costumes of olden days,' wrote Jean-Jacques Waltz under the pseudonym Uncle Hansi. Nevertheless, he managed to find villages where the appearance of a stork in the nest atop the schoolhouse still signalled the arrival of spring in Alsace, and where the women and girls still took pride in wearing the traditional, billowing, butterfly headdress. He remarked that oddly dressed German tourists at the *auberge* unpacked their own strange provisions – veal-liver sausage, smoked eels, marmalades and other *delikatessen* – but that the *Messti*, the *fête patronale*, was still celebrated with rich spice cake and a towering, light *kougelhopf*.

Isolated from Paris and shuttled between French and German rule, Alsace often causes French visitors from outside the province to remark that it feels like a country apart. The culture is different, they say – not French and not German. They are also surprised when they hear French spoken instead of the more popular Alsatian, a German dialect.

'The language made our first years here very difficult,' says Marie-Noëlle. 'I'm Lyonnaise, Dominique is from the mountainous part of the Vosges, and we both felt that we were no longer living in France. In our village, even if people know French, they speak Alsatian. Still, from the beginning we were welcomed into the homes of the Alsatians as if we had always known them. No matter what the time of day, you are always offered a glass of white wine and, this being a region of gâteaux and tarts, some marvellous sweet. That doesn't happen in the Lyonnais, nor anywhere else in France that I know of. I feel at home here now, but even so, it is not France. *Je suis en Alsace.*'

Unlike his wife, Dominique no longer feels a sense of separateness. '*Je suis en France*,' he says.

While the Maurices removed a layer of pebble dash to expose the original half-timbered façade of the Soultz house, and while they kept the building's original dimensions, they divided the interior for

OPPOSITE: *Neatly tied bundles of preselected vegetables and herbs for soup or* pot-au-feu – *this one including celeriac – are sold at Strasbourg's Marché Sainte-Marguerite, which is held every Wednesday and Friday morning. At different times of the year the open market, which brings* paysans *from all around to sell whatever they grow or raise, is also a good source for* foie gras *and* choucroute, *or sauerkraut, the shredded cabbage soaked in brine for which the region is known.*

comfort and practicality rather than for the sake of Alsatian architectural purity. These considerations nonetheless allowed for a *stube* – in old Alsace, the combined living and dining room.

In a traditional *stube* (pronounced 'schtoub'), the dining table was placed in one corner of the room and benches were built into or placed along the walls for the farm workers and *maître de maison*. He determined the rhythm of the meal, cut the bread, and was the first to lift his glass. Chairs pulled up to the two open sides of the table were reserved for the women serving the food.

Since the Middle Ages, Alsatians have been warmed by wood-burning *kachelofens* rather than by open fires. Heat

accumulates and circulates inside these stoves and is slowly and continually diffused through their vast surface area. Installed in the *stube* against the wall that divided it from the kitchen, early *kachelofens* were made of glazed earthenware. Later, in the eighteenth century, more sophisticated examples were built in enamelled faience. A hatch on the kitchen side allowed it to be fed with fuel without dirtying the *pièce de réception*.

The most spectacular *kachelofens* came from Sundgau in southern Alsace, and are distinguished by a *kunscht*, or bench, that recouped the heat from a second stove on the other side of the wall. When it was not occupied by grandparents, the *kunscht* afforded infants a

ABOVE: *Dinner in an Alsatian* stube. *The warm* boiseries *were recovered from an eighteenth-century village house in Kuttolsheim, while on top of the dresser is a collection of regional earthenware pitchers from the town of Soufflenheim.*

warm place to sleep. The *kachelofen* itself heated bricks and packets of cherry stones to warm the beds, and it still serves to keep food hot. Some cooks, like Marie-Noëlle, even use the stove to make *flammekueche*, a local 'flame-licked' onion tart prepared with cream and lardons and served with kirsch.

The *stube* also displays the pottery that has been made for centuries in Alsace for the confection and conservation of food. Production of this pottery today centres on two typical northern towns about 10 kilometres (6 miles) apart. The eighteen ateliers at Soufflenheim are noted for ochre-coloured earthenware, while the eleven ateliers at Betschdorf make the familiar blue–grey stoneware.

Soufflenheim peaked in 1837 and flourished until the end of the last century, leaving a legacy of cooking vessels to Alsatian cuisine. These include the fluted bowl-shaped mould in which the bread-like *kougelhopf* is baked, and the massive oval terrine used for making *baeckeoffe*, a stew of lamb, beef, pork and potatoes. Other shapes are linked to specific holidays: a lamb for Easter, a heart for Lent and Mother's Day, a star for Christmas, the royal fleur-de-lis for epiphany, the symbols of Christ – a fish or an eel – for New Year's Day. Typically, Soufflenheim pottery is thickly and crudely decorated with naïve birds, flowers and hearts.

RIGHT: *The milky light of Alsace in winter.*

More *artisanal* and more familial, Betschdorf's studios are noted for their pot-bellied pitchers with tiny spouts, hefty wide-mouthed pots for storing vegetables, and columnar 'monk-shaped' bottles for eau-de-vie. Cobalt oxide is used to colour the stoneware, and the decoration usually features flowers and animals. The ceramic industry in Betschdorf was practically stamped out by the Franco-Prussian War in 1870, three years after reaching its apogee, when there had been sixty workshops. The arrival of aluminium kitchenware post World War I encouraged the potters to turn to less utilitarian and more decorative forms.

After big-stemmed glasses of *amerbière*, the Alsatian apéritif combining beer with a prepared mixture of gentian bitters, orange and quinine, guests at the Maurices are invited to take their places at a table laid with rare vintage 'Obernai'. The service, showing affectionate and detailed scenes of rural life in turn-of-the-century Alsace, was decorated by Henri Loux. Of the fifty-two motifs he executed for the Utzschneider faience factory in Sarreguemines – 'watermill under the snow', 'poultry pedlar', 'snowball fight' and 'a couple of lovers in a wheat field' among them – twenty-five are still in production. Sadly, the designs have been diluted over the years.

A first course of *presskopf* is served on to Loux's plates, peopled with horsemen and pottery vendors, shepherds and postmen, watchmen and drum majors. Drizzled with vinaigrette, *presskopf* is the Alsatian interpretation of brawn (headcheese). After a crusty *flammekueche*, a bracing Riesling is uncorked to accompany a *baeckeoffe*. Alsace is white wine country (Sylvaner, Riesling, Pinot Blanc, Muscat, Gewürztraminer, Tokay) and there is not reticence about serving one with a dish as hearty and meaty as this. A tender salad of lamb's lettuce, treviso and oak-leaf lettuce is offered next, before the region's one great contribution to the national cheese platter, the odorous Munster, sprinkled with cumin.

Confronted then with a buffet of six desserts (not including the biscuits and fresh meringues), it is difficult to know whether Marie-Noëlle is joking when she says that the mortality rate in Alsace is the youngest of any French province, a rate, she adds, directly related to the popularity of *pâtisserie* and *charcuterie*.

'Real Alsatians have no figures,' says Dominique. 'They are *les bonnes mamans*.'

OPPOSITE: *The bed in one of the Maurices' young sons' rooms is carved with the year 1803. The headboard has a tiny shelf for a Bible and painted just below it, in German, are the words: 'I put myself under the protection of the Lord.'*

ABOVE: *Antique* kelsch *are piled up for repairs in the sewing room.*

MENU
for 8

L'Amer-bière
Alsatian Bitters Mixture and Beer

PRESSKOPF À LA VINAIGRETTE
BRAWN (HEAD CHEESE) WITH VINAIGRETTE

BETTERAVES, CORNICHONS ET PETITS OIGNONS
AU VINAIGRE AROMATISÉ
BEETROOT, GHERKINS AND BABY ONIONS
PICKLED WITH AROMATICS

PAIN TRESSÉ AUX GRAINES DE PAVOT, PAIN PAYSAN NOIR,
PAIN AUX CINQ CÉRÉALES, PAIN EN COEUR À LA BIÈRE
PLAITED BREAD WITH POPPY SEEDS, DARK COUNTRY LOAF
FIVE-GRAIN LOAF, HEART-SHAPED BEER BREAD

FLAMMEKUECHE
'FLAME-LICKED' ONION, CREAM AND BACON TART

Kirsch

BAECKEOFFE
ALSATIAN BEEF, LAMB, PORK AND POTATO STEW

Château d'Ittenviller   Riesling

SALADE MÉLANGÉE DE TRÉVISE, MÂCHE
ET FEUILLES DE CHÊNE
TOSSED SALAD OF TREVISO, LAMB'S LETTUCE
AND OAK-LEAF LETTUCE

MUNSTERS MINIATURES AU CUMIN

UN BUFFET TRADITIONEL DES HUIT DESSERTS ALSACIENS

Café

Liqueur de vieux garçons aux cerises confites, Liqueur d'estragon
'Old Boys' eau-de-vie with preserved cherries, Tarragon liqueur

RIGHT: *Food not to be served until the end*
of the meal is on the table as the guests
take their places: Munster sits on an
antique cabbage shredder.

FLAMMEKUECHE

For the pastry:
21 g ($\frac{5}{8}$ oz) fresh compressed yeast
500 g (18 oz/scant 3$\frac{3}{4}$ cups) flour
2 tsp salt
For the filling:
3 medium onions, thinly sliced
salt and freshly ground pepper
piece of smoked bacon weighing 100 g
*   (3$\frac{1}{2}$ oz), cut into small lardons*
300 ml (10$\frac{1}{2}$ fl oz/scant 1$\frac{1}{3}$ cups) sour cream
*   or crème fraîche*
a pinch of nutmeg

For the pastry:
1. Crumble the yeast in a large deep bowl, add 250 ml (9 fl oz/1 cup) warm water and stir to dissolve. Set aside for 5 mins. Mix in the flour and salt and on a lightly floured surface knead into a smooth ball for 3–5 mins. Return to the bowl, cover with a plate and leave to rise at room temperature for 1–2 hours, or until doubled in volume.
For the filling:
2. Toss the onions with a little salt and set aside for 30 mins. Sauté the bacon until lightly browned but not crisp. Place the oven rack at the bottom of the oven and preheat to 260°C (500°F).
3. Knock back the dough and roll it out as thin as possible, pressing it with your fingers if necessary. Transfer to a heavy baking sheet. Season the cream with pepper and nutmeg and stir in the onions with their liquid. Taste for salt. Spread the mixture evenly over the dough, scatter with bacon, and bake for 15 mins. Move to the top of the oven and cook for approx 10 mins more, or until brown and crisp. Serve immediately.

BAECKEOFFE

Soufflenheim in the north of Alsace still produces the handsome oval earthenware terrines in which *baeckeoffes* are traditionally cooked and served. An enamelled cast-iron casserole would also work well.

1 bottle Riesling or Sylvaner wine
2 cloves garlic, peeled and crushed
2 bay leaves
4 sprigs fresh thyme
4 medium onions, thinly sliced
450 g (1 lb) stewing beef, cut in large cubes
450 g (1 lb) shoulder of lamb, cut in large cubes
450 g (1 lb) shoulder of pork, cut in large cubes
1.5 kg (3¼ lb) waxy potatoes, peeled and thinly sliced
4 medium leeks, trimmed, washed and thinly sliced
salt and freshly ground pepper
1 pig's foot, split and blanched
1 pig's tail, blanched
140 g (5 oz/1 cup) flour

1. In a non-reactive bowl large enough to hold the meat and marinade, combine the wine, garlic, herbs and 1 of the onions. Add the meat, coat well, cover and refrigerate for 24 hours.
2. Preheat oven to 180°C (350°F). Strain the contents of the bowl and reserve the liquid. Layer the bottom of a 3.5 litre (6¼ pint/3½ quart) covered earthenware casserole with one third each of the potatoes, leeks and the remaining onions, and season lightly with salt and pepper. Add the strained solids, season and cover with another one third of the vegetables. Add the pig's foot and tail and cover with the remaining vegetables. Pour in the reserved marinade to half-fill the casserole. If there is not enough liquid, make up the difference with more wine. Season the top of the *baeckeoffe*.
3. Mix the flour with 60 ml (2 fl oz/¼ cup) water to make a doughy luting paste, and seal the casserole cover into place. Bake for 3 hours, breaking the paste and lifting off the cover in front of your guests.

KOUGELHOPF

Cake to some and bread to others, *kougelhopf* is traditionally served toasted for breakfast, in the afternoon with local white wine, or as a light dessert.

21 g (⅝ oz) fresh compressed yeast
250 ml (9 fl oz/1 cup) milk, warmed
100 g (3½ oz)/½ cup) granulated sugar
1 tsp salt
230 g (8 oz/¾ cup plus 2 tbs) unsalted butter, softened
500 g (18 oz/scant 3¾ cups) flour
2 large eggs, beaten
60 g (2 oz/generous ⅓ cup) dark raisins, soaked in warm water until swelled, then drained
60 g (2 oz/½ cup) sliced almonds
Icing sugar for sprinkling

1. Crumble the yeast into a small bowl, dissolve in half the milk and set aside for 5 mins. In a second bowl, stir together the remaining milk, granulated sugar, salt and 200 g (7 oz/¾ cup) of the butter.
2. Place the flour in another, large bowl and make a well. Add the eggs and both milk mixtures, and work the dough with your hands until smooth and elastic. Work in the raisins.
3. Rub the remaining butter into a 1.5 litre (2½ pint/1½ quart) ring mould, and press the almonds into the bottom and sides. Transfer the dough to the mould (to half-fill it), cover, and leave to rise at room temperature for approx 2 hours, or until doubled in volume.
4. Preheat oven to 205°C (400°F). Bake the *kougelhopf* for 35–45 mins, or until a skewer inserted in the middle comes out clean. Turn out onto a rack. When cool, sprinkle with icing sugar and serve.

TARTE AUX POMMES AU STREUSEL

For the *pâte brisée*:
125 g (4½ oz/9 tbs) unsalted butter, chilled and cut into pieces
250 g (9 oz/scant 1¾ cups) flour
2 egg yolks
½ tsp salt
For the filling:
approx 1 kg (2¼ lb) Golden Delicious apples, peeled, cored and thinly sliced
1 tsp cinnamon
100 g (3½ oz/½ cup) granulated sugar
175 ml (6 fl oz/¾ cup) double/heavy cream
2 eggs
For the streusel:
30 g (1 oz/scant ¼ cup) flour
30 g (1 oz/¼ cup) ground almonds
2 tbs granulated sugar
1 tbs cinnamon
30 g (1 oz/2 tbs) unsalted butter, chilled and cut into pieces
caster (confectioners') sugar for sprinkling

For the pâte brisée*:*
1. In a food processor or in a large bowl using your fingertips, a pastry blender or 2 knives, cut the butter into the flour. When crumbly, make a well and add the yolks, salt and 3 tbs iced water. Blend quickly with your fingertips or a spoon, adding more water ½ tbs at a time if the mixture is dry. Gather the dough into a ball and transfer it to a lightly floured work surface. With the heel of your hand, smear the dough away from you a little at a time. Gather it up with a scraper and press into a thick disc. Cover with cling film and chill for 30 mins.
2. Roll out the pastry to line a 25 cm (10 in) high-sided false-bottomed tart tin, pressing with your fingers to repair any cracks. Chill for 30 mins.
For the filling:
3. Preheat oven to 205°C (400°F). Toss the apples with the cinnamon and 25 g (1 oz/2 tbs) of the sugar. Arrange the apples on the pastry and bake for 20 mins.
4. Whisk together the cream, eggs and remaining sugar. Pour the mixture over the partially baked apples and bake for 15–20 mins more, or until the custard just begins to set.
For the streusel*:*
5. Combine the flour, almonds, granulated sugar and cinnamon, and cut the butter into it. Sprinkle the mixture over the tart and bake for 10 mins more. Cool, lift out of the ring, dust with sugar, and serve.

LOOKING for a gardening identity in Provence, Nicole de Vésian was sure that there was a new kind of vernacular garden to be planted. It would ignore the farmhouse cliché of flashy geraniums spilling out of pot-bellied olive oil jars. And it would be unrelated to the formal gardens of clipped box surrounding the eighteenth-century *bastides* of Aix and Marseille.

ABOVE: Vin d'orange *is an apéritif drunk widely in Provence, especially when the sun is high. Traditionally made with white wine, it is here made with* vin gris, *a very pale and refreshing rosé that suggests the colour grey; Nicole de Vésian's version is further distinguished by the inclusion of grapefruit.*

RIGHT: *Rosemary, lavender, laurustinus, lonicera and box helped Mme de Vésian realize her vision of a new kind of vernacular garden in Provence. Nicole, who says that stones are as important to her as plants when she is designing, lives in the medieval hill-town of Bonnieux.*

'I wanted to give my new garden the same qualities of austerity and wildness that I like this region for,' she says. Planted on four levels on the edge of Bonnieux, a winding hill-town in the *département* of the Vaucluse, the garden attached to Nicole de Vésian's medieval house was designed to go unnoticed. Even the benches and chairs were painted the pale silver–grey of maritime cineraria so that they would blend unremarked into their setting.

'What and how I plant is always guided by the Lubéron mountains opposite me. Almost everything I have put in – laurustinus, lavender, sage – grows naturally here on the wild *garrigue*, the arid, chalky land you find all over the Mediterranean. Mine is basically an evergreen garden of green and grey with a handful of white- and blue-flowering plants. The principal shapes – spheres and waves – echo the rhythm of the landscape. By creating an extension of the Lubéron, I feel like it all belongs to me now.'

Nicole's aim was to make a garden that could not be traced to herself or the present. 'The plants and trees look like they've been here forever. The only thing

I have given them is an air of false sophistication. This has always been a poor place and that's the way I've kept it. Despite the work done on it, the house still retains the spirit of what in the patois of the *paysans* is called a *masure* – a hovel, a tumbledown cottage.'

The rigorous new style of garden Nicole has dug out of Bonnieux's inhospitable calcareous soil has made her an extremely popular figure in the Lubéron: everyone is phoning her to design their gardens. These clients, who are also friends, are introduced to one another at her brunches, *goûters* and '*verres-dinatoires*' – stylish and novel buffets like the one pictured here.

'I don't consider what I do entertaining, and I don't have parties, but I do have a house that is always open,' says Nicole. 'The idea of calling people and inviting them eight days in advance for the Saturday after next makes me very nervous. How do I know what I'll be doing eight days from now? I prefer something more improvised. On Sundays I sometimes give what I call a "come-for-breakfast", and in winter instead of brunch I often have a *goûter*, the equivalent of afternoon tea in

ABOVE: *Failing an invitation from Nicole de Vésian to a 'come-for-breakfast', a* gôuter *or a 'verre-dinatoire', a visit to Bonnieux is nonetheless worthwhile – for its Musée de la Boulangerie, for M. Tomas's excellent* patisserie *and bakery, and for the picnics to be enjoyed on the grassy platform near the summit.*

OPPOSITE: *A long summer room with sliding glass walls was built onto Mme de Vésian's village house to give her the impression of being in the garden even when she is inside. Hollyhocks, wheat, lavender, thistles, olive branches shaped into wreaths and decorative weeds picked along the side of the road are all hung to dry against the wall – a giant pegboard for baskets, hats and an English portrait, dating from around 1830.*

ABOVE: *The walls of the house were all plastered in subtly different shades of grey, pink and white – 'There's not a stroke of paint anywhere,' says Mme de Vésian. Beside the calla lily is an eighteenth-century* faïence de Rouen *cachepot; with its simple toile draperies, the salon was designed as a reprieve from the harsh light and brusque landscape of the Lubéron.*

ABOVE RIGHT: *Discovered embedded in the garden wall when the property was reclaimed in 1987 after decades of neglect, this ivy became the object of Mme de Vesian's artistic attention. Stones were packed in tightly behind the plant to hold back the earth and to show its handsome twisting trunk to best advantage.*

OPPOSITE: *Tufts of thyme, lavender, santolina, lonicera, box, rosemary – and stone – jostle for space and attention in one of Nicole de Vésian's characteristic plantings. One of her favourite techniques is to put several identical shrubs in a single plot and to clip them, more or less severely.*

England. If the weather's bad, it's only for as many people as can fit around the kitchen table, but otherwise we're in the garden, even in the middle of January. This is the south of France after all. The only other time I have friends in is for a "*verre-dinatoire*". There is plenty to eat and it all looks good, but I would never dare call it a real dinner. Actually, I do it this way out of laziness. Taking time over the preparation of a meal is not my idea of a day well spent. I am queen of the microwave. There is no better artichoke in the world than the one you make in seven minutes in the microwave in a plastic bag, no salt, no water. In any case, twenty minutes on top of the stove is out of the question. I am the same way with anything to do with houses and homes as I am with gardens: it has got to be right away or not at all.'

Nicole is accustomed to fearlessly wrenching homes out of unsuitable properties in Bonnieux. In 1979 she bought and converted a chapel that had originally belonged to one of the penitent brotherhoods based in and around nearby Avignon between the thirteenth and seventeenth centuries. Each of the orders was identified by the colour of its hood

and sackcloth; the brothers in Bonnieux, the most aristocratic of all these sorrowful sinners, wore white. More recently, Le Pénitent had served as a cinema, where an ambulant projector was set up once a week for the villager's distraction.

What kind of woman decorates the heart of an impractical old chapel like a barn, paves it with loose grey stones from the bottom of the Durance, and uses it as her salon, building a tool shed into one corner? Magnificently thin and perpetually bronzed, Nicole wears her white hair scraped back into a severe chignon, revealing features as powerful as those of an American Indian. She tours her garden carrying a rope shoulder bag and wearing a Rolls-Royce lap rug over a long Hermès-orange leather gilet. Her perfume, the same one with which she sprays the entire house, is a confidential home-made mixture of lavender essence and good name-brand eau-de-toilette. Born in Wales to a French mother and a Welsh banker, she was raised in Paris. Living out World War II in different parts of France, always on the move, Nicole says she learned to be ruthlessly inventive and to rely only on herself. 'My family had a manor in Normandy, and though I wasn't daring

ABOVE: *It took Mme de Vésian only a few hours to decorate this guest room as a fantasy camp site for her grandchildren. The headboards resembling wagon wheels are actually fanlights, the blankets are flokati rugs, and the tin lanterns are from Morocco. The décor was such a success that she has never dismantled it. The box on the left contains Nativity figures with barbotine heads that Nicole made for her family more than thirty years ago.*

enough to use the actual curtains, I was able to make quite a decent jacket with the lining and wadding. The collar was cut out of a rabbit pelt. That was my Scarlett O'Hara period. The Occupation taught that I can survive anything and make anything out of nothing.'

In another life Nicole had a big house in Paris – staff, grandchildren, a dining room hung with Gobelins tapestries and all the other trappings. And she had 'this capacity for getting things done, my best quality. Once I have an idea for something, or see the solution to a problem, the idea is as good as realized and the solution

as good as implemented. The only thing left for me to do is do it, the easy part.' In 1962, never having worked before, Nicole set up her own industrial design firm in the basement of 20, rue de l'Elysée in Paris. Seated at a desk beside a coal passage that connected with the Presidential Palace, she drew cooking utensils, textiles, perfume bottles, shoes and knitwear. Embroiderers working on *haute couture* dresses for Christian Dior were commissioned by Nicole to design the motifs she stamped on plastic table cloths with the look of handwoven linen. Later she developed home furnishings for

RIGHT: *In the Middle Ages a village road passed directly under the arch in what is now the entrance hall. The floor is covered with loose grey stones from the bottom of the Durance river. Nicole used the same stones to cover a large part of the garden. The seventeenth-century walnut chest in the foreground is Provençal, and the pew opposite is from the church in nearby Ménerbes. The branch against the back wall is dried ilex.*

ABOVE: *All the doorways that give onto the garden are hung in late spring with curtains made out of old hand-woven linen sheets bought at the Sunday flea market at L'Isle-sur-la-Sorgue. Hanging curtains out-of-doors is another of Mme de Vésian's methods of bringing the outside in and the inside out. This room, the pantry, formerly housed rabbits.*

Hermès and fabrics designed by Sonia Delaunay. 'My whole career was based on trying to dress houses like people and people like houses,' she says.

Le Pénitent served as a kind of bachelor's crash pad for Nicole during her last years as a stylist. The chapel had more character, she admits, but a tiny garden. She had not been thinking of moving in 1987 when her present house came up for sale, but the standard *coup de foudre* experienced when she visited it, plus the fact that it had more land and a well, had her rushing to sign the papers the same weekend.

'The old man who lived in the house until a few days before I first saw it was in fact born here when it belonged to his grandmother,' say Nicole. 'It had been a working farm – at one point all the land in the valley below went with it. In the end I became so tired of clearing away demi-johns and horseshoes, and tools for cultivating asparagus, vines and olive trees, that I just threw them out. The kitchen was a stable with a hole in the floor through which grain was passed to the cellar. The *entrée* was a kind of hut with linoleum on the floor – I was the one who uncovered the stone walls and vaulted ceiling. In the Middle Ages a road passed directly through here on its way from the village into the fields, which explains the ramp that takes you into the garden today. There were 3,300 people living in Bonnieux then; today there are only 1,400. When we were renovating the house, we found four *foyers* – four hearths in which meals would have been prepared and which prove that once four families lived here in not a very large space.'

Box and pine visibly planted rather than simply growing wild also suggested to Nicole that the farm had known a certain period of prosperity. Harshly cut back, much of the box was moved to square stone-bordered plots that are the brawniest expressions of her new vision of the Provençal garden. Bumping up against these shrubs in close plantings that trap moisture and protect against the cold are lavender, rosemary, thyme, santolina and nepeta. Stones fill in the gaps.

'I could never make a garden without stones,' says Nicole. 'I need the stones to justify the plants; they go in first and the plants come afterwards. I can't disassociate the two. The stones are a pretext and at the same time a constraint, something that limits me. I like the discipline they impose and I like the difficulty. They divide up the garden visually and, apart from anything else, they are terrifically useful when a big plant dies and you haven't had the time to replace it. I think I like stones as much as I like plants.'

Conceived as a series of rooms to be lived in rather than looked at, Nicole's garden is a natural setting for her hastily organized brunches, teas and buffets. For a 'come-for-breakfast', guests are invited for between ten and two, before Mass or after, for jugs of coffee, freshly squeezed orange juice, buttery croissants and brioches from M. Tomas, the very good village baker, and jam and honey – the celebrated honey of the Lubéron. For those who arrive later, or who have already had breakfast, a small table is set up on one side with *saucisson* and attractive jeroboams of Mas de la Dame, a hot, earthy red. Although they have requested their own *appellation*, Mas de la Dame and eight other vineyards in and around the Alpilles mountains between Avignon and Arles are currently grouped under a sub-*appellation* of Côteaux d'Aix-en-Provence called Côteaux des Baux-en-Provence. There are three qualities of *vin d'appellation* and in 1985 all the Côteaux d'Aix wines graduated from the middle to the top category, to become *vin d'appellation d'origine controllée* (AOC).

Friends who are invited for a *goûter* by Nicole can expect a *galette* of flaky pastry filled with frangipane; a *tourte Michel*, coarse orange marmalade and a mixture of lavender honey and almond cream between a biscuit crust and almond meringue; and three sorts of tea – bitter orange, lemon verbena and the unavoidable Earl Grey.

A '*verre-dinatoire*' very often includes clove- and grapefruit-flavoured *vin d'orange* as an apéritif, pesto quiche, ham pierced with garlic, a jellied rabbit terrine made with black olives, ham-and-Gruyère-filled loaves made with a mixture of croissant and brioche dough, and several *tourtes Michel*.

M. Tomas and a talented young village girl make it possible for Nicole to see her friends without for a moment neglecting her garden. 'I live outside,' she says. 'The house for me is an extra. If I built a new house today, it would have two ground-floor rooms and a garden marching right inside. The garden here has *un air de rien*, a feeling of melting into the village; but I would like it to be even more invisible. At the moment it's showing a bit too much.'

ABOVE: *The famously small, tender and fragrant Charentais melons are known locally as* melons de Cavaillon, *named after the nearby town, where an important market is held every Monday.*

MENU
for 8

Vin gris d'orange macéré aux pamplemousses
Orange-flavoured *vin gris* macerated with grapefruit

QUICHE AU PISTOU
PESTO QUICHE

PAINS EN DUO DE PÂTES AU JAMBON ET AU GRUYÈRE
DOUBLE-DOUGH LOAVES WITH HAM AND GRUYÈRE

LAPIN EN GELÉE AUX OLIVES NOIRES
JELLIED RABBIT TERRINE WITH BLACK OLIVES

JAMBON CUIT AU TORCHON PIQUÉ D'AIL
HAM PIERCED WITH GARLIC AND COOKED IN A TEA TOWEL

CORBEILLE D'ASSORTIMENT DE PAINS SECS SUÉDOIS
BASKET OF ASSORTED DRY SWEDISH BREADS

Mas de la Dame
Côteaux des Baux-en-Provence rouge

TOURTE MICHEL
PROVENÇAL ALMOND AND ORANGE MARMALADE *TOURTE*
SCENTED WITH LAVENDER HONEY

Café

(The quiche, terrine and *tourte* make a complete meal for 8 people)

VIN GRIS D'ORANGE MACÉRÉ AUX PAMPLEMOUSSES

On the kind of deliciously parched days the Lubéron knows in July, Nicole de Vésian serves her home-made *vin d'orange* with sparkling water over ice. The *vin gris* is a lovely peach–grey colour that flatters the clove-stuck oranges.

200 g (7 oz/1 cup) sugar
3 bottles vin gris, *or dry white wine such as Côtes du Lubéron*
3 oranges, washed and stuck with cloves
1 grapefruit, washed, cut into thick slices and pips removed
1 lemon, washed, cut into thick slices and pips removed
1 vanilla pod, split
1 cinnamon stick
475 ml (17 fl oz/2 cups) fruit eau-de-vie or cognac

Stir the sugar into the wine. Place the remaining ingredients except the eau-de-vie in a large decorative glass jar, beaker or jug and pour both the liquids over them. Cover and macerate for at least 48 hours, and for up to 3 weeks, in a cool, dark place. Strain through a paper coffee filter and return to the jar with the oranges, vanilla pod and cinnamon.

LEFT: *A reference to the Scottish way of keeping game is made by slicing ham onto a slate tile. Also on the menu are rabbit terrine and loaves filled with cheese and ham.*

ABOVE RIGHT: *Stylish buffets are held in the summer room, a space that comes closest to Nicole de Vésian's ideal of reconciliation of house with garden. Part of her gastronomic education was undertaken by Alice B. Toklas – 'my neighbour near Belley in 1940 and the one who introduced me to a dish I will never forget – escalopes of veal with fresh spinach and raisins.' Mme de Vésian was also given books to improve her English by Toklas and her friend Gertrude Stein.*

QUICHE AU PISTOU

Always pound pesto in a mortar.

pâte brisée *(see page 185 for recipe) lining a 25 cm (10 in) false-bottomed flan tin, chilled*
approx ⅓ cup fresh basil leaves, chopped
100 g (3½ oz/½ cup) grated Parmesan
5 eggs
500 ml (18 fl oz/2 cups) double/heavy creame *or* crème fraîche
salt and freshly ground pepper
3 thin slices lean boiled or baked ham

For the pâte brisée:
1. Place a baking sheet in the oven and preheat to 190°C (375°F). Line the pastry shell with foil or parchment paper and weight with pie weights, rice or dried beans. Bake for 15 mins, then remove the weights and cook for approx 10 mins more, or until golden brown. Repair any cracks with the reserved trimmings and leave the oven on to finish the quiche.
For the filling:
2. Pound the basil, oil and half the cheese in a mortar. Whisk together the eggs, cream, remaining cheese, half the pesto and seasoning, keeping in mind that the ham and cheese are quite salty. Place the partially baked pastry shell on the baking sheet and line with the ham. Pour in the custard and bake for approx 30 mins, or until the centre is set.
3. Cool slightly, lift out of the ring and transfer to a serving dish. Decorate, dragging the remaining pesto across the surface of the quiche in three bands with a fork. Serve warm.

LAPIN EN GELÉE AUX OLIVES NOIRES

Refreshing and savoury as a first course or as part of a buffet.

3 medium onions, thinly sliced
2 tbs olive oil
salt and freshly ground pepper
½ bottle dry white wine such as Côtes du Ventoux
250 ml (9 fl oz/1 cup) home-made chicken stock
1 bouquet garni
1 rabbit weighing approx 900 g (2 lb), cut into 10 pieces
100 g (3½ oz/¾ cup) black olives, pitted
1½ tbs (1½ envelopes) unflavoured powdered gelatin
3–4 slices bacon

1. In a large non-reactive pot, sauté the onions in the oil with the seasoning until soft but not brown. Add the wine, stock and bouquet garni, bring to the boil, and then simmer for 2 mins. Cool slightly. Add the rabbit and olives, bring to a low boil and skim off any impurities. Lower the heat to a simmer, placing a plate on top of the pot to keep the rabbit submerged. Cook for 1 hour. Leave the meat to cool slightly in the liquid.
2. Sprinkle the gelatin over a little cold water and leave to stand for 5 mins. Strain the contents of the pot, discarding the bouquet garni and reserving the other solids. Measure out 500 ml (18 fl oz/2 cups) of the liquid and simmer, skimming off any fat and impurities. Off the heat, stir in the gelatin until completely dissolved. Set the pot aside in a cool place.
3. Bone the rabbit, shredding or chopping the meat into small pieces. Chop half the olives and combine with the rabbit and onions. Pour a little of the liquid into a 1 litre (1¾ pint/1 quart) loaf-shaped terrine and add the meat mixture. Pour over the remaining broth, knocking the terrine on the counter to bring any air bubbles to the surface. Press the whole olives and bacon into the top and chill for 6–8 hours, or until firmly set.

TOURTE MICHEL

The ingredients here sing of Provence. Good straight out of the oven, the *tourte* is even better the following day.

For the *pâte brisée sucrée*:
100 g (3½ oz/6½ tbs) unsalted butter, chilled and cut into pieces
200 g (7 oz/scant 1½ cups) flour
80 g (3 oz/generous 6 tbs) sugar
3 egg yolks, 2 whites reserved for the meringue
a pinch of salt
ground almonds for rolling out the pastry
For the filling and meringue:
100 g (3½ oz/6½ tbs) unsalted butter, softened
150 g (5¼ oz/1½ cups) ground almonds
60 ml (2 fl oz/¼ cup) lavender honey
2 eggs, plus 2 egg whites reserved from the pastry
50 g (scant 2 oz/⅓ cup) caster sugar, plus enough icing sugar for sprinkling
2 tbs rough-cut orange marmalade

For the pâte brisée sucrée:
1. In a food processor or in a bowl, using your fingertips, a pastry blender or 2 knives, cut the butter into the flour. When the mixture is crumbly, make a well and add the sugar, yolks and salt. Blend quickly and gather dough into a ball.
2. On a lightly floured work surface, smear the dough away from you a little at a time with the heel of your hand to further blend the flour and butter. Gather it up with a scraper and press into a thick disc. Cover with cling film and refrigerate for 30 mins.
3. Sprinkle the work surface with ground almonds and roll out the pastry to line a 25 cm (10 in) false-bottomed tart-tin, pressing with your fingers to repair any cracks. Refrigerate for 30 mins.
For the filling and meringue:
4. Place a baking sheet in the bottom third of the oven and preheat to 160°C (325°F). Stir together the butter, honey, whole eggs and two-thirds of the almonds. Beat the egg whites reserved from the pastry until soft peaks form, then whisk in the sugar until stiff and shiny. Gently fold in the remaining almonds.
5. Spread the marmalade over the chilled pastry shell, fill with the almond mixture and cover with the meringue. Place on the baking sheet and bake for 40 mins. Lift out of the ring when still slightly warm. When cool, sprinkle with sugar and serve.

16 The shuttered life of a Riviera villa

LA PROUVERESSE was acquired as a house in an olive grove in the middle of nowhere, but Riviera-style encroachment, maybe the worst in the world, will ensure that it ends up as a house in an olive grove ringed by commerce, billboards and brassy neighbours. The fourteen-hectare basin that cradles the property will always give Jean and Irène Amic a luxurious sense of privacy and protection. But many of the other qualities, emotions and rituals attached to the 1769 farmhouse – transformed by his parents into a glamorous villa during the Second World War – have already disappeared or are gradually dying out.

ABOVE: *Canvases such as this one in the entrance hall were produced by Aubusson in the eighteenth century to furnish the designs for tapestries. The moss topiaries are from David Hicks, Paris.*

LEFT: *Zohra, Jean and Irène Amic's Moroccan housekeeper, lays the table for lunch at La Prouveresse on the penultimate of thirteen terraces leading up to the house, in the shade of olive and pistachio trees. She has worked for the couple in different parts of the world for more than twenty years.*

199

ABOVE: *La Prouveresse was built in 1769; a stone marked with the year is set into the façade above the walnut front door. Following Provençal custom, a* scourtin, *or olive oil filter, is used as a door mat. Young rosemary bushes are planted in the shade of a grapevine which, thickly entwined with heavy-scented jasmine, is trained against the wall.*

'When I first knew La Prouveresse thirty years ago the bed linen was still laundered by hand in vast tubs, and then spread out on the ground to dry over the wild herbs,' says Irène Amic. Born in Paris to a French mother, and Romanian father, Prince Alexandre Cantacuzène, Irène certainly knew luxury, but not this sensual southern variety. 'When you pulled back the sheets at night to get into bed there was the most wonderful smell... We would spend the day in the sea at Cannes, then lazily drive home to Grasse through open fields of flowers. You could smell the jasmine. But we haven't been in the Mediterranean for years.'

People like the Amics barely comment on the wounds inflicted on a Riviera they knew in another time in a different way. It is difficult anyway to add anything original to the existing catalogue of horror stories and complaints: the infections contracted at the beach instead of suntans; the visually insulting concrete blocks; the exhausting inelegance of the people; the noise. The noise – a steady hum of cars trapped in the hills below – even reaches La Prouveresse.

Like Dirk Bogarde, who has known the Riviera since 1948 and who lived on its periphery for nearly twenty years, the Amics have always benefited from its gentler flip-side. This *arrière-pays*, or back country, offers extremely good restaurants and honestly priced hotels, and takes in such villages as Fayence, Mons, Bargemon, Caille, Auribeau-sur-Siagne, Seillans, Cabris and Moustiers-Sainte-Marie. If Bogarde's Nice, 'that old whore down the coast... wears a tremendous necklace of diamonds', the hill-towns only half an hour away are *demoiselles* in modest strings of small glass beads.

'I look at La Prouveresse as a country house, not as a seaside place,' says Jean Amic. 'Although I'm not a misanthrope, and I'm not a hippy, my greatest pleasure is taking off for two hundred kilometres on one of my big Hondas. In the countryside behind the coast you get the real smell of lavender and thyme and rosemary, not the synthetic fragrance. I get enough of the bogus thing at work.'

Roure, founded by his family in 1820 and headed today by Jean, is one of the top suppliers of raw materials to the perfume industry in the world. His grandfather ran it when he was senator of the Alpes-Maritimes, and under his father the firm popularized the now-routine marriage of scent to fashion, with fragrances by Cris-

tobal Balenciaga and Elsa Schiaparelli. Jean has done very well himself with big moneymakers by Yves Saint Laurent and Oscar de la Renta among others.

Jean's father Louis already had an apartment in Paris and one in Grasse when he purchased La Prouveresse – 'The Provider' in Provençal – in the late 1930s for the price of two bicycle wheels. Charles de Noailles bought the property on which he would plant his famous garden at about the same time and the two men became neighbours. La Prouveresse was so isolated then that railway tracks had to be laid to transport the building materials for the additional bedrooms and a kitchen and larder at the back.

Jean and his parents moved to the country full-time for part of the war, worked on the house and waited. Pigs, goats, barley and a bread oven, and sheep in what would become the dining room, made them completely self-sufficient. When La Prouveresse was completed, a poky farm dwelling had been turned into an impressive villa, fitting for one of the country's great old-style perfume barons. Plaster coloured a juicy shade of pink was smoothed over a stone façade interrupted by pale blue *stores à l'italienne*, slatted shutters that open upwards instead of outwards and that create the most beautiful shadow play. Access was still difficult, however, so the good cars were parked more than a mile away at the bottom of the hill and an old wrecked one used as a shuttle for the stony climb.

The new design gave the house a buzzing upstairs–downstairs life for which it was never destined. Directed by Jean's half-American mother, a former curator of the Musée des Arts Décoratifs at the Louvre who still works occasionally for the museum, a great number of *bonnes* and *serveuses* properly dressed in black dresses and starched white aprons moved silently through the pantries, polished the silver serving platters, and made sure the right Bordeaux – no Provençal plonk – was on the table. In a house that used to keep sheep in the middle of an olive grove under the lashing Mediterranean sun Madame Amic's original formula of good staff, good silver and good wine caused many of her visitors to catch their breath.

While meals at La Prouveresse today are served from contemporary Moustiers faience and the wine is a more sensible Côtes de Provence, Bastide des Bertrands, the staff remains first-rate, if reduced. The whims and wants of guests are attended to by two Moroccan maids. One of them, the famously discreet Zohra, also does the job of major-domo. She has worked for the Amics for more than twenty years and travels most places with them. A visitor's idea of what his stay in the country house of an important international perfume executive will be like is never disappointed. Zohra is always stocking and restocking the bathrooms with fragrant goodies – René Desvaux Bitter Spice Bath Essence, Village Celebrated Cucumber Bath Powder, Crabtree & Evelyn Gardenia Dusting Powder, Sisley Country Water.

Henri Colla, first employed in 1952 to maintain the olive trees that are still cultivated for oil, is now caretaker. 'I arrived between the two generations of Amics,' he says, 'so I have known the old and the new. With Louis Amic, lunch was at exactly half-past one and not a single moment later. The president of the Republic could be expected and even if he was late, the order would still come: "Henri, serve the meal." Everyone else I knew trembled before him, but we were always friends. Compared to his father, Jean is a *bon garçon*. His mother once kept her

distance from the servants, but she has become modern now, following Irène. There is more contact.

'For me, the house changed forever the day we were burgled. I no longer think of it as La Prouveresse. There was a beautiful commode on every floor; there were at least seven *secrétaires*. It was all eighteenth-century Provençal and extremely rare. There was so much they had to come twice. After the second time, it was decided not to put in anything of value. It would have been crazy to furnish it the same way again.'

Henri Colla's wife Josette, once the scullery maid and now the loudly applauded cook, was born to Italian parents who came to France as immigrants in the early 1920s to pick flowers for the perfume distilleries. 'Jojo's great talent is for making a good dish out of nothing,' says Jean. She is also good at remembering foods favoured by regular guests and making sure they have them. Betty Catroux, the wife of the decorator, is regularly invited to stay by the Amics, but she never fails to be charmed by the way Josette always obliges her love of garlic and tomatoes.

BELOW: *Another view of the entrance hall. The companion Aubusson* toile à peint *to the one across the room is hung between rush-seated eighteenth-century Provençal chairs.*

ABOVE: *The proximity of coastal Provence to Italy accounts for the popularity in the region of shutters the French call* stores à l'italienne. *The writhing form of the olive tree is for Jean Amic a metaphor for the Provençal people: 'Their pessimism – and they are the greatest pessimists on earth – goes with the poor and difficult land.'*

LEFT: *The Amics' cook Josette Colla arrives at La Prouveresse every morning with baskets of ingredients for the day's meals. Many of them come from her own kitchen garden. The marjoram and onions are for a* pissaladière, *the cherries for a cherry cake.*

These and other provisions – rabbits and pigeons, potatoes (for hand-made gnocchi) and herbs – are grown and raised by the Collas at their home nearby, packed into open baskets and delivered to La Prouveresse daily. Whatever they cannot supply themselves they shop for at the kitchen gardens of neighbours. Vegetables, including *mesclum*, are harvested in the morning and on the Amics' table at noon. *Mesclum*, a mixture of delicate, individually grown salad greens, is one of the elements that distinguishes the Riviera table from that of inland Provence. Typically, it combines oak-leaf lettuce, endive, rocket, romaine, chervil, escarole, dandelion and red treviso, but there is no standard formula.

Henri Colla likes to guide guests to the fragmentary remains of a monastery in an oak grove at La Prouveresse, testimony to the antique presence of an order of monks founded on the Iles de Lérins by Saint Honoratus, who died in 429 as the Bishop of Arles. These two pine-covered islands, lying opposite Cannes in the Golfe de la Napoule, had served the Romans as guard-posts, but when Honoratus discovered them, they were abandoned. He chose the smallest and furthest on which to establish his seminary of sacred learning, and for five hundred years it was untouched. As the order's adherents grew in number so did its possessions on the mainland. The land around La Prouveresse was claimed and farmed, and flour

RIGHT: *Goblets and tumblers in the bubble glass of Biot are paired with modern faience from Moustiers-Saint-Marie; both towns are located near Grasse. Moustiers is traditionally decorated with grotesques, revolutionary motifs, and mythological scenes.*

FOLLOWING PAGE: *When cooking with courgette flowers, which have an elusive arrière-gout of honey, only the male is used; the shorter-stemmed female is left attached to the ripening fruit to nourish it. Deep-fried here, the blossoms have a very short life in the kitchen garden and must be picked the morning they open, and eaten the same day.*

and wood were processed at mills nearby in Mougins and Pegomas. In Vallauris, also just set back from the coast, vines were planted and a small summer palace was built for the abbots, who found their own rocky island too hot. Picasso produced his great body of ceramics in Vallauris and decorated the palace chapel with a fresco-on-plastic entitled *War and Peace*, that may still be seen.

Medieval pilgrims journeyed to Saint-Honorat, as the island was later known, but after them it became infected with corruption. By 1787, by which time La Prouveresse had been established as a working farm for almost twenty years, Pope Pius XI was so annoyed by the abbey's moral sloppiness that he ordered it to be absorbed by the Bishopric of Grasse. The next year it was dissolved entirely. When in 1791 the monastery came up for auction, it was bought, crazily enough, by the nephew of its last accountant for his daughter, an actress with the Comédie Française. After the actress came *les pères tranquilles*, Cistercians from the abbey of Sénanque in the Lubéron. They installed themselves in

1871 and found it so agreeable that they stayed on. There are still fathers living there today.

Saint-Honorat tempts the Amics. In *The Golden Riviera* published in 1975, Roderick Cameron wrote that the best way to approach the island was by yacht, dropping anchor in the early morning in order to steal a look at the monks in their smart black and white habits: 'They can be seen as stooping figures, weeding in between their vines or, if it is June, scything their acres of lavender.'

Lavender, sage, anise, rose geranium and coriander are among the forty or so plants distilled to produce the island's two liqueurs, both marketed under Saint-Honorat's original name of Lérina. One is green and tonic, the other yellow and digestive.

If perfume had not planted the Amics in the hills facing Saint-Honorat in the last century, something else might have: fashion. The Riviera had become the place to be. Before 1839 it was a backwater. But following the plutocrat Lord Brougham's discovery that it made a pleasant resort, it became the one place where the English

BELOW: *Hidden in a terraced olive grove far from the house, the pool at La Prouveresse was built in the late 1940s, making it one of the first in this part of the Côte d'Azur. 'My father wanted a pool that didn't look like a pool,' says Jean Amic. 'It was conceived more like a basin – no diving board, no ladders. And he wanted it integrated into the landscape. The idea was not to transplant Miami or Hollywood to Grasse.'*

ABOVE: *Of the many bedrooms at La Prouveresse, this was the one preferred by the present owner's father, who refurbished the house during the war. Thick plaster walls defeat the Mediterranean sun, guaranteeing coolness for the ritual* sieste *which follows a long and late lunch. Draped over the footboard of the simple Provençal bed is an antique hand-quilted* boutis, *simply patterned with a traditional geometric design.*

and Russian aristocracy wanted to winter. It was Cole and Linda Porter who introduced the idea that the Côte d'Azur could also be attractive in the warmer months. In 1921 the Porters rented Château de la Garoupe on Cap d'Antibes, and their guests were Sarah and Gerald Murphy. Four years later the Murphys were back on the Cap in a much humbler house they called Villa America. The visitors now included writers, composers and painters – the Fitzgeralds, Hemingway, Stravinsky, Léger, and Picasso, and they all needed somewhere to stay. The local hotels had to be persuaded to stay open for 'just one summer', and that was the summer the Riviera was launched.

The only people who do not find this romantic chapter in the history of this chameleon coast irresistible are those who have never found a way to live with the vulgar compromises imposed on them since World War II. Like Jean and Irène Amic, however – stretching out every summer beside the pool that his father insisted dissolve into the landscape – others are still susceptible.

It is early July, just before two o'clock. Zohra lays the wicker luncheon table, placed in the shade of olive and pistachio trees on the penultimate of thirteen terraces marching up to the house. Green paper napkins that say 'La Prouveresse' match the bubble-glass goblets from Biot. Everyone is on their way up from the pool, the usual crowd: banker Nicky Worms, Betty and François Catroux, the painter Guy de Rougement and his wife Anne-Marie. Zohra and the junior *bonne* appear from the back of the house carrying successive courses of a meal carefully conceived by Josette as a demonstration of textbook Provençal cooking: big, fleshy, deep–fried courgette blossoms; the anchovy and onion tart showered with fresh marjoram known as *pissaladière*; tiny violet-coloured artichokes *à la barigoule*, filled with ham, breadcrumbs, garlic and cheese; and cherry cake for dessert.

'The onions in the *pissaladière* are the big *oignons blancs de Midi*,' says Josette. 'They don't keep very long, but no other variety is as tender. Their smell as they cook is so sweet that in Grasse we say, "*Fais frire tes oignons et rendre les voisins jaloux*" – Fry your onions and make the neighbours jealous.'

MENU
for 6

BEIGNETS DE FLEURS DE COURGETTES
DEEP-FRIED COURGETTE BLOSSOMS

Bastide des Bertrands
Côtes de Provence rouge, blanc et rosé

ARTICHAUTS À LA BARIGOULE
SMALL STUFFED ARTICHOKES

PISSALADIÈRE
ONION AND ANCHOVY TART

FROMAGES DE CHÈVRE FRAIS EMBALLÉS
EN FEUILLES DE LAURIER ET CUITS SOUS LA BRAISE
FRESH GOAT'S CHEESE WRAPPED IN BAY LEAVES
AND COOKED OVER COALS

SALADE DE MESCLUM DE CHEZ JOJO

GÂTEAU AUX CERISES NON-DÉNOYAUTÉES
CHERRY CAKE WITH UNSTONED CHERRIES

Café
Infusion de menthe à la marocaine
Moroccan mint infusion

BEIGNETS DE FLEURS DE COURGETTES

In summer, young courgettes with their trumpet-shaped flowers still attached are found in markets throughout Provence. For a heartier dish than this one, the blossoms can be stuffed with chicken mousse and baked in stock. When filled with chopped mushrooms or minced meat, they may be either deep-fried or baked.

70 g (2½ oz/½ cup) flour
1 egg
2 tbs finely chopped flat-leaf parsley
1 small garlic clove, peeled and finely
  chopped
1 tbs olive oil, plus 1 part olive oil to 4
  parts vegetable oil for deep frying
salt and freshly ground pepper
24 courgette blossoms, trimmed

1. Place the flour in a bowl, make a well and add the egg, herbs, 1 tbs olive oil, seasoning and 75 ml (2½ fl oz/⅓ cup) water. Whisk to blend, adding more water if necessary to make a batter that coats a spoon very lightly.
2. Heat the deep-frying oil in a deep pot until it sputters when a drop of water is added. Holding the stems, dip the blossoms in the batter. Carefully drop them into the pot, frying as many as will fit in a single layer without crowding. Cook until golden on both sides and drain on brown paper bags. Sprinkle lightly with salt and serve at once.

LEFT: *The tough leaves attached to the stems of baby artichokes are used to line a crowded platter of the vegetables prepared à la barigoule. The filling is a mixture of ham, breadcrumbs, garlic, Parmesan cheese and parsley.*

OPPOSITE: *'Be careful where you buy your* pissaladière,*' cautions a Niçoise cookbook. 'The industrial versions have onions that look as if they were applied with a brush. Stay away from those sold in* les drugstores *of Nice and on the sidewalks.' The book also says that a good anchovy and onion tart, such as those found at the city's food markets, has a filling of onions equal in thickness to that of the crust.*

ARTICHAUTS À LA BARIGOULE

If you are lucky enough to find extremely small violet-hued artichokes, they may be too young to have grown chokes. If the fuzzy centres have developed, however, you will need patience and slim fingers to extract them.

12 small violet artichokes
2 lemons
100 g (3½ oz) lean ham, diced
4 tbs home-made unflavoured breadcrumbs
2 tsp finely chopped garlic
15 g (½ oz/1 tbs) unsalted butter, softened
1 egg, lightly beaten
5 tbs finely chopped flat-leaf parsley
50 g (scant 2 oz/¼ cup) grated Swiss cheese or Parmesan or Sbrins
salt and freshly ground pepper

1. Cut the stems from artichokes and tear off the tough outer leaves. Cut the artichokes approx in half horizontally, keeping in mind that the leaves must be high enough to contain the filling. Carefully remove the chokes with your fingers or with the end of a spoon. Place the artichokes in a bowl of water containing 1 tsp lemon juice for every 2 litres (3½ pints/2 quarts) of water.
2. Combine the ham, 3 tbs of the breadcrumbs, half the garlic, the butter, egg, 2 tbs of the parsley, the cheese and seasoning. Stuff the artichokes, placing the mixture in the centres and between the leaves.
3. Scatter the remaining breadcrumbs, garlic and parsley in a non-reactive straight-sided pan just large enough to hold the artichokes tightly so that they stand up straight. Add enough water to reach two-thirds of the way up the sides of the artichokes and place in the pan. Boil vigorously, uncovered, for approx 5 mins. Cover and simmer, adding more water if it evaporates before the artichokes are done – cooking time will depend on how big and tender they are. Alternatively, if at the end there is more than a few tbs of liquid in the pan, remove the lid and turn up the heat until almost all of it evaporates. Transfer to a serving platter, sprinkle with the remaining parsley and serve.

PISSALADIÈRE

The most authentic version of this tart is made with *pissalat*, a purée of tiny, salt-cured fish known as *poutine* and caught off the coast between Cannes and Menton.

For the pastry:
300 g (10½ oz/2 generous cups) flour
1 tsp baking powder
a pinch of salt
freshly ground pepper
1 tsp dried marjoram, or 2 tsp fresh
1 egg
115 ml (4 fl oz/7½ tbs) olive oil
For the filling:
1 kg (2¼ lb) Spanish onions, cut into medium slices
75 ml (2½ fl oz/⅓ cup) vegetable oil
3 bay leaves
110 g (4 oz) tinned anchovy fillets
2 tbs olive oil
freshly ground pepper
approx 20 whole unpitted Niçoise olives or 10 large oil-cured ones, pitted and halved
½ tbs dried marjoram, or 1 tbs fresh

For the pastry:
1. Sift the flour, baking powder, seasoning and marjoram together. Form a well, break in the egg, and combine with 100 ml (3½ fl oz/6½ tbs of the oil, trickled in a little at a time. Finish by working in approx 3 tbs water. The resulting ball of dough should be quite firm. Chill for 30 mins. Rub a 30 cm (12 in) ovenproof glass flan dish with the remaining oil and roll out the pastry to line it, folding back the edges so that the walls of the shell are twice as thick as the base. Chill for 30 mins.
For the filling:
2. Sauté the onions in vegetable oil with the bay leaves over a low heat without browning them. Cook for approx 20 mins, or until the volume has been reduced by half. Add half the anchovies, season with pepper and sauté for approx 10 mins more; the onions should be very soft. Remove the bay leaves. Preheat oven to 190 °C (375 °F).
3. Fill the shell with the onion mixture and distribute the olives and remaining anchovies over the top. Sprinkle with pepper and the marjoram, and drizzle over the remaining olive oil. Bake for approx 40 mins. Serve hot or warm.

GÂTEAU AUX CERISES NON-DÉNOYAUTÉES

Leaving the cherries unstoned gives this simple cake a pleasant hint of bitterness.

110 g (4 oz/7 tbs) unsalted butter, softened
100 g (3½ oz/⅔ cup) sugar
¼ tsp vanilla essence
1 tbs brandy
2 eggs
200 g (7 oz/scant 1½ cups) flour
1 tsp baking powder
300 g (10 oz) fresh black cherries

Preheat oven to 190 °C (375 °F). Grease a square 18 cm (7 in) cake tin with ½ tbs of the butter and sprinkle with 1 tbs sugar. Cream the remaining sugar and butter. Add the vanilla, brandy and, one at a time, the eggs. Incorporate the flour by degrees, then the baking powder. The batter will be very thick. Fold in the cherries and transfer to the cake tin. Bake for 40 mins, or until a knife inserted in the centre comes out clean. Cool, turn out and serve.

A TYPICAL fireplace in the Dordogne, wide and deep enough to sit in and often tall enough to stand in, makes easy work of cooking and keeping warm. For Adrianne Beauvieux it is the only place to prepare a *mique*, a giant leavened dumpling simmered in a cast-iron kettle that is filled with vegetable broth and hung from a *crémaillère*, or pot hook. In winter a chest containing a ham covered in cinders is set inside the hearth just to the side of the fire – no easy chair but nonetheless the best seat in the house for watching television. In spring the ham is taken out and wrapped in a tea towel, before being hung in a muslin sack in the chimney for further curing.

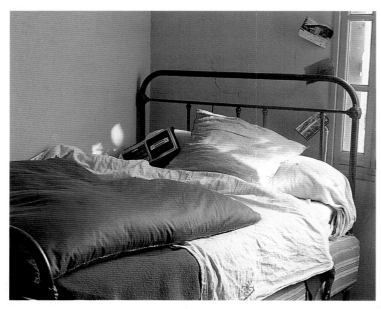

ABOVE: *Adrianne Beauvieux's bedroom at L'Oeil-la-Garde.*

RIGHT: *The decision of Mme Beauvieux's sons not to take on the running of the farm from their mother is typical; like many small land-holders in Périgord, Adrianne will be the last generation to work the soil, which gives her back practically everything she needs – including vegetables for the broth in which the traditional* mique *will be cooked. 'Cooking's all right,' says Mme Beauvieux, trimming a leek. 'Like everything else,* Je le fais parce qu'il faut le faire ... *I cook and eat what we have with no preference for any one thing over another ... there has never been any question of having a taste for a particular dish.'*

17 Madame Beauvieux, a *paysanne* in Périgord

Old ways have not survived nearly as well elsewhere in the Dordogne as they have here. While the fireplaces in many farmhouses are no longer used to prepare the afternoon and evening meal, others have been retired completely. As chimneys offer a ready-made escape for smoke, fuel-burning stoves with bright aluminium flues are frequently seen rudely blocking up old and once-beautiful fireplaces. When Adriannne Beauvieux decided she needed one of these Godin stoves to help heat the house, she installed it just outside the hearth so that her cooking was not interrupted.

By even the simplest standards, Adrianne's holdings in the four-family hamlet of L'Oeil-la-Garde in the hills 10 kilometres (6 miles) north of Sarlat do not add up to what is considered a *propriété*, The humblest *propriété* in the Dordogne might once have included a horse, one or two cows, ten or so sheep, some fowl and three or four pigs to be slaughtered for the table each year, plus a little corn, wheat and perhaps tobacco. But in the 1960s the *paysans* found that these assets could no longer sustain them. Television also changed their ideas about what they needed to live. Men and women who had never imagined what the inside of a Paris apartment might look like learned about mysterious but compelling concepts like comfort and convenience.

ABOVE: *Adrianne Beauvieux's farmhouse in the hamlet of L'Oeil-la-Garde in the hills east of Sarlat was built in around 1840 and acquired by her family in 1928. The luminous façade so characteristic of the Dordogne is of limestone, while the terra-cotta tiled roof replaced one of local grey* lauze *between the two world wars. The new, less steeply pitched roof resulted in a loft with a larger floor surface for drying walnuts and storing fruit.*

MADAME BEAUVIEUX, A *PAYSANNE* IN PÉRIGORD

Apart from a SEB coffee grinder and a bottle-gas stove for making dishes like jugged rabbit, comfort and convenience still do not seem to have reached L'Oeil-la-Garde. Raising and slaughtering two pigs a year, one for the *charcuterie* in Carlux, and one for herself, Adrianne Beauvieux otherwise has only corn, sheep and fowl. Rabbits, which she also keeps, are not significant enough to be considered an asset. Before 1975 there was no toilet in the farmhouse, and before 1957 only one bedroom served the entire family, which in those days numbered four boys, including an infant. That room today is an infinitely intriguing larder and junk room, accumulating mail, old sweaters, a handful of onions, a perfectly new toaster won years ago in a post-office raffle, a plastic tub of rotting apples, baskets of walnuts and hazelnuts, a giant stoneware jar of pig's feet and ears curing in salt, and a vinegar barrel that is also used as a hatstand. On the other side of the kitchen, where a shed once stood, are the bedrooms – one for Adrianne and one for the two sons who still live with her. Aged thirty-two and forty-two, one is a mason and the other, this being *foie gras* country, works in the nearby Delpeyrat *foie gras* factory.

Sentimentally it is usually assumed that the kind of cooking done by Adrianne is that which has traditionally been practised by most farmers' wives in the Dordogne, but history tells a grimmer story.

RIGHT: *The October harvest at L'Oeil-la-Garde completed, walnuts dry on the floor in the loft, where air circulates freely. Fires are often lit in the ground-floor room directly below such a loft in wet weather to eliminate the damp. Machines, however, are increasingly replacing this drying method in the Dordogne: a machine can achieve in twenty-four hours what it takes two months to accomplish naturally.*

MADAME BEAUVIEUX, A *PAYSANNE* IN PÉRIGORD

Until the nineteenth century their lives were characterized by want and even starvation. In Périgord they say that when God made France he filled a sack with châteaux, placed the biggest in the Loire and scattered the rest all over the Dordogne. While one ate copiously and well at the tables of the châteaux, it was not until after the Revolution that acceptable and interesting food was finally made available to the peasantry. With no aristocrats left to fatten, chefs who had kept the castle pantries flush set themselves up in restaurants, *pâtisseries* and *charcuteries*. Their bourgeois clientele, seeking the same quality in their own homes, hired the daughters of tenant farmers to staff their kitchens. These women, who measured every gesture and knew only savage necessity, encountered for the first time sophisticated techniques and an unthinkable food philosophy founded on pleasure. A generally improved standard of living and greater access to raw materials after 1789 enabled them to return home and make for themselves what they made for *monsieur*. This meeting of culinary traditions resulted in an exchange, and out of this exchange a new

cuisine was forged – the one on which the modern cooking of the Dordogne is based.

Adrianne Beauvieux says food is not a subject she has ever reflected on. 'I cook and eat what we have, with no preference for one thing over another. Being as poor as we are, there has never been any question of having a taste for a particular dish, though I suppose it's all completely different now with the young. I cook like my mother did – a little of everything. Perhaps the châteaux have specialities but she didn't have any and neither do I, not in a house like ours. If it's potatoes, they'll be *pommes de terre sarladaise* – sautéed in goose fat or lard with garlic and parsley, and with *cèpes* if they're in season. Otherwise it's a purée. In the summer we eat a lot of carrots and peas; pigeons and chickens are plucked, drawn, seasoned with salt and pepper, trussed and roasted. At Christmas there might be a *poule au pot*, but we're not really in the habit of marking holidays in the country.

'Until 1984 I made my own *foie gras* but after I fell over on the road in front of the house, I had to stop. Force-feeding with a hand-cranked funnel meant kneeling on the ground and straddling the

BELOW: *Mme Beauvieux's fireplace is typical of those in the Dordogne; it is hung with twin banners of fabric to keep smoke from entering the room, and it is wide enough and deep enough both to cook and sit in. The Godin wood-burning stove to the left provides additional heat in the winter. Through the doorway are the bedrooms.*

ABOVE: *The drawers of farm tables in Périgord are still used to hold leftovers, including perishables. When Adrianne Beauvieux serves* mique, *any uneaten dumpling is stored here, to be eaten stale the following morning spread with jam.*

birds, and it was my knee I hurt. So, I get my *foie gras* from my cousin now. But *foie gras* would only be for Sunday or, as I say, the odd *fête*. Forty years ago we made our own bread too but the bread oven has been demolished and so now we buy whatever we need in Carlux. The only time we ever treat ourselves to a meal in a restaurant is for a baptism. Otherwise we just don't have the means. Cooking's all right. Like everything "*Je le fait parce qu'il faut le faire*" – I do it because I have to.'

Adrianne was born in neighbouring Calviac, moving with her family to the typically Louis Philippe farmhouse in L'Oeil-la-Garde in 1928. While her father was employed to maintain roads in the Dordogne, her mother worked the land around their home. Her two brothers suffered untimely deaths, one in the war and the other from meningitis.

Built around 1840, the family's new home was still untouched when they arrived, with a stone roof of local grey *lauze* and a low façade of luminous ochre limestone. Between the two wars the exterior walls were heightened to support a new, less steeply sloping roof, thus creating a more useful loft for storing fruit and

drying walnuts. The roof itself was redone with machine-made terra-cotta tiles, the heavy uneven *lauze* being rejected as too hard on the beams and too difficult to lay. Today the rare roofer who works in this stone covers only a square metre a day. Farmhouses all over the Dordogne were renovated in this manner, and their owners benefited in every way except one: their new homes are less beautiful.

Nuts are pocket money for Adrianne but big business in the Dordogne. Terrasson in the Nontronnais is famous for them, and one nut mill near Belvès in the south of the *département* is fed by 80 hectares (200 acres) of walnut trees – the fruit there still being harvested by hand, one by one. Part of Adrianne's yearly crop of 100 kilograms (weighed in their shells) is sold to one of the nut merchants in the area and part is held back for eating on the farm. Traditionally, old peasant women called *ennoiseuses* who work at home are hired by the merchants to do the shelling, a static and tedious fate Adrianne has escaped. Each walnut is placed on a round board and gently attacked with a wooden mallet – gently in the interests of extracting the meat in just

OPPOSITE: Chez *Adrianne Beauvieux, guests* faire chabrol, *the old Dordogne custom by which a splash of red wine is added to a nearly finished plate of soup. The wine is swirled around so that it is heated through, and then drunk straight from the plate. Mme Beauvieux always makes* mique *in the fireplace, which is also used for preparing most meals in cold weather; the stove is used in warmer months and for dishes such as jugged rabbit. The water heater above the sink does not work, so hot water for washing dishes is carried from the bathroom.*

BELOW: *Folded into a cotton pillow slip, the* mique *is left to rise in front of the fire before being eased into the broth for poaching. A basic dough enriched with eggs,* mique *draws on the Dordogne's tradition of severely economical peasant cooking.*

BELOW RIGHT: *The* mique *will be added to an iron kettle hung over the fire containing a broth of pumpkin, carrots, green beans, leeks and tomatoes.*

two pieces. As these half-kernels earn for the women about twice the amount that broken ones do, and as they are cradled against the seam of the shell, one learns quickly to take aim at the nut's wrinkled face rather than the seam.

Walnuts are sold at village markets throughout the Dordogne: plain, suspended in honey, grilled and glazed, macerated in eau-de-vie, confected into bonbons. Walnut oil is also sold, which is most often used in vinaigrette for green salads – watercress, dandelion, lamb's lettuce, chicory and above all endive. To tempt the wary with no experience of this oil it is sometimes suggested that it be cut with peanut oil, but this is nonsense – and disrespectful to a virgin oil of great character.

Adrianne's source for walnut oil is the Huilerie du Moulin de la Tour, where it has been made without a lapse in production and according to the same methods since the early sixteenth century. Located across the Dordogne river in Sainte-Nathalène, the mill has stone grinding wheels that are powered by the River Enea; a large key set into the back wall regulates the flow of water and ultimately the speed at which the wheel

turns. A first grinding of nuts produces a *pâte* which is carefully heated in a huge open cauldron over a wood-burning fire to encourage the release of the oil. The *pâte* is then transferred by shovel to a burlap-lined press. The raw walnut oil that trickles through the burlap is cloudy; at La Tour it is left in a barrel for three days to settle before being filtered and bottled.

Typically, 30 kilograms of kernels are pressed at a time, 2 kilograms (or 5 kilograms before shelling) being needed for one litre of oil. Nothing is wasted. The *tourteau*, or oil cake that remains after pressing, is re-ground and sold as fish bait; it is also excellent fodder for livestock.

The mill is owned today by a committed young woman named Francine Bordier; it was a wedding present from her grandfather to her mother. In her own home, attached to the *huilerie*, Madame Bordier uses walnut oil to fry fish, especially gudgeon, whiting and hake; in *brandade de morue*, usually made with olive oil; and in a salad of sautéed duck or goose gizzards, avocado and hearts of palm.

In a memorable recipe from *The Silver Palate Good Times Cookbook*, Brussels sprouts are steamed and tossed with chopped walnuts in a vinaigrette of wal-

ABOVE: *Adrianne Beauvieux's jugged rabbit, locally famous with the postmaster and schoolmistress, is made with one of her own eighteen-month-old rabbits, chosen at this age for its firm flesh. The wine sauce is made gelatinous with bits of pork rind, and a square of dark chocolate tempers the acidity of the alcohol.*

RIGHT: *Until 1984 when she fell and hurt her knee, Adrianne made* foie gras *the old way – kneeling on the ground with a goose between her legs and a hand-cranked funnel down its neck. These top-quality creamy blonde* foies gras *were obtained from geese fed with maize for three weeks, three times a day. The maize is cooked with salt, goose fat and water just to the point where it can be pierced with a fingernail.*

OPPOSITE: *The room where Adrianne Beauvieux and her four sons slept until 1957 acts as a larder and junk room.* Queues de renard *spill limply from a vase, and a* vinaigrier *wears three hats. The figure on the table is a plastic Virgin – a souvenir from Lourdes – filled with water for the steam iron.*

nut oil, maple syrup and sherry vinegar. *Chez* Adrianne, the oil is simply drizzled on white *haricots*.

Adrianne is well-liked. 'She is *une bonne femme classique*,' says Henri Dos Ramos, the postmaster at Carlux, a friend for whom she has cooked many times. As Adrianne has an account at the post office, M. Dos Ramos is also her banker. 'Madame Beauvieux is extremely generous, the sort of woman who would give you her shirt, or in my case a chicken or firewood put aside for herself. She would refuse you nothing. Well thought of by everyone, always ready with a favour, she is content and happy, someone who does not think of herself as unfortunate. Madame Beauvieux is *une brave femme* – not *brave* in the sense of being courageous, but *brave* in her willingness and readiness to do good. She is an excellent woman, *bonne comme le bon pain*.'

Adrianne does not have a great repertoire of recipes; the meal pictured here is the one the postmaster can expect to be served whenever he is invited to lunch. To start with, the broth in which the humble *mique* has cooked and swelled is ladled with the vegetables over slices of crusty and stale *pain de campagne*. While carrots, cabbage and onions and/or leeks are traditionally used to flavour the liquid, Adrianne uses all of these plus whatever is around, which may include pumpkin and tomatoes. The *mique* itself takes the place of bread with the main course of jugged rabbit. To ensure it does not collapse the loaf is sliced the moment it comes out of the kettle to release the steam. The dumpling is often eaten the

next day for breakfast, spread with jam.

In less time than it takes to strike a match Adrianne kills one of her eighteen-month-old rabbits. Holding its hind legs in one hand and its head in the other, her thumb pressing on the base of its skull, she stretches the animal out; in an abrupt snap its vertebrae are ruptured and death is instant. Skinned and cut into pieces, the rabbit spends the next twenty-four hours in a drunken marinade perfumed with cloves, onions and carrots. Well dried, the meat is browned in duck fat, and simmered with the marinade and most of another bottle of wine. The sauce is thickened with bits of pork rind and a square of chocolate. Both the wine in the casserole and that on the table is made in a portable grape press bought jointly in 1949 by all the inhabitants of L'Oeil-la-Garde, each of whom has his own vines. Jugged rabbit cannot be made without wine, of course, but Adrianne says that the sauce also benefits from a small glass of the animal's blood, mixed with a little vinegar to prevent it coagulating.

Both desserts depend on the walnut harvest: a gâteau covered with melted dark chocolate, and a delicate tart with a biscuit crust. Coffee is strong and black.

'I don't have anything to complain about,' says Adrianne. 'If something or someone pleases me, okay, otherwise I never say a word. I never argue with anyone; not my neighbours, whom I like, and not my sons. I get on well with everyone. As for *l'art de recevoir...* someone comes by, you say hello, you talk. Sometimes they stay and eat, and sometimes they go.'

MENU
for 8

LA MIQUE LEVÉE SARLADAISE
DANS UN BOUILLON DE LÉGUMES
LEAVENED DUMPLING IN A VEGETABLE BOUILLON,
FROM THE REGION OF SARLAT

Vin nouveau de la ferme
Young wine made on the farm

———————

CIVET DE LAPIN SANGUINAIRE AU VIN DE BERGERAC
JUGGED RABBIT IN A BLOOD AND BERGERAC WINE SAUCE

———————

GÂTEAU AUX NOIX NAPPÉ AU CHOCOLAT AMER
WALNUT CAKE COVERED WITH BITTER CHOCOLATE

TARTE AUX NOIX DE LA RÉSERVE DE MADAME BEAUVIEUX
WALNUT TART, MADE WITH MADAME BEAUVIEUX'S
SPECIAL RESERVE WALNUTS

———————

Café

BELOW: *Conserves for winter. The hand-cranked funnel is left over from the days when Mme Beauvieux force-fed geese for her own foie gras.*

LA MIQUE LEVÉE SARLADAISE DANS UN BOUILLON DE LÉGUMES

In this *mique* recipe duck or goose fat replaces butter in a brioche-like dough that is cooked in a full-flavoured bouillon. Others use stale bread or corn meal and are simply steamed or poached in salted water.

For the *mique*:
21 g ($\frac{5}{8}$ oz) fresh compressed yeast
125 ml (4$\frac{1}{2}$ fl oz/$\frac{1}{2}$ cup) milk, warmed
500 g (18 fl oz/scant 3$\frac{3}{4}$ cups) flour
3 eggs
75 ml (2$\frac{1}{2}$ fl oz/$\frac{1}{3}$ cup) rendered goose or
  duck fat, melted
2 tsp salt
For the bouillon:
50 g (scant 2 oz/3$\frac{1}{2}$ tbs) unsalted butter
2 medium leeks, trimmed, washed and
  thinly sliced
2 medium carrots, trimmed, peeled and
  thinly sliced
salt and freshly ground pepper
100 g (3$\frac{1}{2}$ oz) green beans, trimmed
100 g (3$\frac{1}{2}$ oz) fresh pumpkin flesh, diced
1 small wedge green cabbage
2 medium tomatoes, cored and diced

For the mique:
1. Crumble the yeast into a large bowl, add the milk and stir to dissolve. Set aside for 5 mins. Incorporate the remaining ingredients and knead on a lightly floured surface for 3–5 mins, forming a smooth ball. Wrap loosely in a clean tea towel and leave to rise at room temperature for 2 hours, or until doubled in volume.
For the bouillon:
2. While the *mique* is rising, make the soup in a covered pot large enough to hold both *mique* and bouillon. Melt the butter and sauté the leeks and carrots, seasoned with salt, until soft but not brown. Add the cabbage and approx 2 litres (3$\frac{1}{2}$ pints/2 quarts) water and bring to a simmer. Add the beans, pumpkin and tomatoes and cook for 30 mins. Season.
3. Leave the *mique* in its towel to transfer it carefully to the pot. Gingerly lower the dough into the soup without deflating it. Cover and simmer gently for 30 mins – the bouillon must not boil. Carefully flip it over, re-cover and cook for 15 mins more. Ladle the soup and vegetables over slices of stale *pain de campagne* as a first course. Remove the *mique* to a warm place, pierce with a knife to release the steam, cover with a damp towel, and serve with the rabbit (recipe follows).

CIVET DE LAPIN SANGUINAIRE AU VIN DE BERGERAC

If blood worries you, go ahead and make this dish without it. The stew will still be good, if less rich and with a less interesting texture. If rabbits's blood cannot be obtained, pig's blood may be substituted. Gelatinous pork rind, also not critical, adds body to the final sauce. Chocolate brings out all the flavours and takes the acidic edge off the wine.

1 freshly killed rabbit weighing approx
  1.5 kg (3¼ lb), cut into 10–12 pieces
2 onions, sliced
1 carrot, peeled and sliced
2 cloves garlic, peeled and crushed
2 sprigs fresh thyme
1 bay leaf
1–1½ bottles Bergerac red wine
salt and freshly ground pepper
3 tbs rendered duck fat or vegetable oil
3 tbs flour
30 g (1 oz) pork rind, diced into very small
  pieces and blanched
60 ml (2 fl oz/¼ cup) rabbit's blood, mixed
  with 3 tsp red wine vinegar
30 g (1 oz) bitter chocolate, chopped

1. Combine the rabbit, onions, carrot, garlic and herbs in a glass or stainless steel bowl and add wine to cover. Cover and marinate in the refrigerator for 24–48 hours.
2. Strain, recouping the liquid. Dry the rabbit thoroughly with paper towels and season. Heat the fat and brown the meat evenly on all sides, in as many batches as necessary so as not to crowd the pan. Reserve.
3. Preheat oven to 180°C (350°F). Sauté the carrot and onions from the marinade until soft. Sprinkle with the flour and cook over a low heat, stirring, for approx 3 mins. Whisk in the marinade and cook until the sauce thickens. Skim off any impurities. Add the rabbit and pork rind, add wine to cover, and simmer, covered, for 1 hour.
4. Transfer the meat to a serving platter, cover and remove to a warm place. Stir a little of the warm sauce into the blood and then, off the heat, whisk this mixture into the sauce. Return the pan to a very low heat – the sauce must not simmer – stirring continuously until it thickens slightly. Stir in the chocolate and correct seasoning. When the chocolate has melted, ladle the sauce over the meat and serve.

GATEAU AUX NOIX NAPPÉ AU CHOCOLAT AMER

A biscuit-like cake rich in the famous walnuts of Périgord.

125 g (4 oz/1 scant cup) flour
170 g (6 oz/⅔ cup plus 1½ tbs) unsalted
  butter, chilled and cut into pieces
200 g (7 oz/2 cups) ground walnuts, plus
  enough to dust the cake tin
1 tsp baking powder
200 g (7 oz/1 cup) sugar
4 eggs, separated
100 g (3½ oz) bitter chocolate
12 walnut halves

1. Pulse the flour and 125 g (4½ oz/½ cup) of the butter in a food processor until crumbly. Transfer to a bowl and stir in the ground nuts, baking powder and half the sugar. Incorporate the egg yolks with a spoon – the batter will be quite sticky. Preheat oven to 180°C (350°F).
2. Whisk the egg whites until stiff peaks form and beat in the remaining sugar.

Gently fold the meringue into the nut mixture. Butter a 25 cm (10 in) round cake tin, dust with ground nuts, and pour in the batter. Bake for approx 30 mins, or until the centre springs back when tested. Remove to a cooling rack.
3. Melt the chocolate and remaining butter in a bain-marie. Stir until smooth. Turn out the cooled cake onto a serving plate and glaze. When the glaze has set, decorate with the walnut halves and serve.

BELOW: *Truffles, foie gras, confit and walnuts are among the great specialities of the Dordogne. Adrianne Beauvieux sells part of her annual 100-kilogram harvest of walnuts (weighed in their shells) to one of the region's nut merchants, but holds back the rest for her own use in simple tarts and dark chocolate-covered gâteaux.*

TARTE AUX NOIX DE LA RÉSERVE DE MADAME BEAUVIEUX

This rich tart can easily be made for a large group by doubling or tripling the recipe. Use a Swiss roll tin, and then cut the finished tart into small squares.

pâte sucrée brisée (see page 197 for recipe)
2 eggs, lightly beaten
100 g (3½ oz/¼ cup) sugar
100 g (3½ oz/1 cup) ground walnuts, plus
  enough for sprinkling
12 walnut halves

1. Flour a work surface and roll out the pastry to line a 25 cm (10 in) false-bottomed tart tin, pressing with your fingers to repair any cracks. Refrigerate for 30 mins. Preheat oven to 180°C (350°F).
2. Stir together the eggs, sugar and ground walnuts, and pour into the pastry shell. Bake in the bottom third of the oven for 25–30 mins, or until set. Cool slightly, lift the tart out of the ring and transfer to a serving plate. Decorate with the ground walnuts and walnut halves and serve.

18 A harvest *fête*
in the Bordelais

W INE dealers greet François Mitjavile today with the greatest affability, but that was not always the case. When he first began making wine at Château Le Tertre Roteboeuf in Saint-Emilion in the Bordelais, they bought it at prices that were not only insulting but almost certainly ruinous. 'The *négociants* wanted my *grand vin* at a *bon prix*,' he says, 'but I decided I would do without them.'

ABOVE: *30 September 1989: grape pickers on the last day of the harvest. It was to be the finest vintage since the Mitjaviles started making wine at Le Tertre in 1978.*

LEFT: *A blind horizontal tasting at Le Tertre assembles eight Saint-Emilions grown on the southern* côte, *or slope. The one judged to be the best is decanted and evaluated further. Whereas 'horizontal' indicates that all the wines are from the same year, a 'vertical' tasting would sample several vintages from a single grower. Tastings are also organized to determine whether a wine should be admitted into an* appellation, *and to analyse the style of casks from different suppliers and from the wood of trees from different forests.*

OPPOSITE: *The elements of the*
dégustation aveugle, attended by the
owners of each of the châteaux
represented, are set out on a scrubbed
nineteenth-century English table. The
estates are Larcis-Ducasse, Ausone,
Cheval Blanc, Pavie, Figeac, Canon,
Beauséjour-Bécot and Le Tertre.

When in 1978, at the age of twenty-six, François Mitjavile took over Le Tertre, it produced an unremarkable wine that did not even carry the name of the estate. After two years of training at neighbouring Château Figeac and a year at technical school, he bypassed the *négociants* by driving around markets and camp sites in the Bordelais with his trunk full of Le Tertre, and by travelling up to Paris to stage tastings and stir up interest. The obsessive years of developing a *grand cru* while stalling the bank manager were more or less over when Robert Parker, whose dryly professional newsletter makes him the most powerful journalist in the wine world, discovered the 1982 *millésime*, or vintage. Shocked that there was not even an entry for the château in Feret's *Bordeaux et Ses Vins*, Parker was so excited that he referred to Le Tertre's fruitiness twice in his review, calling it a 'ripe, richly fruity, well-structured, deep, spicy wine which shows plenty of black cherry fruitiness and full body'. When Parker wrote that François, with his 'fanatical commitment to quality', wanted to make a Saint-Emilion 'in the image of Pétrus' – the king of Pomerols –

he meant that he sought the same depth and intensity of flavour. He said of the 1985 that it seemed 'to want to out-Pétrus Pétrus' and that it was in a class with every other Saint-Emilion except Ausone, Cheval Blanc and Canon. On Parker's rating scale of 50 to 100, the 1986 was given 91 points.

The site of this rather bohemian *vigneron*'s success is a severely beautiful 1730 stone *chartreuse* – the designation in the Bordelais for a country house belonging to the gentry. The purpose originally served by Le Tertre, however, is unclear. It may have been designed strictly for *fêtes*, as a shooting *relais*, or as the seat from which the surrounding land was managed. According to François, early owners of the estate would have journeyed here the 32 kilometres (20 miles) from Bordeaux for the day but they would not, in all likelihood, have stayed the night. With only three rooms, all for receiving and all paved with handsome square and octagonal terra-cotta *tommettes*, it simply did not offer the right sort of comfort. The typical *chartreuse* is built on one level and so indeed is Le Tertre, a fact lost on visitors who have not been

BELOW: *Freshly painted chairs dry among*
the vines on the morning of the fête.

told that the first floor, now given over to small charming bedrooms for the Mitjaviles and their school-age children, was in the first years nothing more than an attic. While there are sinks in four of five of these rooms, there is no question of a toilet or shower or bath. The only bathroom is downstairs at one end of the house and to reach it you have to pass right through the dining room and kitchen. This is quite a trek in your bathrobe and slippers, but worth it if the weather is good and your object happens to be a long lazy soak. The bathroom has a door leading directly into the garden and nobody will think you strange for leaving it open and spending the entire morning splashing around with an old number of *Jours de France.*

A *chartreuse*, a pure *maison de réception*, a *maison de maître* and a *maison noble* – Le Tertre answers to all these descriptions. But as François says, it is just as much a farm. The vines march right up to the house, and its integration into the life of the vineyard is complete. The main building, the worker's cottage where François's assistant Antonio lives, and the *chai* where casks are stacked together form the classic 'U'. In the eighteenth century meals would have been walked over from the worker's house, a bit of history that is replayed every autumn, when François and his wife Miloute host a lavish lunch for seventy-five friends and grape-pickers to celebrate the end of the harvest. Gas rings on iron tripods are scattered on the floors of both the Mitjaviles' and Antonio's kitchens to handle all the cooking. The relay across the back lawn of pots and platters the size of large children goes on merrily all day. Because the party is mainly for the pickers, and because eighty per cent of the agricultural workers in the Bordelais today are Arab, the meal is all-Moroccan, prepared by Assna Lachohab, a former Le Tertre harvester who now works locally as a private caterer. Her *repas de vendange* for the Mitjaviles, loaded with ginger and cinnamon and saffron, includes two *tajines*, the traditional mutton stew, one of them savoury with quince and the other sweet with prunes; *mqualli* chicken, prepared with violet olives and preserved lemons; a raw salad of grated carrots and orange slices dressed with oil and lemon juice, another marrying tomatoes, cucumbers and onions, and a third of cooked minced tomatoes and aubergines spiced with cumin. After litres of fresh fruit juice, and as the meal wears on, the bottles of Le Tertre get older – 1987, 1986, 1985, 1981.

Even if Miloute Mitjavile did long for her old job at a photographic agency in Paris and did not enjoy entertaining, what choice would she have? You cannot make one of the most thrilling new wines in France and send buyers and journalists into town after a tasting for a Big Mac and chips. And she gets it exactly right, serving these professionals, who are invited into private wine estates for a living, the kind of food they want instead of the kind of food they have been dulled into expecting. 'It can be thirty-five degrees outside,' says Miloute, 'and for eight days in a row the only dishes they're given are those which show off the wine: *foie gras*, *confit*, and a lot of rich, heavy, buttery sauces. On the same sort of occasions at Le Tertre I will serve chilled beetroot and cucumber soup, plain grilled pigeons, *croquant* green beans and coconut gâteau. In my opinion, the trouble with entertaining in the Bordelais is that too much of it revolves around wine.'

Yet even the Mitjaviles find it hard to escape their *cru*. When dinner at Le Tertre is among friends François is usually working in the *chai* as they arrive, so that is where the party begins, with the current vintage always being offered as an apéritif. It is also where the party usually ends, with the guests sampling the older *millésimes* until two or three in the morning. 'The *chai* is our salon,' says Miloute.

It is easy now to say that François Mitjavile was destined to make the wine he describes as having the percussive style of a great boogie-woogie. His father directs Banyuls and Côtes du Roussillon vineyards, though that is hardly the same thing as actually making one of the top Saint-Emilions; and before rescuing Le Tertre, François worked for the company in Paris founded by his great-great-grandfather for the transport of *vin de table*. While the tankers that roar down the motorways filled with inexpensive wine have made Mitjavile a familiar name in France, they have also perhaps made making a Bordeaux *grand cru* a little more difficult for François than it might otherwise have been. Nor is the name of the château very compelling. Translated literally, it means 'the hill of the belching ox', a reference to the animals that worked the *côte* – rather unhappily it would seem – until the early 1950s.

ABOVE: *The grape pickers are rewarded on the last day of the harvest with a long lunch served on a wide terrace overlooking the vineyards at Le Tertre. Elsewhere on the lawn additional tables are made by laying dozens of wine crates end to end and side by side. When the sun goes down the party continues with dancing in the salon.*

RIGHT: *The Mitjaviles say that because the* fête de vendange *is principally for the grape pickers, many of whom are Arab, they should honour them with their own cuisine.* Briouats, *deep-fried pastries filled with ground almonds, are among the desserts. At the other end of France, in Alsace, the same occasion is observed with* choucroute *and* baeckeoffes.

227

François says that his greatest tool in relaunching Le Tertre was the yawning black hole that represented his knowledge of just what it was he was supposed to be doing. 'Many people were surprised that I started to make exciting wine,' he told Jancis Robinson of the English magazine *A La Carte*. But lack of experience worked to his advantage. He said that unlike those who are raised to be wine-growers, whose confidence is guaranteed, his insecurity made him almost unreasonably eager and questioning.

Agronomically, the Pétrus connection that both shadows and flatters François is based on grape variety and soil. All of Pétrus and eighty per cent of Le Tertre is planted with Merlot, the balance of vines at the latter being Cabernet Franc. And both properties are rich in clay. 'Our philosophies are the same,' says François. 'We both share the idea that with this soil, these grapes, old cement vats and a classic press we can produce a *grand vin* – a wine both powerful and fleshy, potent and luxurious.'

Like Jean-Pierre Moueix at Pétrus, François harvests his grapes at their absolute last-gasp, optimum ripeness. A daredevil making wine from a high wire without a net, he risks rain and rot but says picking late is precisely what gives Le Tertre its opulence and deliciously opposing softness and strength. In 1985 his *vendange* took place eight days after the attending oenologist told him it ought to, and it was his best vintage until 1989. 'I prefer to pick ripe fruit in the rain than unripe fruit in the sun,' François told Robinson. 'If I had allowed myself to be influenced, I would never have made the wine I have. At first people said I was crazy. They said no one would buy such powerful wine. [But I learned that] no one notices the power of alcohol in wine if you make it well. Once you have understood this, you realize you are obliged to make very strong wine here. You must first look for power and then elegance on top. I am proud of picking last of all. ... When you pick you play your [trump] card. I want to have just a little bit of overripe red-fruit character, something like liquorice, almost raisin-y. Just a little bit.'

François is not the first to make good wine at Le Tertre, a south-facing amphi-theatre of 5 hectares ($12\frac{1}{2}$ acres) yielding 20,000 to 25,000 bottles in an average year.

ABOVE: *The dovecote is used as a larder to store conserves, including that rather odd speciality of the Bordelais, lamprey – like an eel but more terrifying-looking. With white flesh similar to veal, lampreys take in food through big gaping openings at one end of their bodies. Their own blood is the most important ingredient in their preparation. Shallots, wine and leeks are stewed on and off for three days before the fish is added for poaching. Finally, the blood is stirred in, and the mixture transferred to preserving jars. Lampreys, never eaten fresh, are sold in the region not by fishmongers but by* charcutiers.

OPPOSITE: *The sober chairs around the pine table in the kitchen at Le Tertre are from the Haute-Loire while those with sweeping lines are from Morocco. Miloute Mitjavile painted them all a blue she identifies with Chechaouen in North Africa. The walnut buffet to the right is Louis* XVI. *In winter, a shallow cooking vessel with three legs known as a* tourtière *is placed in the fireplace over coals to make a pastry-covered dish of veal sweetbreads, wild mushrooms and salsify.*

BELOW: *When the Mitjaviles have Le
Tertre full of houseguests, their young son
Henri is obliged to give up his room and
sleep in the corridor. The window
overlooks vines that are planted right up
to the front door. The bedspread was
woven in the Côte d'Ivoire.*

In the 1920s Miloute's father, a marine
officer, married into the family which
owned the château, and on the death of
his wife he bought it. He and his second
wife, the schoolmistress in Saint-Emilion,
produced a wine their daughter Miloute
remembers as 'rich and black'. When she
and François moved down to Saint-
Laurent-des-Combes and took over the
estate in 1975, it was these qualities they
sought to recapture. It took them three
years to produce their first vintage, which
is not one they speak of. Before that they
were occupied by clearing up the long
period of indifferent wine-making which
had followed her father's death in 1960,
when the property was rented out by
cousins.

'When we first arrived Le Tertre was
a little abandoned because it had always
been just a vacation house, a *maison de
belle saison* used from the fifteenth of July
to the first of October and then again at
Easter,' says Miloute. 'Growing up, the
salon was like a sixteenth-century common room where my sister and parents
and I all slept together and even ate.
There were no cows or chickens, but
almost. Father hated small bedrooms and
even after we moved upstairs he con-
tinued to sleep in the salon like some aged
student. Mother had a house provided by
the school in the old ramparts of Saint-
Emilion and it was there that we actually
lived.'

Miloute says the décor at Le Tertre
was much less evolved in 1975 than it is
now and that there was no bathroom, no
hot water, and no heating. 'The kitchen
was there but it was never a place we
spent any time in as children. After we
grew out of the salon, meals were always
respected by being served in the dining
room. My memory is of an old *bonne*
lighting the fire and preparing dinner and
a *chambre froide* upstairs where provisions could be kept cold. My mother was
born in North Africa so the cuisine we ate
at home was always quite *chaleureuse*,
with fresh vegetables twice a day. It was
François who inaugurated the kitchen as
a real room, and it has become the heart of
the house.'

When she became *maîtresse de
maison* Miloute in a very un-French gesture dipped Le Tertre in colour. The
dining room was painted the mauve–blue
of Chechaouen in Morocco, and the bedroom doors and frames along the narrow
sisal-covered corridor were painted coral,
the blue of the Aegean, and hunter green.

ABOVE: *The bathroom off the kitchen was originally the scullery. Before the room was refurbished, a live gas flame was placed under a zinc bath tub like a casserole to heat the water. The faux bamboo mirror was part of a turn-of-the-century armoire.*

FOLLOWING PAGE: *Living on a wine estate has many culinary advantages, including the ready availability of verjuice, the sour juice of underripe grapes that goes so well with fish. Here it flavours a whole salmon stuffed with a mixture of mushrooms and breadcrumbs, although it is more frequently used in the area with shad and carp from the Dordogne river. Verjuice, which can replace lemon juice in many recipes, works especially well with* foie gras *and partridge.*

The massive amount of bamboo furniture that serves as catch-alls for books and lamps and bath towels throughout the house was bought in Morocco for next to nothing and driven home in a truck. And while the charming old fittings which fill the bathroom were bought cheaply and locally, some of the nicest things at Le Tertre came free from the rubbish tip, including a beautifully weathered *épi de faîtage*, or pottery finial, typical of those crowning rooftops all over the Bordelais.

The *épi* found an instant home on the mantelpiece in the dining room, where the menu pictured here is shared with just two good friends on a Saturday evening in front of the fire in early autumn. For the first course, a whole fresh salmon is stuffed with a mixture of breadcrumbs, mushrooms and the sour juice of unripe grapes straight off the vine. The *beurre blanc* sauce is made with a Monbazillac sweet white wine, and the red on the table is the most recently bottled Le Tertre. The main-course pigeons scented with a *mélange* of twelve herbs and spices including lavender and cardamom are sent out from the kitchen surrounded by exquisitely tiny vegetables and an elaborate sauce of

raisins and preserved lemons. The wines here are two top Saint-Emilions which François always hoped that his would be classed alongside: Figeac and Pavie. Water is served with the *blanc-manger*.

With Le Tertre running at full throttle and accumulating more and more Parker points, François has also moved into the Côtes du Bourg *appellation*, making wines at vineyards he owns at Château Roc de Cambes. Bourg is not Saint-Emilion but the estate does have two things Francois knows about: clayey soil and south-facing vineyards. The first time he picked there, in 1988, he was three weeks 'late'. With long experience of the vines there, François's workers were sceptical and needed a lot of assurance that harvesting after everyone else would in fact benefit the vintage.

Writing a year after his 'little tour in France' in 1882, Henry James noted that 'good wine is not an optical pleasure, it is an inward emotion.' He was also tempted to 'trace an anology between good claret and the best qualities of the French mind.' In a glass of the right Bordeaux, he observed, 'there is a touch of French reason, of French completeness.'

MENU
for 8

Château Le Tertre Roteboeuf 1989   Saint-Emilion

SAUMON AU VERJUS EN PAPILLOTTE
SALMON *EN PAPILLOTTE* WITH VERJUICE
BEURRE BLANC AU MONBAZILLAC

UNE BOTTE DE PETITS LÉGUMES BLANCHIS
A BUNCH OF BLANCHED BABY VEGETABLES

Château Figeac 1982   Saint-Emilion

PIGEONS FROTTÉS AUX AROMATES MAROCAINS,
CUITS AUX CITRONS CONFITS
PIGEON RUBBED WITH MOROCCAN AROMATICS
AND BAKED WITH PRESERVED LEMON

Château Pavie 1986   Saint-Emilion

BLANC-MANGER AUX FRAISES
ET AU COULIS DE FRAMBOISES
ALMOND CREAM MOULD WITH STRAWBERRIES
AND RASPBERRY SAUCE

Café

Château Le Tertre Roteboeuf 1982   Saint-Emilion

PIGEONS FROTTÉS AUX AROMATES MAROCAINS, CUITS AUX CITRONS CONFITS

Pigeons are a very successful vehicle for this Moroccan-inspired mixture of herbs and spices. Preserved lemons can be found in shops specializing in Middle Eastern foods.

3 tbs mélange d'aromates marocains (recipe below)
8 pigeons weighing approx 250 g (9 oz) each, dressed
45 g ($1\frac{1}{2}$ oz/3 tbs) unsalted butter
8 small leeks or spring onions (scallions), trimmed, washed and thinly sliced
4 shallots, finely chopped
4 cloves garlic, peeled and finely chopped
salt
125 g (4 oz/$\frac{3}{4}$ cup) golden raisins
1 tbs green peppercorns in brine, strained
$1\frac{1}{2}$ small preserved lemons, $\frac{1}{2}$ cut in small dice, and 1 cut in wedges
2 tbs cider vinegar
250 ml (9 fl oz/1 cup) home-made chicken stock
a pinch of saffron

1. A day in advance, spoon a bit of the blended aromatics into the cavity of each pigeon and shake out the excess. Rub the outsides with this excess. Cover with cling film and refrigerate overnight.
2. In a heavy roasting pan large enough to hold all the ingredients, melt the butter and sauté the leeks, shallots and garlic. Season with salt and add the raisins, peppercorns, diced lemon and vinegar, and simmer for 5 mins. Preheat oven to 180°C (350°F).
3. Place the pigeons on the bed of vegetables and cook for 35–45 mins, basting every 10 mins with the stock. The meat is medium-rare when the juices run pale pink and well-done when they run clear. Arrange the birds on a serving platter, cover, and remove to a warm place. Add the saffron to the pan with the vegetables and reduce the liquid until slightly thickened. Serve separately or spoon around the pigeons, decorating the platter with the lemon wedges and brightly coloured blanched baby vegetables.

LEFT: *Moving back to Le Tertre in 1975, Miloute Mitjavile discovered the tablecloth embroidered with hirondelles she remembered from her childhood, and the same Lunéville service too, each plate decorated with a different fish.*

SAUMON AU VERJUS EN PAPILLOTTE

Verjuice, the juice of under-ripe grapes, is a tart and refreshing flavouring for rich salmon. If under-ripe grapes are not available, use ripe green ones and combine their juice with a pinch of tartaric acid. The subtle sweetness of Monbazillac wine in the *beurre blanc* marries well with the bread stuffing.

300 g (10½ oz) under-ripe grapes
200 g (7 oz) mushrooms, thinly sliced
15 g (½ oz/1 tbs) unsalted butter
salt and freshly ground pepper
100 g (3½ oz/1 cup) home-made unflavoured breadcrumbs, dried
1 whole salmon weighing approx 1.5 kg (3¼ lb), cleaned
2 tbs olive oil
4 sprigs fresh basil
2 egg whites, lightly beaten with a little salt

1. Reserve 60 g (2 oz) of the grapes, purée the rest in a food processor and strain, recouping the juice; there should be approx 180 ml (6 fl oz/¾ cup). Measure out 60 ml (2 fl oz/¼ cup) for the mushrooms, 90 ml (3 fl oz/6 tbs) for the fish, and 30 ml (1 fl oz/2 tbs) for the sauce.
2. Toss the mushrooms in their verjuice. Melt the butter in a saucepan, add the mushrooms and their liquid, season, and cook over a very high heat until tender. Combine the breadcrumbs with the mushrooms. Preheat oven to 180°C (375°F).
3. Measure the salmon to see if it will fit in the oven. If it does not, cut off the head and tail. Brush the oil on a sheet of parchment or greaseproof paper large enough to generously cover and fold over the fish (2 sheets may be used if necessary). Place on the baking sheet, oiled-side up. Cut the reserved grapes in half and place them down the centre of the paper with 2 of the basil sprigs as a bed for the salmon. Lay the fish on top. Sprinkle the cavity with some of the verjuice reserved for the fish, season, and fill with the stuffing. Sprinkle the remaining fish verjuice over the salmon, season and lay the remaining basil on top.
4. Brush the egg whites over the edges of the paper. Roll tightly together and twist the ends closed. Bake for 35 mins for salmon that is slightly rare at the bone and 45 mins for well-done. Transfer to a serving platter and cut open the *papillotte* in front of your guests.

BEURRE BLANC AU MONBAZILLAC

200 g (7 oz) shallots, finely chopped
250 ml (9 fl oz/1 cup) Monbazillac wine
30 ml (1 fl oz/2 tbs) verjuice, reserved from the salmon recipe above
200 g (7 oz/generous ¾ cup) unsalted butter, cut into small pieces

While the salmon is baking, simmer the shallots and wine until all the wine has evaporated. Stir in the verjuice. Over a low heat whisk in the butter a few pieces at a time until it is all incorporated. Season and reserve in a warm bain-marie. Serve separately.

MÉLANGE D'AROMATES MAROCAINS

The mixture made with the following quantities of dried and ground herbs and spices will allow you to keep some to try with other dishes. Pretty vials filled with the *mélange* also make an original gift that would delight any cook.

1 tbs each of cayenne pepper, cardamom, lavender, rosemary and cinnamon
2 tbs each of cloves, white pepper, nutmeg, cumin, ginger and summer savory
3 tbs coriander

Combine all the ingredients and store in airtight containers in a cool, dark, dry place.

BELOW: *Le Tertre, a* chartreuse *built in 1730, at dusk.*

BLANC-MANGER AUX FRAISES ET AU COULIS DE FRAMBOISES

For the custard:
200 g (7 oz/2 cups) ground almonds
500 ml (18 fl oz/2 cups) milk
200 g (7 oz/1 cup) sugar
1¼ tbs (1½ envelopes) unflavoured powdered gelatin
250 ml (9 fl oz/1 cup) double/heavy cream, whipped
For the sauce:
300 g (10½ oz) fresh raspberries
juice of ½ lemon
2 tbs sugar
300 g (10½ oz) fresh strawberries

For the blanc-manger:
1. A day in advance, combine the almonds, milk and sugar and let the mixture stand for 1 hour. Warm through over a low heat, stirring continuously, then strain through a sieve lined with damp cheesecloth. Sprinkle the gelatin over a little cold water and let it stand for 5 mins.
2. Warm the liquid again, remove from the heat, add the gelatin and mix thoroughly. Strain into a bowl and chill until the mixture begins to set. Fold in the whipped cream and transfer to a 1.5 litre (2¾ pint/1½ quart) ring mould. Refrigerate overnight. Run a small knife around the edge of the mould, dip it in warm water for a few seconds, and turn out.
For the sauce and to assemble:
3. Purée the raspberries, sugar and lemon juice in a food processor and pass through a sieve. Surround the *blanc-manger* with the sauce, fill with the strawberries, and serve.

DIRECTORY

Many resources will fill orders by post or telephone. *Italics* denote *départements*.

ANTIQUE TABLEWARE
ARTS PRIMITIFS ARGILES (spoons), 16 rue Guénégaud, 75006 Paris (46-33-44-73)

BOUTIQUE MARIE-PIERRE BOITARD, 9–11 place du Palais-Bourbon, 75007 Paris (47-05-13-30)

LE CHEMIN DE TABLE, 10 rue de Grenelle, 75006 Paris (42-22-40-21)

DANENBERT & CIE (art nouveau and art deco specialists) 2 place du Palais-Royal, 2 and 5 Allée Boulle, 75001 Paris, (42-61-57-19)

DÎNERS EN VILLE, 27 rue de Varenne, 75007 Paris (42-22-78-33)

MADAME EST SERVIE, 92 boulevard Malesherbes, 75008 Paris (42-25-89-49)

MANUFACTURE DU PALAIS-ROYAL, 54 Galerie Monpensier, 75001 Paris (42-96-83-38)

LE PAS PERDU, 4 rue du Pas de la Mule, 75003 Paris (42-71-87-83)

AUX PUCERONS CHINEURS, 23 rue Saint-Paul, 75004 Paris (42-72-88-20)

SÉPIA, 96 rue de la Faisanderie, 75016 Paris (45-04-08-06)

LA VIE DE CHÂTEAU, 157 Galerie de Valois, 75001 Paris (49-27-09-82)

ANTIQUE DOMESTIC ARTS
ART DOMESTIQUE ANCIEN, 231 rue Saint-Honoré, 75001 Paris (40-20-94-67)

CHAQUE CHOSE EN SON TEMPS, 46 rue de Saussure, 75017 Paris (42-27-60-70)

ERIC DUBOIS, 9 rue Saint-Paul, 75004 Paris (42-74-05-29)

FAIENCE
ATELIER DE POTERIE ARTISANALE DE PONTY (jaspé earthenware), R.N. 100, Le Ponty, 84220 Goult *Vaucluse* (90-72-22-79)

FAIENCERIE MONTAGNON, 10 porte du Croux, 58000 Nevers *Nièvre* (86-57-27-16)

SIMONNE FAVIER (Moustiers), Couvent des Capucines, Route de Moustiers *Alpes-de-Haute-Provence* (92-77-80-29)

LORRAINE FAIENCE, 44 rue de l'Alsace, 54950 Saint-Clément *Meurthe-et-Moselle* (83-72-43-83)

PAUL LAMBERT (*faïence de Rouen*), 3 rue du Hameau du Canal, 27460 Alizay *Eure* (35-23-02-83)

MASSÉ-ARTISANS FAIENCIERS, 39 rue Rodolphe-Minguet, 62240 Desvres *Pas-de-Calais* (21-91-63-99)

MUSÉE DES ARTS DÉCORATIFS (boutique), 107 rue de Rivoli, 75001 Paris (42-60-32-14)

POTERIE D'ALSACE, 3 rue des Frères, 67000 Strasbourg *Bas-Rhin* (88-32-23-21)

POTERIE CHRISTIAN KRUMEICH (Betschdorf stoneware), 23 rue des Potiers, 67660 Betschdorf *Bas-Rhin* (88-54-48-00)

POTERIE FOUCARD-JOURDAN, 65 bis, avenue Georges-Clémenceau, 06220 Vallauris *Alpes Maritimes* (93-63-74-92)

POTERIE FRIEDMAN (Soufflenheim earthenware), 3 rue Hagueneau, 67620 Soufflenheim *Bas-Rhin* (88-86-60-63)

POTERIE MÉDECIN, Mas Saintes-Puelles, 11400 Castelnaudary *Aude* (68-23-17-01)

POTERIE PROVENÇAL (also garden pots), 1689 route de la Mer, 06410 Biot *Alpes Maritimes* (93-65-63-30)

POTERIE DE TERRE VERNISSÉE, Sampigny-les-Maranges, 71150 Chagny *Saône-et-Loire* (85-91-12-99)

JEAN-CHRISTOPHE HERMANN (traditional Savoyard earthenware), Poterie de la Côte, 74570 Evires *Haute-Savoie* (50-62-01-90)

CLAIRE DE LAVALÉE (by appointment), 11 rue de Saint-Simon, 75007 Paris (42-48-46-25)

RAVEL-DELACROIX ET FILS (also cookware and 'Roman' garden pots), avenue Goums, 13400 Aubagne *Bouches-du-Rhône* (42-03-05-59)

TERRAILLES ET FAÏENCES DU MIDI, 15 rue Tour du Fabre, 13200 Arles *Bouches-du-Rhône* (90-93-02-37) *also at the Sunday market at L'Isle-sur-la-Sorgue Vaucluse*

LA TUILE À LOUP, 35 rue Daubenton, 75005 Paris (47-07-28-90)

ANTIQUE GLASSWARE
LES VERRES DE NOS GRAND-MÈRES, 3 marché Biron, 93400 Saint-Ouen *Seine-Saint-Denis* (40-12-72-19)

LA BROCANTE DE MARIE-JEANNE, 14 rue Saussier-Leroy, 75017 Paris (47-66-59-31)

CONTEMPORARY GLASSWARE
HENRI CIMETIÈRE (crystal), 26 rue Max-Boirot, 71140 Bourbon-Lancy *Saône-et-Loire* (85-89-01-28)

SIEGFRIED HARTWIG (engraved crystal), 33 vieille route d'Ouzouer, 45260 Lorris *Loiret* (38-92-31-23)

LA ROCHÈRE, Passavant-La Rochère, 70210 Vauvillers *Haute-Saône* (84-68-08-12)

LA VERRERIE DE BIOT, 47 rue Paradis, 75010 Paris (45-23-15-07) *glassworks and boutique at*: chemin des Combes, 06410 Biot *Alpes Maritimes* (93-65-03-00)

CONTEMPORARY TABLE SILVER
ODIOT, 7 place de la Madeleine, 75008 Paris (42-65-00-95)

LE VIEIL ORFÈVRE, 22 rue du Vieux Colombier, 75006 Paris (45-49-11-40)

CONTEMPORARY CUTLERY
CLAUDE CAPUT-THÉVENOT (table and professional kitchen knives), 19–21 rue de Chaumont, 52340 Biesles *Haute-Marne* (25-31-93-53)

PETER, 191 rue du Faubourg Saint-Honoré, 75008 Paris (45-63-88-00)

ANTIQUE TABLE, BED AND BATH LINEN
CHRISTIAN BENAIS, 18 rue Cortambert, 75017 Paris (45-03-15-55)

FUCHSIA, corner of rue Saint-Paul and rue de l'Ave-Maria, 75004 Paris (48-04-75-61)

JANINE GIOVANNONI, Marché Vernaison, Stand 141, 93400 Saint-Ouen *Seine-Saint-Denis* (40-12-39-13)

LES MUSES D'EUROPE, 64 rue de Seine, 75006 Paris (43-26-89-63)

NOSTALGIE, 23 rue Descombes, 75017 Paris (42-67-07-66)

PEAU D'ANGE, 1 rue Mesnil, 75016 Paris (45-53-78-11)

CLAUDINE PELTOT, Marché Malassis, Stand 52, 142 rue des Rosiers, 93400 Saint-Ouen *Seine-Saint-Denis* (40-10-85-82)

LE JARDIN MOGHOL (Indian designs), 53 rue Vieille du Temple, 75004 Paris (48-87-41-32)

NUITS BLANCHES, 55 rue Bossière, 75016 Paris (47-04-42-43)

PÉNÉLOPE, 19 avenue Victor Hugo, 75016 Paris (45-00-90-90)

JEAN VIER (traditional jacquard Basque designs), R.N. 10, 64122 Urrugne *Pyrénées-Atlantiques* (59-47-07-77)

CONTEMPORARY LINEN
THE WHITE HOUSE (exquisite table linen; also porcelain, crystal and fine English silver) *as featured on page 8*, 51/52 New Bond Street, London W1Y 0BY (071-629-3521)

FABRICS
ALSACE AUTHENTIQUE (kelsch), 3 rue Engel, Muttersholtz, 67600 Sélestat *Bas Rhin* (88-85-12-69)

ATELIER DU BROUTEL (custom-woven seat coverings and draperies), 1 rue Ernest-Dumont, 80120 Rue *Somme* (22-25-00-04)

LES INDIENNES (antique textiles & clothing), 10 rue Saint-Paul, 75004 Paris (42-72-35-34)

MUSÈE DE L'IMPRESSION SUR ÉTOFFES (museum & boutique) 3 rue des Bonnes-Gens, 68100 Mulhouse *Haut-Rhin* (89-73-74-74)

MUSÉE OBERKAMPF (toile de Jouy museum & boutique), Château Montebello, 78350 Jouy-en-Josas *Yvelines* (39-46-80-48)

NOUVEL ESPACE MICHEL BIEHN (antique Provençal textiles), 7 avenue des Quatre Otages, 84800 L'Isle-sur-la-Sorgue *Vaucluse* (90-38-49-62)

RESTAURANT-SUPPLY KITCHEN EQUIPMENT
DEHILLERIN, 18 rue Coquillère, 75001 Paris (42-36-53-13)

ISLER (knives), 44 rue Coquillère, 75001 Paris (42-33-20-92)

A. SIMON, 48 rue Montmartre, 75002 Paris (42-33-71-65)

COOKWARE
ÉTABLISSEMENT VERGNES (copper), Dufort, 81540 Sorèze *Tarn* (63-74-10-52)

JEAN MATILLON (copper), 45 rue du Général-Huard, 50800 Villedieu-les Poêtes *Manche* (33-61-02-37)

SODIFREUX 'LE CAPUCIN' (iron), Nallier, 86310 Saint-Savin *Vienne* (49-48-03-72)

PEWTER
LES ETAINS DU MARAIS, 26 rue des Gravilliers, 75003 Paris (42-78-73-70)

ROBERT VOLLET, Marchastel, 15400 Riom-ès-Montagnes *Cantal* (71-78-41-83)

LES ETAINS DU CAMPANILE, 138 rue des Rosiers, 93400 Saint-Ouen *Seine-Saint-Denis* (40-10-07-33)

ANTIQUE BISTRO FURNISHINGS AND ACCESSORIES
DÉCO BISTRO, Marché Paul-Bert, Allée 6, Stand 87, 93400 Saint-Ouen *Seine-Saint-Denis* (40-10-92-73) *also at:* avenue du Clos Mouron, Porte de Chalon, 71700 Tournus *Saône-et-Loire* (85-32-10-52)

BISTROS D'AUTREFOIS, Marché Serpette, Allée 4, Stands 1 and 2, 93400 Saint-Ouen *Seine-Saint-Denis* (40-12-90-06)

BASKETWORK
LES AMIS DE L'ART PAYSAN (baskets for harvesting olives, apples, cherries and wine grapes), La Ratranche, Bat. L 147, 83340 Le Luc *Var* (94-60-91-47)

CHÂTEAU FRÈRES SA (baskets for draining cheese), rue Rebis, 53500 Fayl-Billot *Haute-Marne* (25-88-66-34)

ALBERT BERTON, Route de La Rochelle, l'Ile d'Elle, 85770 Vix *Vendée* (51-52-00-75)

ROGER HERISSET ET FILS, Les Grands Ormeaux, Rannée, 35130 La Guerche-de-Bretagne *Ille-et-Vilaine* (99-96-32-31)

PATRICK LAMBERT, L'Auzizière, Saint-Marsault, 79380 La Forêt-sur-Sèvre *Deux-Sèvres* (49-80-82-41)

CLAUDE LE CORRE (fish, oyster and vegetable baskets), rue de la Gare, 35350 Saint-Méloir-des-Ondes *Ille-et-Vilaine* (99-89-12-06)

JEAN-CLAUDE CAMUS (wicker-covered demijohns), Chigny, 02120 Guise *Aisne* (23-60-21-73)

HUBERT MARTIN, La Pagerie, 79340 Vasles *Deux-Sèvres* (49-69-05-95)

JEAN-CLAUDE PERNÉE (grape-harvesting baskets and bottle carriers), 3 rue Saint-Crépin, 02400 Château-Thierry *Aisne* (23-83-28-22)

VANNERIE BUSSIÈROISE, 52500 Bussières-lès-Belmont *Haute-Marne* (25-88-62-75)

NEEDLEWORK
L'ART DE L'AIGUILLE, 9 quai aux Fleurs, 75004 Paris (46-34-76-33)

TAPISSERIES DE FRANCE, 25 rue Paul-Fort, 75014 Paris (45-41-77-92)

TAPISSERIE AU POINT, 128 Galerie de Valois, 75001 Paris (42-61-44-41)

CANDLES
PATRICE CHARTON, Le Bourg, Vion, 72300 Sablé-sur-Sarthe *Sarthe* (43-95-48-10)

CIERGERIE DES PRÉMONTRES, 2 avenue du Lieutenant-François-Atger, 13690 Graveson *Bouches-du-Rhône* (90-95-71-14)

DIPTYQUE (scented candles; also La Rochère glassware), 34 boulevard Saint-Germain, 75005 Paris (43-26-45-27)

YVES GÉRARD (beeswax), Les Girauds, Billezois, 03120 Lapalisse *Allier* (70-99-06-26)

FRANÇOIS GUÉDON, 113 Grand'Rue, 86000 Poitiers *Vienne* (49-41-07-43)

MARCEL LANDRIN, 17 rue du Général-de-Gaulle, Sainte-Anne-d'Auray, 56400 Auray *Morbihan* (97-57-63-84)

DRIED BOTANICALS
RENÉ DHOMBRES, Porte des Autrichiens, 07240 Chalençon *Ardèche* (75-58-03-12)

JULE DES PRÉS, 46 rue du Roi de Sicile, 75004 Paris (48-04-79-49)

REPRODUCTION PROVINCIAL FURNITURE
AU SIÈGE D'AUTREFOIS, Les Bas, Rancy, 71290 Cuisery *Saône-et-Loire* (85-74-26-33)

BERNARD ET JEAN-CLAUDE BLIN, 5 rue Saint-Marie, 50400 Granville *Manche* (33-50-17-51)

MOISSONNIER, 67 avenue Maginot, 01000 Bourg-en-Bresse *Ain* (74-23-15-31)

VINCENT MIT L'ANE (Provençal furniture specialists), route d'Apt, 84800 L'Isle-sur-la-Sorgue *Vaucluse* (90-38-07-37)

TILES
AURÉLIEN ET CLAUDE RIVIÈRE, Raujolles, Creyse, 46600 Martel *Lot* (65-60-14-03)

EDOUARD ET LUCIENNE SISMONDINI (terra-cotta *tommettes*), Route Sillans, Quartier des Mudes, 83690 Salernes *Var* (94-04-63-06)

TUILERIE FRANÇOISE MAYLE DAVID, Morizès, 33190 La Réole *Gironde* (56-71-45-56)

FLOOR COVERINGS
MAISON DU VILLAGE SAVOYARD (straw mats; also bowls, baskets), 73670 Saint-Pierre-d'Entremont *Savoie*

LES NATTIERS-TEINTURIERS (hand-sewn sisal, coco), Entrecasteaux, 83570 Carcès *Var*

LA SCOURTINERIE (coconut floor and table mats), 26110 Nyons *Drôme* (72-26-33-52)

ANTIQUE FIREPLACES AND FLOORING MATERIAL
JACPIERRE, 'Le chêne vert', R.N. 23, 61260 Male *Orne* (37-49-69-71)

JEAN LAPIERRE, rue Vieille du Temple, 75003 Paris (42-74-07-70) *also at*: Sennece-les-Mâcon, 7100 Mâcon *Saône-et-Loire* (85-36-01-08)

PIERRES D'ANTAN, La Forêt, 78550 Houdan *Yvelines* (30-59-72-77)

FOR THE GARDEN
COOPÉRATIVE DES FOURCHES (nettlewood pitchforks), 30160 Sauve *Gard* (66-77-56-12)

HERVÉ BAUME (furniture), 19 rue Petite-Fusterie, 84000 Avignon *Vaucluse* (90-86-37-66)

POTERIE BOUAT (footed green-glazed pots; also tableware), 65 rue de Dunkerque, 11400 Castelnaudary *Aude* (68-23-00-03)

LE JARDIN DE SAINT-PAUL (furniture; also fireplace accessories), 24 quai des Célestins, 75004 Paris (42-78-08-89)

POTERIE D'ANDUZE (traditional 'drip-glazed' Anduze garden pots), 30140 Anduze *Gard* (66-61-80-86)

FOOD
BERNACHON (chocolate), 42 cours Franklin-Roosevelt, 69006 Lyon *Rhône* (78-24-37-98)

BOUTIQUE MAISON DE L'ALSACE (products of Alsace; also pottery, table linen), 10 rue du Colisée, 75008 Paris (45-62-54-85)

PIERRE BRESC (honey), Le Village, 84750 Viens *Vaucluse*

LE CASTELAS (goat's cheese), 84400 Sivergues *Vaucluse* (90-74-60-89)

CHARCUTERIE DES ARCADES (stuffed duck neck), Arcades du Consulat, 12200 Villefranche-de-Rouergue *Aveyron* (65-45-06-46)

ALBERTE CHAVOUTIER (herbs, flavoured olive oil), Route des Baux, 13990 Fontvieille *Bouches-du-Rhône* (90-54-73-24)

COOPÉRATIVE AGRICOLE D'OUESSANT (*wakame* seaweed), 29242 Ouessant *Finistère* (98-48-84-69)

COOPÉRATIVE FOIE GRAS PÉRIGORD-QUERCY, rue de l'Abbatoir, 24200 Sarlat-la-Canéda *Dordogne* (53-59-16-21)

GANACHAUD (bread), 150 rue Ménilmontant, 75020 Paris (46-36-13-82)

LES HERBES DU PALAIS ROYAL (tisane), 4 rue de Passy, 75016 Paris

IZRAËL (products of North Africa; exotic spices), 30 rue François-Miron, 75004 Paris, (42-72-66-23)

LA MAISON DU CHOCOLAT (chocolate) 52 rue François Premier, 75008 Paris (47-23-38-25)

LA MAISON DU MIEL (honey), 24 rue Vignon, 75009 Paris (47-42-26-70)

MAS DE BEDARRIDES (olives and olive oil), 13990 Fontvieille *Bouches-du-Rhône* (90-97-70-04)

MARRIAGES FRÈRE (tea & tea accessories), 30 rue Bourg Tibourg, 75004 Paris (42-72-28-11)

PIERRE MILHAU (*saucisson d'Arles*), 11 rue Reattu, 13200 Arles *Bouches-du-Rhône* (90-96-16-05) *also at the Wednesday morning market opposite Monoprix and at the Saturday morning market on boulevard Emile-Combes near the post office*

MOULIN DE LA TOUR (walnut oil), Sainte-Nathalène, 24200 Sarlat-la-Canéda *Dordogne* -53-59-22-08)

P. PÉBEYRE (truffles), 66 rue Frédéric Suisse, 46000 Cahors *Lot* (65-22-24-80)

LE PETIT MANUSCLAT (organic brown rice, rice cakes), Le Sambuc, 13200 Arles *Bouches-du-Rhône* (90-97-20-29)

SOLEIL DE PROVENCE (products of Provence; also soaps), 6 rue du Cherche-Midi, 75006 Paris (45-48-15-02)

WINE
Sold directly to the public; enquire about cellar visits and tastings.
BONNELLY PÈRE ET FILS, route de Roussillon, 84220 Roussillon *Vaucluse* (90-05-61-40)

CAVE DE VACQUEYRAS, 84190 Vacqueyras *Vaucluse* (90-65-84-54)

CHÂTEAU BELLEVUE, La Forêt, 31620 Fronton *Haute-Garonne* (61-82-43-21)

CHÂTEAU DE LA CHAIZE, Odenas, 69460 Saint-Etienne-des-Oullières *Rhône* (74-03-41-05)

CHÂTEAU DU PETIT THOUARS, Saint-Germain-sur-Vienne, 37500 Chinon *Indre-et-Loire* (47-95-96-40)

CHÂTEAU LE TERTRE ROTEBOEUF, Saint-Laurent-des-Combes, 33330 Saint-Emilion *Gironde* (57-24-70-57)

CHÂTEAU VIGNELAURE, route de Jouques, 83560 Rians *Var* (94-80-31-93)

DOMAINE RICHAUD, route de Rasteau, 84290 Cairanne *Vaucluse* (90-30-85-25)

MAS DE LA DAME, Les Baux, route de Saint-Rémy 13520 Maussane-les-Alpilles *Bouches-du-Rhône* (90-54-32-24)

PRODUCTEURS PLAIMONT (Colombar), 32400 Saint-Mont *Gers* (62-69-62-87)

BOOKSHOPS
Specializing in food and wine titles.
LIBRAIRIE GOURMANDE, 4 rue Dante, 75005 Paris (43-54-37-27)

LA VERRE ET L'ASSIETTE, 1 rue du Val-du-Grâce, 75005 Paris (46-33-45-96)

EDGAR SOETE, 5 quai Voltaire, 75007 Paris (42-60-72-41)

TEA SALONS AND A RESTAURANT GASTRONOMIQUE
SUZEL, rue du Bain aux Plantes, 67000 Strasbourg *Bas-Rhin* (88-23-10-46)

LE CAVAIGNAC, Place Saint-Pierre, 46300 Gourdon *Lot*

RESTAURANT CHRISTIAN MABEAU, Odenas, 69460 Saint-Étienne-des-Ouillières *Rhône* (74-03-41-79)

DIRECTORY & BIBLIOGRAPHY

FOLK AND SPECIALISTS MUSEUMS

ECOMUSÉE D'ALSACE, B.P. 71, 68190 Ungersheim *Haut-Rhin* (89-48-23-44)

ECOMUSÉE DU NIO, 29242 Ouessant *Finistère*

MAISON DE L'OUTIL ET DE LA PENSÉE OUVRIÈRE, 7 rue de la Trinité – rue Larivey, 10000 Troyes *Aube* (25-73-28-26)

MAISON RÉGIONALE DES ARTS DE LA TABLE, 15 rue Saint-Jacques, 21230 Arnay-le-Duc *Côte-d'Or* (80-90-11-59)

MUSÉE ALSACIEN, 23 quai Saint-Nicols, 67000 Strasbourg *Bas-Rhin* (88-35-55-36)

MUSÉE DE L'ART CULINAIRE, 06270 Villeneuve-Loubet *Alpes Maritimes* (93-20-80-51)

MUSÉE DES ARTS ET TRADITIONS POPULAIRES, 6 avenue Mahatma Gandhi, 75016 Paris (40-67-90-00)

MUSÉE DE LA BOULANGERIE, 12 rue de la République, 84480 Bonnieux *Vaucluse* (90-75-88-34)

MUSÉE CAMARGUAIS, Mas du Pont-de-Rousty, 13200 Arles *Bouches-du-Rhône* (90-97-10-82)

MUSÉE CHARLES DEMÉRY, 29 rue Proudon, 13150 Tarascon *Bouches-du-Rhône* (90-91-08-80)

MUSÉE DE LA GASTRONOMIE, Château de Thoiry, 78770 Thoiry *Yvelines* (34-87-40-67)

MUSÉE DU VIEUX MARSEILLE, 2 rue de la prison, 13002 Marseille *Bouches-du-Rhône* (91-55-10-19)

MUSÉE DU VIN, 5 square Charles Dickens, 75016 Paris (45-25-63-26)

MUSÉON ARLATEN, rue de la République, 13200 Arles *Bouches-du-Rhône* (90-96-08-23)

TOOLS, POTS, FURNITURE, ACCESSORIES

LE CÈDRE ROUGE, 22 avenue Victoria, 75001 Paris (42-33-71-05)

JARDINS IMAGINAIRES, 9 rue d'Assas, 75007 Paris (42-22-88-02)

UGHETTI (tools), 14 avenue Pasteur, 13100 Aix-en-Provence, *Bouches-du-Rhône* (42-23-28-32)

BARRELS, BROOMS AND . . .

ROGER ALLARY (wine, alcohol and vinegar barrels), 17520 Archiac *Charente-Maritime* (46-49-14-59)

ATELIER LES ENFANTS (olivewood bowls, platters), chemin des Bachettes, 06410 Biot *Alpes Maritimes* (93-65-01-82)

BACHELIER ANTIQUITÉS (wine-related antiques), Marché Paul-Bert, Allée 1, Stand 17, 93400 Saint-Ouen *Seine-Saint-Denis* (40-11-89-88)

BILLIARDS CHEVILLOTTE (billiard tables), 133 rue du Faubourg Saint-Antoine, 75011 Paris (43-63-67-13)

DOMINIQUE DERIVE (custom-made decorative screens), 46 rue Albert Thomas, 75010 Paris (42-01-72-18)

GILLES FRÉRES (brooms), 84840 Lapalud *Vaucluse* (90-40-33-91)

DIDIER GARDILLOU (fine porcelain: by appointment), La Peline, 24110 Saint-Astier *Dordogne* (53-04-91-30)

ROLAND KEIFLIN (*kachelofens* – Alsatian heating stoves), 112 rue de Saint-Louis, 68220 Hésingue *Haut-Rhin* (89-67-58-01)

LAVANDE 1100 (lavender and lavender oil), 88400 Lagarde d'Apt *Vaucluse*

LA MAISON DES ARTISANS CRÉATEURS DE BRETON (diverse Breton crafts), Ferme Mont-Saint-Michel, Brasparts, 29190 Pleyben *Finistère* (98-81-41-13)

LA MAISON DES DINANDIERS (metalwork), 14–16 rue du Parc-Royal, 75003 Paris (42-74-02-35)

MANOIR DE QUERVILLE (cider and Calvados), Prêtreville, 14140 Livarot *Calvados*

MERCERIE ARLÉSIENNE (Arlésien costumes), 10 rue du Président-Wilson, 13200 Arles *Bouches-du-Rhône* (90-93-28-05)

MONTAIGNER (lanterns and hurricane lamps), 24 rue de Grenelle, 75007 Paris (45-48-16-41)

MY-GWENN (roof finials), Huellau-Plounerin, 22160 Callac-de-Bretagne *Côtes-du-Nord*

PIERRE PATEL (wooden butter moulds), Le Bourg, 72670 La Fresnaye-sur-Chedouet *Sarthe* (43-97-80-52)

RAMPAL PATOU (savon de Marseille – palm coconout and olive oil soaps), 71 rue Felix-Pyat, 13300 Salon-de-Provence *Bouches-du-Rhône* (90-56-07-28)

JEAN POMMIER (alcohol stills), avenue de la République, 17770 Burie *Charente-Maritime* (46-94-90-49)

A. SIMON (restaurant-supply tableware), 36 rue Etienne Marcel, 75002 Paris (42-33-71-65)

BIBLIOGRAPHY

BARRY, ANN 'Fare of the Country', *The New York Times*, 28 April 1985

BENTLEY, JAMES *Life and Food in the Dordogne*, Weidenfeld & Nicolson, London, 1986

BOYER, MARIE-FRANCE 'Ushant', *The World of Interiors*, London, April 1985

CARLISLE, OLGA 'Arles's Summer Costume Party', *The New York Times*, 14 June 1987

COURTINE, ROBERT J. *Cuisine des Provinces de France*, Pierre Bordas et Fils, Paris, 1979

DOERFLINGER, MARGUERITE *Petit Recueil de la Gastronomie Alsacienne*, Vol. I, Editions S.A.E.P., Colmar, n.d.

GLENDINNING, VICTORIA *Vita*, Weidenfeld & Nicolson, London, 1983

GRUENAIS-VAN VERTS, MONIQUE A. *Cuisine de Provence Lubéron*, Denoel, Paris, 1982

HERTZOG, JEANNE *Petit Recueil de la Gastronomie Alsacienne*, Vols II and III, Editions S.A.E.P., Colmar, n.d.

JULLIAN, PHILIPPE 'The Château de La Chaize', *Architectural Digest*, Los Angeles, March–April 1986

MAHON, CATHERINE *Poteries d'Alsace*, Editions des Dernières Nouvelles d'Alsace, Molsheim, 1988

MALENFANT, PIERRETTE *L'Ecomusée d'Alsace*, Editions La Nuée Bleue, Strasbourg, 1989

OLNEY, RICHARD *Simple French Food*, Penguin, London, 1983

PEREIRE, ANITA and VAN ZUYLEN, GABRIELLE *Private Gardens of France*, Weidenfeld & Nicolson, London, 1983

PERON, FRANÇOISE *Ouessant, L'Ile Sentinelle*, Editions de la Cité, Brest-Paris, 1985

ROSSO, JULEE and LUKINS, SHEILA *The Silver Palate Good Times Cookbook*, Workman Publishing, New York, 1985

SAVAGE, GEORGE and NEWMAN, HAROLD *An Illustrated Dictionary of Ceramics*, Thames and Hudson, London, 1974.

SPURRIER, STEVEN *French Fine Wines*, Willow Books, London, 1984

WILLAN, ANNE *French Regional Cooking*, Hutchinson, London, 1984

WILLAN, ANNE *The Reader's Digest Complete Guide to Cookery*, Dorling Kindersley, London, 1989

WOLFERT, PAULA *The Cooking of South-West France*, The Dial Press, New York, 1983.

INDEX

Page numbers in **bold type** denote recipes. Page numbers in *italics* denote pictures.